**The Great Awakening
and the American Revolution:
Colonial Thought in the 18th Century**

The Rand McNally Series on the History of American Thought and Culture

The Great Awakening and the American Revolution: Colonial Thought in the 18th Century

Cedric B. Cowing
University of Hawaii

Rand McNally & Company · Chicago

The Rand McNally Series on
the History of American Thought and Culture

David D. Van Tassel, series editor

To Anne Cowing
and the memory of
George Cecil Cowing
(1885–1960)

Editor's Preface

The Great Awakening was a religious revival that not only shook the foundations of the established churches throughout colonial America, but affected all other areas of life and thought prior to the Revolution. Although many historians have suggested and some have asserted the relationship between the Great Awakening and the revolutionary movement, here for the first time in a single volume are gathered specific threads linking "New Light" religion to the Revolution. In the case of New England, especially Rhode Island, some of these connections are printed here for the first time. The evangelical Calvinists—Baptists and Presbyterians in all the colonies as well as New England Congregationalists—because their otherworldliness was coupled with political activism, were more important in advancing civil and religious liberty and converting Indians and Negroes than were rationalists whose ideas sprang from the European Enlightenment.

The Great Awakening and the American Revolution, surveys the whole range of colonial thought showing how the religious outlook is inextricably related to and helps explain economic, legal, social, scientific, and political theory and events of the period. In so doing, this volume admirably fulfills the major purpose of the Rand McNally series on the *History of American Thought and Culture.* The series aims to give the general student a synthesis, a means of tying together developments in religion, education, philosophy, science, literature, and the arts through a series of short readable volumes covering broad chronological periods. Each volume is designed to help bridge the gap between topical surveys and monographic studies by giving conceptual framework to significant periods and drawing together the burgeoning knowledge of this vast area of the American past. The authors are experts in their fields, but they do not represent any one school of intellectual history. Each author has chosen his own approach or emphasis, although the general aim is to present the ideas in depth and to point out the significant relationships between developments in all areas of intellectual and cultural expression within the period.

In this volume, Cedric Cowing not only synthesizes the most recent secondary literature on colonial thought and culture but also supplies stimulating insights and new interpretations based upon his original research. This is a thoughtful book about important and involved themes ranging from the development of religious and civil liberty to incipient nationalism. The writing sparkles with mica-dry humor and lively vignettes about such figures as John Wise and Solomon Stoddard. It should not only inform but appeal to every student of American civilization.

DAVID D. VAN TASSEL

Author's Preface

Certainly a major theme, if not the theme of 18th century American history is civil and religious liberty. This book is a social history of the century before American Independence, with an emphasis on evangelical religion and its effect on those liberties. I have seized upon illuminating insights, ideas and phrases wherever I could find them, including the most recent monographs, journal articles, and in some cases, unpublished doctoral dissertations. My great debt to the authors of these works is, I hope, fully revealed in the annotated bibliography. I can only hope that this small volume will prove informative and readable to a broad spectrum of readers.

I would like to acknowledge the helpful suggestions received from the series editor, David Van Tassel, my colleagues—James McCutcheon, Gavan Daws, and Herbert Margulies—and from my wife Sue Brown Cowing, who is also largely responsible for the index. My thanks go to the staffs of the Hamilton Library of the University of Hawaii and the Sterling Library at Yale University where much of the work was done, and to the University of Hawaii Research Council; their support over several years has made it possible for me to contribute my own research to several chapters. Mrs. Judy Horio has cheerfully and efficiently typed several drafts of this manuscript.

CEDRIC B. COWING

Honolulu, Hawaii
October, 1970

Contents

Chapter 1

Colonial Religion in the "Glacial Age"

The first signs of the religious upheaval known as the Great Awakening appeared among some Dutch Reformed churches in East Jersey in the 1720s; fifty years later, on the eve of the American Revolution, there was still some fervor left in the Carolina backcountry. One estimate of the results claimed 250,000 converts and 350 new churches. There is general agreement that the effect of this revival on American culture must have been profound; the majority have tended to view it as an over-reaction to the influx of rationalistic ideas from the European Enlightenment; as a "reactive nationalism," that in the long run facilitated democracy. Scholars, however, have tempered their praise of its democratic ethos by pointing out that reliance on God's sovereignty and grace was also conducive to anti-intellectualism.

Obviously such a widespread movement in the decades preceding 1776 must have had considerable effect on the quarrel between the Crown and the colonies and on the resulting American Revolution. While this has been conceded in a general way, direct connections between religion and the more evident political and economic forces have been hard to establish. Was the energy released by evangelism transferred to reinforce the struggle for natural rights and generate a will to take up arms for liberty?

The Awakening was the greatest revival in American history, but what exactly was being revived? For most of the participants, it was not merely primitive Christianity or the spirit of the Reformation but rather the courageous days of the first settlers in the early seventeenth century, and the religio-political ethos of the reign of the first two Stuart kings. Those were the days when religious and political reformers—the partisans of Puritanism and Parliament—were acting in concert to define and protect ancient British liberties against despotic monarchs. After the defeat of Charles I in the Civil War, that harmony between the religious and political spheres was broken by quarrels among the victors, and it was never to return. The religious pattern of the settlements before 1649 is therefore more than a prelude to an understanding of the 18th century; this "golden age" is a key to interpreting the behavior of the colonists between the Great Awakening and the Revolution.

In examining religious culture in this century it is helpful to distinguish carefully between creed and church government; that is, between theology and polity, and note how they complement each other. A good knowledge of theology, as distinct from knowledge of the Bible, has been confined to an elite most of the time, and the extent to which these systematic beliefs affect the whole society has fluctuated; conversely, the way the polity[1] affects church life has been more important to the mass of the people, at least if they are literate. One of the major themes of this book is that Calvinistic doctrines, whatever their cosmic truth, suited the New World wilderness and served to reinforce "soul liberty" and congregationalism better in the 18th century than the rationalistic and gradualistic Christianity that denied predestination[2] and sudden conversion. (This latter viewpoint of free will is loosely described as Arminianism, after the Dutch theologian Arminius who endorsed conditional rather than absolute predestination and brought on a schism in the Dutch Reformed Church by challenging Calvin's basic tenet.) The conflict between Calvinistic and Arminian views was latent in all the colonies from the beginning, but was not obvious until the Great Awakening.

The Pattern of Settlement

The joint stock company chartered to develop Virginia (The London Company) sent to Jamestown colonists who represented a fair cross-section of the English population, even though conscientious Roman Catholics were excluded by the oath of supremacy to the king, and there were far more men than women. At this time tensions between the conforming "high church" and nonconforming Puritan elements in the Church of England were dividing the English people and this schism was reflected within the Company. The promoters came to favor the Puritans and Parliament against the divine right pretensions of the king. The leader of the Company's Puritan faction was Sir Edwin Sandys, the son of an archbishop of York, who had studied abroad and was impressed by Calvin's system in Geneva. Sandys encouraged Pilgrim separatists who were restless in Holland to seek a land patent in Virginia. It was because of the dissenter[3] sympathies of Sandys and his friends that the king dissolved the London Company and made Virginia a royal colony in 1624. The first settlements in Virginia were designated as "cities," suggesting analogies both with the Genevan city-state and with the basic unit used later in New England, the township.

The Company established the Church of England in Virginia; this had been indicated in the charter and was approved by the colonists who, like all subsequent immigrants to America, wanted to be reassured by an old institution in their new clime. The first few clergymen seem to have been dutiful and sincere in their missionary efforts towards the Indians. Their sermons were quite doctrinal, but Governor De La Warr attempted to inject some Old World pageantry into the Anglican worship. Morning and evening prayers were offered, and days of fasting, humiliation, and thanksgiving were observed. The ministers were expected to spend their Sunday afternoons catechizing the young. The Virginians also put on the books the kind of restrictions on public morals and Sabbath day activity that we call "blue laws" and associate with the New England Puritans. Despite all these manifestations of religion, and some pious words in the 1606 charter, evidence of strong piety was lacking, and has justified historians in reporting that Virginia was settled by those whose motives were very largely secular. More important than the established Church was the guarantee of the rights of Englishmen and the meeting in 1619, without authorization, of the first deliberative body in America, the House of Burgesses. The colonists were eager to implement the liberties they had been accorded, to ensure that they would have the full measure of rights enjoyed by Englishmen at home.

The transfer of control from Company to king coincided with the concentration on tobacco culture and led to a decline in interest in the colony in several quarters. The initial curiosity about Virginia on the part of gentleman naturalists and soldiers of fortune connected with the Company had been satisfied and their attention turned elsewhere. The young Church, in facing the class of self-made planters that assumed leadership, was weak because it was not part of any diocese and had no bishop or ecclesiastical courts. The royal governor therefore assumed some of the episcopal functions; at the local level prominent planters used the vestries to choose the rectors and dominate the parishes. In addition, an early shift from the compact "cities" to the sprawling counties and parishes also made Virginia less attractive to a town-oriented clergy from the Old World. A desperate shortage of rectors developed; in some cases, even dissenting clergymen were allowed to officiate. Vestries felt justified in offering contracts to ministers on a year-to-year basis because of the low quality of those willing to cross the Atlantic. In the meantime vestrymen took to filling vacancies in the vestries themselves without a parish vote and thus became self-perpetuating oligarchies controlling social and political as well as religious life.

When Archbishop Laud began to press a relentless conformity on the Puritans in England, there was a corresponding, but much milder, pressure in Virginia to follow the orthodox liturgy, the Book of Common Prayer. Piety among the planters was private and gentlemanly but not altogether absent; perhaps a quarter of the books in their libraries were on religious subjects. The colony did not reveal any symptoms of early evangelism, however, and was conservative enough to uphold the House of Stuart through the Civil War and Interregnum. Cavalier refugees came to settle with their families, and slavery of the Africans was legalized. Yet despite this aristocratic trend, the trappings and culture of high churchmanship did not gain a hold; after the Glorious Revolution of 1688, there were no Jacobite upholders of the Stuarts as there were in England. A "low church" puritanical type of Anglicanism took shape before mid-century in the Old Dominion and was not materially altered by the hardening social lines of subsequent decades, the founding of William and Mary College, or the arrival of a commissary, the representative of the Bishop of London.

Eighteenth century Virginians, looking back, would take most pride in the early assertion of the rights of Englishmen; insofar as religion was mingled subtly with these feelings, it would serve to stiffen resistance to high church liturgy as well as to a bishop for America. On the eve of the Revolution, Virginia was not only the oldest and biggest among the southern colonies, but the most puritanical and libertarian.

The Pilgrims who landed at Plymouth Rock in 1620 had the characteristics of religious sectarians. They preferred sermons yet would accept a lay ministry; a number of their pastors had no college degree. They held many notions that were Calvinistic, but these were not systematic enough to constitute a theology. They were individualistic Protestants who, like the Lollards of pre-Reformation England, took their Bible literally and sometimes quarreled over scriptural passages, but very few of them had any love for theological exegesis.

Polity, of course, was much more important to them than theology. They were pure congregationalists who distrusted any kind of hierarchy at all; they could barely tolerate associations for advice and fellowship. Most significant of all was their Separatism, their willingness, despite strong latent nationalism, to defy tradition and the state by breaking with the national establishment, claiming that the Church of England was not a "true church." This willingness to break clean, to "come out and be separate" from sinful English society differentiated the Pilgrims from the Puritans, or at least from the Puritan leaders, who were anxious to maintain formal links with the establishment and avoid the stigma of outright separation.

The Pilgrims had the sectarians' narrow concern for morals reflected in the minutiae of conduct. In pride and envy they had raised the luxurious vices of the English upper classes to the level of sins against God. It may be that these Separatists represented an ancient resentment of Saxon-Celtic yeomanry against the Romanized culture brought over in the Conquest by the Normans. While such ethnic cleavage seems plausible, class differences alone could have accounted for the antagonism. The Pilgrims and other dissenters of this class were sensitized to idolatry; the trappings of Anglo-Catholicism were distasteful to them. In Holland the Pilgrims campaigned unsuccessfully to reform the Dutch Sabbath. In America, when "Regular Singing," a reform advocated by the young Puritan clergy which substituted singing by note for rote, reached Plymouth, the Old Colony was conspicuously reluctant to make what appeared to be a serious concession to formality and popery. The passengers on the *Mayflower* and its successors were from two groups: the Leyden contingent, whose forebearers were chiefly from the English Midlands, and the London group, young artisans from dissenter enclaves in the city. In either case, their roots were in the English yeomanry, which may explain their particular vices of drunkenness and premarital sex.

Although the Pilgrims did not come to America specifically to erect a model religious community, they did not come merely to fish and farm, either. What they sought was livelihood in a place where they could retain their simple amorphous faith and sectarian ways in isolation and peace yet remain under the British flag. For a time they found it in a corner of southeastern Massachusetts; later their descendants and dissenter brethren found it on the moving frontier.

While they were relatively conformist in their attitude toward behavior, sectarian vagueness of creed made it easier for them to tolerate at least the "non-essentials" in the beliefs of others. Because they stood for "soul liberty" and voluntarism, they had some flexibility, and sectarians generally, in order to strengthen their own freedom, have assumed pragmatically a "live and let live" position. Each successive immigrant group in America has reacted initially to the American situation by trying to invoke remembrance of its Old World creed and practice. In the case of the Pilgrims and English dissenters, this reaction was not so much a reversion to a formal creed—because they did not have any—but, rather, to a vague Calvinistic evangelism coupled with a renewal of the congregational form and a vigorous re-assertion of "soul liberty," namely the importance of individual consent to an idea or program. These sectarian yeomen may bear some resemblance to the peasants and common people of other countries, but their modicum of literacy gave them a confidence in their own common sense that was generally lacking elsewhere.

During the colonial era the Pilgrims spread out, settling on the Maine coast, in the Connecticut River Valley, and in eastern Connecticut, while kindred immigrants from England became an underclass in Puritan strongholds. Although normally people of "steady habits," they could be aroused to memorable moments of religious and political fervor by evangelism and real or fancied threats to liberty, which were, perhaps, more often defined in physical than mental terms. These Pilgrims, and other English and Scottish dissenters made more alike by the frontier environment, have actually constituted a kind of silent majority in America through most of its history.

French-speaking Netherlanders (Walloons) were the first permanent settlers in the New Netherlands of North America. They were sent by the Dutch West Indies Company which in the previous decade had maintained only trading stations on Manhattan Island and on the Hudson River at Fort Orange. Until 1638, most immigrants were not freemen but tenants employed by the Company. By the time the Company finally realized that it must settle many families from the homeland or succumb to the encroachments of populous New England, it was already too late.

It was also too late to give the Reformed Church in America the special position it enjoyed in the mother country. The first few clergymen were fiery Calvinists called to work among the Mohawk Indians. One of them protested unsuccessfully against the undemocratic character of the patroonships whereby the Dutch Republic offered wealthy entrepreneurs feudal privileges to develop large estates along the Hudson, but the aggressiveness of these clerics was exceptional. In general, the domines were educators respected for their learning, but neither they nor their Church were very influential in colonial affairs. The period of settlement of New Netherland coincided with the Dutch drive for independence from Spanish rule and an accompanying renaissance in arts and letters; this was the half-century of Huygens, the poet, and Grotius, the jurist. Fifty percent of Europe's books were printed on Dutch presses, yet in New Netherland, there was no press and only a few devotional tomes on the shelves.

The predominantly masculine and maritime atmosphere on Manhattan from the beginning created an atmosphere of religious indifference. Although at home Dutch law provided that dissenters from the Reformed establishment could worship only in private, Baptists and Lutherans had been holding public services for years. This happened in New Netherland too when the Lutherans demanded it. Governor Peter Stuyvesant tried to reverse this trend by favoring the Reformed service and suppressing public worship by dissenters, but Company officials overruled him; they pointed to the commercial advantages of a tolerant religious policy, and the heterogeneous make-up of the traders already active in the colony because of this understanding. So long as the Dutch settlements consisted largely of sailors, trappers, and traders, the Calvinistic element was more than offset by the Company and the atmosphere of indifference; this was the case throughout the Dutch period. When the British seized New Netherland and parceled it out to proprietors, of course they were inclined to continue the Dutch policy of religious toleration in the hope of populating this vast acquisition quickly. Except for the nationalistic Stuyvesant and a few domines, Calvinistic sentiment remained latent during Dutch rule, stymied by the early and spontaneous cosmopolitanism of New Amsterdam, the port city. The Calvinistic potential among the Dutch in the New World was not realized until the next century, when they had dispersed to the countryside and Theodore Frelinghuysen answered God's call to preach to phlegmatic farmers in East Jersey.

When the Puritan migration to North America began in 1630, Virginians, Pilgrims, and Dutchmen were already on the scene. The Puritans, unlike their predecessors (the Pilgrims had not suffered persecution in Holland) were religious refugees. They were being harried out of England by Archbishop Laud's campaign for strict conformity. The Primate was seeking not only acquiescence in the Anglican ritual, but compliance with a shift from a Calvinistic to an Arminian interpretation of the creed. Because of this, the Puritan flocks brought their shepherds over with them; many of these clergymen had been educated at Emmanuel College, the Puritan stronghold at Cambridge University.

The Puritans derived their name from their goal of purifying the Church of England from within. They regarded themselves as nonseparating congregationalists and disapproved of the "rigid separation" of sectarians like the Pilgrims. They drew upon the same authorities for their congregationalism, however, and when they arrived, extended fellowship to the Plymouth colonists. Yet they could not join them in going all the way and incurring the stigma of schism. While the Puritans were convinced that the congregational and not the episcopal polity was what God intended, they engaged in casuistry to demonstrate that the Church of England, despite its hierarchy, contained enough of a substratum of congregationalism to warrant classification as a "true church" from which it was wrong to separate. At Massachusetts Bay, the Puritans had a rare opportunity; they could profess communion with the Church of England but, out of reach of Laud and the king, set up an autonomous congregational model of what the Church should be and hope their brethren at home would follow it in attempting to reform the Church of England. For many Puritan settlers, the religious motive may have been secondary to secular considerations, but the leaders were on an "errand into the wilderness." John Winthrop spoke of building a "city on a hill" that would be a beacon to the world.

Scholars who have labeled the Massachusetts Bay government of the first generation a "theocracy," have probably been misled by the analogy with ancient Israel so often made by the Puritans. The charter of 1629 clearly put the power in civil hands and company leaders were careful to maintain secular supremacy and a separation at all times. The church was subordinate, the clergy being consulted only intermittently on important religious matters. The state did strive to enforce godliness and interfered in church affairs on occasion, but the reverse did not occur; the church did not intervene in secular affairs unless invited. Pastors were circumspect in their election sermons and did not seek to challenge the power of the state directly. In the oft-quoted phrase of a contemporary, the Puritan society was a "speaking aristocracy in the face of a silent democracy"; this suggests not so much an all-powerful ministry as an oligarchy of elders, pious laymen who were good administrators determined to hold to a middle course between episcopal regimentation and sectarian anarchy in the New World.

This system of semi-presbyterianism was possible because the Puritan leaders had commercial and political experience; wealth and education was diffused among them to a greater extent than among the sectarians. The Puritans were not yeomen but townspeople, including a number of gentlemen. So many of these self-reliant folk sailed over in the Great Migration of 1630–40 that, although disease and the frontier took their customary toll, the New England settlements were populous from the outset and never in real economic straits. Many of the newcomers were from London, but the chief source was East Anglia, a region of England with a noticeable genetic and intellectual infusion from the Continent because of the proximity of Holland and northern France just across the Channel. East Anglia had already felt the first ripples of the coming industrialism, as the techniques of textile manufacture were carried across the Channel from the Low Countries and mills were set up, creating larger towns and an urban style of life.

One of the significant Continental influences the Puritans brought from East Anglia to the New World was the logic of Petrus Ramus. The Puritans were not Biblical literalists but theologians inclined to build their creed by extracting axioms from the scriptures. Ramus, the Calvinistic controversialist from Picardy, provided them with an improved method of reasoning, an alternative to the Aristotelian system that was largely the property of scholars in the Anglo-Catholic tradition. The Puritans needed a less metaphysical scheme that would regulate conduct, that was practical and self-evident, yet remained abstract enough to be respectable when combined with revealed religion. Ramus' logic fulfilled this requirement; he relied on fewer deductions and syllogisms than Aristotle and therefore claimed to be more "natural." The Ramists assumed the pre-existence of truth, and sought to fashion their arguments so precisely and congruently that these formulations would become self-evident, actually standing for the truths themselves. The Ramist logic was essentially a system for classifying individual, self-evident propositions in such a way that one led inexorably to another. By means of Ramus' "golden rules of art," axioms were laid out in schematic sequence; instead of erecting a pyramid of deductions from a few premises at the top, the Ramists offered a road to reality with self-evident axioms as reassuring signposts along the way.

The Puritans revered logic as a divine gift; they accepted it as the work of God even from pagan philosophers. When young Harvard undergraduates studied the trivium of the liberal arts, Ramist logic was pre-eminent, and rhetoric was put in a subordinate position, reduced to gestures and ornaments that would increase receptivity to arguments already contrived. By this separation, the Puritans ensured that the arguments were intrinsically sound, and not affected by the mode of presentation. Consequently, theology buttressed by the liberal arts was not only good intellectual exercise but excellent preparation for organizing the world outside. As long as the New England Puritans could sustain their piety, harnessing Ramist logic and congregational polity to it, they could energize their followers for God, for learning, philanthropy, government, business—and war.

In building a rationale for independence, patriots always give heightened emphasis to the roots of their prospective nation; for 18th century Americans, the relevant pattern was, therefore, the one set by the first generation. Settlers had come to Virginia, Massachusetts, and New Netherland; they had dispersed to Connecticut, New Hampshire and Rhode Island. These colonists had in common a nagging fear of Spanish Catholicism; although the Armada against England had failed in 1588, the Spanish were still aggressive and

English and Dutch Protestants arriving in the New World retained their strong prejudices. Partly as a result, the American settlements also had in common a Calvinistic outlook; this was reinforced by the Geneva Bible of 1560, which was not supplanted in popularity by the King James Version until the 1640s. The Protestants in England and Holland, after freeing themselves from Rome, had later to face major controversies within their ranks between Calvinists and Arminians. While these divisions did not come to America in the early years, they seemed in the long run to have been conducive to an awareness of individual conscience, to civil as well as religious liberty, and to the separation of powers in government. These tendencies *did* filter across the Atlantic and were intensified by the American wilderness.

The Glacial Age

The phrase, "Glacial Age," has usually been applied to New England after the passing of the first generation. The term suggests not only that the Puritans became preoccupied with frontier hardships and the things of this world, but that their religious orthodoxy contributed to a cultural stagnation in these years. Historian James Truslow Adams, who took an extreme libertarian and anti-Puritan view, claimed that progress in New England stopped early—in 1637, with the expulsion of Mistress Anne Hutchinson for heresy—and did not resume until 1761 when James Otis asserted the natural rights of man against the King's general warrants. Actually, a Glacial Age of varying length has been common to all immigrant groups to America and was not solely a phenomenon of colonial New England. It may be defined as a second, third and fourth generation pause (even longer if the cultural barrier is great) when newcomers are concentrating on gaining a livelihood while assimilating into a new environment; this is simply the price of emigration and relocation into a new society or different culture. For the first settlers in the 17th century, dates for the onset of the Glacial Age would vary slightly from colony to colony: in Virginia, 1625, when it became royal; in Plymouth, 1657, when William Bradford, lone college graduate and perennial governor, died; in New Netherland, 1664, when the British navy first conquered the region; in Puritan New England, 1649, when Charles I was beheaded and the colonists were disappointed in Cromwell's dictatorial regime in Britain.

Even in their Glacial Age, the Puritans produced more ideas and writings than the other colonists, as will be indicated. It is, of course, possible that the New Englanders would have flowered even more with a different type of religion, but the converse seems more likely: that the cultural superiority of the region was *because* of their religiosity, theology, logic and polity and the subtle effects these engendered, and not *in spite of* these influences.

The Nadir of Puritan Piety

By 1649 it was already apparent that the military victory of the Puritans over Charles I did not augur the peaceful triumph of a purified, Calvinistic and congregational national church in Britain. Cromwell was a Calvinist, but he was harried on the right by Arminian Anglicans, and much more on the left by antinomian sectarians who had emerged during the war and posed the threat of millennial anarchy. Yet the emigration of Puritans to New England had stopped, and Puritan leaders in the New World with university educations were dying off, being replaced by native-born graduates of Harvard College. There was no religious utopia to go home to, and Puritans of the American variety were all alone in the world.

Isolated from England, and with piety declining, the Puritans were put more and more on the defensive. This was reflected particularly in their fast day sermons. From the beginning, the Massachusetts Bay General Court had deemed days of collective humiliation important; the first pastors had taken such occasions to remind the people of their special covenant obligations and to enumerate and "improve" upon the various afflictions—storms, droughts, pestilence, shipwrecks and Indian raids—that God imposed on his Chosen People because of their lapses. The second generation clergy made this device of the fast day sermon a major weapon in resisting the "declension" of the Wilderness Zion, but altered the emphasis. Instead of dwelling on the details of the disasters provoked by the Puritans' sins, the ministers treated the sins themselves as disasters; they examined directly the failings of the people. They took their doctrine from the prophets of the Old Testament, holding that the colony was being pursued for its sins because the inhabitants were falling away from their covenant pledges. With less imagery and subtlety than their predecessors, the clergy outlined God's controversy with

New England and offered for "uses" or applications, various plans of reformation. Pastoral skill was measured by the ability to evoke tears, arouse guilt and depict the judgments that might yet befall an unrepentant society. These lamentations were voiced increasingly on public occasions and were refined and stylized into a ritual with a definite literary form. This type of sermon has been called, after the prophet, a "jeremiad."

Despite the efforts of the pastors, these jeremiads, even on the eve of 1684 when the sacred Massachusetts charter was revoked, did not seem to produce the desired results. Often they drew yawns instead of tears. Some churchgoers were "sermon-proof," and others felt a certain pride at hearing themselves compared unfavorably with their saintly forebears. Nevertheless, in printed form the jeremiads sold well enough to monopolize the lone printing press at Cambridge, and the pastors concentrated on them to the exclusion of more ambitious or speculative theological tracts.

The clergy, after enduring many years of the protracted downswing in piety, adjusted to it by conceding that there could be cycles in Protestant Christian history. Whereas the earlier Puritans had confidently penned narratives depicting more or less steady progress toward the Kingdom, punctuated only by brief and minor afflictions, Puritan scholars of the late 17th century acknowledged wider swings and longer setbacks. Cotton Mather, in his history of King Philip's War, claimed that the Indians were successful in the war until their depredations exactly matched New England's transgressions; only then did God relent and bring the Puritan victory. Decline and recovery, rather than the progressively upward slope of history, fitted New England's condition and expectation at this time.

The Reforming Synod of 1679 examined but did not arrest the decline in piety. For a long time afterward, however, the Jeremiahs used the synod's catalogue of sins to arraign the people. At the top of this list was "secret apostasy," meaning outward conformity that concealed lack of commitment—dutiful behavior and the confusion of morality with grace that suggested a drift to popery. While there was virtually no overt opposition to the leaders, public spirit was weak, and the clergy resented popular indifference toward churchly and scholarly matters. The majority of Puritans were evidently guilty, above all, of the synod's tenth indictment, "inordinate affection for the world."

With the advent of the new charter in 1691, political alignments became much more secular, and the Mather faction invoked the jeremiads with greater intensity. The religious message had to be accommodated to the new conditions: a royal charter and toleration. But the Mathers did not think that the liberty of conscience associated with William and Mary and the Act of Toleration meant the liberty to sin. They believed that the royal governor, although an Anglican, was still obliged to enforce support of the locally orthodox clergy, and to insist that "true" doctrines be taught. The people had to be reminded that there had been no real break between the old charter and the new, between 1684 and 1691; they were still in special covenant with God.

During this time of troubles, foreign critics actually took the New Englanders' sermons at face value and concluded that New England was a decadent society. The Puritans, convinced that actually they were morally superior to most societies in the world at that time, reacted by de-emphasizing past shortcomings that outsiders might misconstrue and concentrating on the future—issuing dire prophecies for an unrepentant New England. Faced with mounting apathy, some pastors became shrill and catastrophic in their predictions.

Of course, only a fraction of the sermons took this form. By the early 18th century, preaching in most churches had become instructional rather than exhortatory. The zealous first generation clergy had memorized their sermons for "live" delivery, but in later years, notes and manuscripts appeared. Some young clerics were even facetious at the expense of their bewildered flocks. Pleasant discourses coincided with the empty pews universally reported after 1700.

When the 100th anniversary of Massachusetts Bay arrived in 1730, the jeremiad was still in use. There were new sins—gaming, fraud, indebtedness, female drunkenness—to be added to the 1679 list and pastors spoke more often about sins in the business world, although details were avoided. They recommended moderation and condemned idleness yet were careful not to decry economic progress, only its evil consequences.

The principal effect of the jeremiad was the reinforcement of filiopietism. For almost three generations Puritans had heard their history retold and their ancestors praised in extravagant terms. While the founders would have been revered in any case, the peculiar conjunction of the covenant theology with the errand into the wilderness intensified this attitude. In seeking to conserve as much as possible of the original piety and polity, the clergy turned themselves into a caste and turned their followers—the relatively few who took them seriously—into moralistic antiquarians.

Fortunately for the orthodox party, the jeremiad was not their only device for resuscitating the Puritan spirit; Cotton Mather had another that proved somewhat more effective: the reform society. He saw the need, particularly after the decline of clerical power under the new charter, to reach beyond church members into the barns and countinghouses of many erstwhile Puritans. To move these practical folk, he would have to eschew scholastic speculation and sectarian dogmas, and concentrate on the heart of Christianity. By making common objects "engines of piety," by teaching people to see God in everything about them, perhaps he could broaden and eventually reunite the Puritan community. Mather was reacting to the "declension" in New England, but he was encouraged and re-assured in this policy when he learned of the flowering of Pietism in Germany, and the blossoming of reform societies in Britain, or-ganized by the Nonconformists to rally devotional spirit in the pop-ulace there. His decision to dispense with theological disputation and seek a pietistic consensus was in accord with the trend of Euro-pean Protestantism a generation after the religious upheavals of the English Civil War.

To this end Cotton Mather directed much of his prodigious energy and talent for "scribbling." In manual after manual he sought to reduce the vitals of Christianity to the lowest capacity and the briefest compass—he got it down to a single sheet. He prepared pamphlets of instruction for each occupation, showing people how to find God while on the job, and among the tools of their trade. To revive piety Mather was, in practice, ready to forgo his Calvin-ism. He urged people to perform good works for subjective satis-faction, the sheer joy of it. He did not remind them that good works without grace were not saving.

With this practical godliness, Mather and his colleagues hoped not only to return New England to its errand, but to regain their pastoral status and influence by bringing back into subordination a world that had grown beyond their control. To promote godliness, Mather recommended reform societies on the British model, urging pastors to support them as a force for virtue in the community, and also as a means to dampen antiministerial sentiment, a greater problem in some places than simple apathy.

In these reform societies we see the prototypes of the volunteer associations that foreign commentators later praised as distinctive in American life. But the societies not only diffused piety and benevolence; they also spun a web of interdependence and conformity. Thus, the Puritans bequeathed America not only the guided democracy of the town meeting, but a version of the reform society. The legacy was civic pride and moral busybodyism, the social gospel of the Rotarians and the Babbittry of Main Street. The societies promoted more efficiency than godliness; in the dynamic New England of Mather's last days, do-good organizations could only check the religious ebb tide, not reverse it. It was later, during the the 19th century, when the jeremiad was a vestige and when separation of church and state had become official, that the reform society finally came into its own.

Another strategy for halting the decline was to modify standards for church membership. The Puritans settling in America had established a requirement for admission that was unique and excruciating; public relation of the experience of saving grace. Could this test, set in the fervid days of persecution and exodus, be maintained in the following generation after the Spirit withdrew and the Saints developed some attachment to their corner of the New World? Within a generation it became clear that the answer was no. Baptized children of the Saints—the term used for those in communion—were reaching adulthood and even begetting children without the conversion experience that would confirm them as members of the church and the community. The problem became acute when these baptized but unregenerated heirs requested baptism for *their* children, the third generation.

A synod tried to solve this problem in 1662. The clergymen agreed that baptized but unconverted adults, although not communicants, had not lost their connection with the church. If they could not testify to their conversion, they were urged instead to publicly "own the covenant." That is, they were asked to demonstrate some understanding of Christian precepts, assent to the church creed and discipline, and acknowledge the obligation on them deriving from their baptism in infancy. The synod made the incentive for "owning" a strong one; only those renewing their baptismal covenant in this manner could receive baptism for their children. The compromise came to be known as the Half Way Covenant because persons who "owned" might never go on to full communion.

The opponents of the halfway plan were numerous and vocal. Generally speaking, they were the surviving English-educated pastors and the older laity, including a majority of the Deputies of the Massachusetts Assembly. Their strongest argument was, of course, that the Synod was betraying the fundamental tenet of the founders by admitting those who were not visible Saints; even though the "owners" would be kept in halfway status, denied the Supper and the vote for church officers, nonetheless, the flock would be diluted by moral neuters. The sacred New England Way of polity would be so modified as to be tantamount to European Presbyterianism wherein everyone who was not of "scandalous conversation" could join the church by mere assent.

The advocates of the halfway plan were less logical and more pragmatic. They were trying to conserve as much as they could of the Holy Experiment. They knew that unless members were added to the churches soon, under a new formula, the rule of the visible Saints, resting on a very small percentage of adult males, would become precarious. Above all, they wanted to be assured that their progeny were not lost to the faith, that their heirs would at least be baptized and grow up under the watch and care of the church.

There were also rationalizations for this seeming innovation. Perhaps the founding fathers in their ardor had veered too far toward separatism; the Half Way Covenant was the way back, a move closer to the practice of European Protestants. There was truth to the argument that after decrying Anglo-Catholic formalism, New England Puritans had fallen into a formalism of their own in their attitude toward public profession, so that what counted was not so much the actual state of a person's soul, but rather what his neighbors thought it was. Since most theologians had conceded that some who professed conversion were hypocrites, and only God knew the list of the truly saved, why not take the additional step and presume grace for the baptized children? And "owning," like the "relation" of the religious experience, still meant testimony in front of the flock and a vote on the "performance," so that the congregational principle of assent was retained. Owners of the covenant, moreover, could be presumed to have more than natural ability, to be "enabled" to respond to the pastor's demands; if they breached their covenants, they could be consigned to a particularly unattractive section of hell. Proponents also claimed that this double track system would preserve rather than lower admission standards:

pastors could relieve the pressure by admitting covenant members but still reserve full communion for the genuinely gracious few.

The liberals forced the compromise through the Synod and then spent thirty years combatting the stubborn opposition. When clerical power drove the resisters out of the government, they took refuge in the small towns. The Pilgrims of the Old Colony never did adopt the Half Way Plan in any numbers.

Despite the enlarged congregations resulting from the halfway plan, the clergy, for a variety of reasons, continued to lose power and prestige. At the turn of the century, the Mathers and their party decided that to protect dissenter churches under a royal charter, it was necessary to presbyterianize the polity, to create a strong ministerial association and impose a system of standing councils on the individual churches. In Massachusetts, the five church associations in the east, and the ministerial association, a social group dating from the foundation, endorsed such a plan, known as the Proposals of 1705. But prominent citizens denounced the scheme as a serious departure from the almost pure congregationalism of the "New England Way" and the legislature, having become quite secular, wanted no renaissance of clerical power. Although proponents argued that powerful councils were needed to settle disputes and restore order in the churches, the Proposals did not pass; this was a major defeat for the Mathers.

In Connecticut, however, the drift to presbyterianism was of long standing. The trustees of the new college (Yale) led the drive for the Saybrook Platform, the counterpart of the Proposals. The colony was not royal and church-state relations were close under the charter, so that when the elected governor, who was a minister, gave his support, the Saybrook Platform was approved in 1708. Ministers had to join associations and churches had to join consociations in each county. When a few obstinate churches refused to consociate and proclaimed the earlier Cambridge Platform, they were denied fellowship and, more significantly, had to support themselves without the taxing power. The consociationism of Connecticut undoubtedly conserved ministerial prerogative and dignity, and protected an increasingly professional clergy from excesses of opinion among the laity, but by itself neither helped nor hindered piety and evangelism.

The crisis over church polity in Massachusetts and Connecticut had already occurred when John Wise published his philippics against consociationism. Nevertheless, *The Churches Quarrel*

Espoused (1710) and *A Vindication of the Government of New England Churches* (1717) were clear and forceful polemics that had some immediate influence and were reprinted on the eve of the Revolution. Wise evidently believed that the best course was to hold fast to the purity of the New England Way of congregationalism and avoid the stultifying effect on religion that would inevitably come with too close an alliance with secular government. On the basis of his two essays, many scholars have hailed Wise—usually in the company of Roger Williams—as a precursor of the American Enlightenment, of separation of church and state, and of modern democracy.

Wise has gained favor with historians of this century partly because of his origins and the positions he took in the many controversies of the day. He was the son of an indentured servant, yet graduated from Harvard College. In 1687, he defied Sir Edmund Andros with the cry of "no taxation without representation" when the hated governor tried to impose taxes without the consent of the Massachusetts assembly. He tried to reverse the convictions of the Salem witches. He sided with the younger clergy against the older laity in favoring singing by note instead of by rote in church. Later in life he supported colonial paper money and agreed with an old adversary, Cotton Mather, that inoculation for smallpox should be tried. This consistently liberal record tended to confirm these modern historians in their generous estimates of his works on church government. They enjoyed his equation of reason and revelation and his promise to "divert" the reader by taking an unbeaten path —supporting congregationalism by natural reason. John Wise's secular tone, lucid style, and anticlerical argument suggested to them a kind of native-born *philosophe*, America's first philosophical democrat.

But Wise, pastor of Chebacco parish in Ipswich, was a rather obscure figure. He left neither diaries nor published sermons so his theology can only be conjectured. Because he used the Light of Nature so skillfully in his essays to buttress his scriptural case for a democratic church polity, liberals have assumed that he was certainly not an orthodox Calvinist, and probably was somewhat deistical.

Circumstantial evidence—a combination of belief and behavior— suggests he may have been orthodox, after all. Wise condemned Arianism, a form of unitarianism, as "damnable." When the Salem witch scare was at its peak, Wise was one of the leaders who sought to save the accused Proctor family not by denying the existence of witches, but merely by arguing that the Devil could not impersonate innocent victims. He was tall and muscular and had a reputation as a wrestler. According to legend, a Captain Chandler challenged the minister, who consented reluctantly because he was a man of the cloth. Wise won the two bouts they had, and in the second, threw his opponent over a low stone wall, whereupon the Captain got to his feet and good-humoredly asked the parson to throw over his horse and he would be on his way. As a chaplain, Wise took an active part in King Philip's War and in an expedition against Quebec; in the latter campaign he accused the commander of cowardice. Generally in colonial history, such vigor and aggressiveness in a minister indicated Calvinistic leanings. And Wise's eldest son, the scholarly Jeremiah, who graduated from Harvard in 1700, lived up to his name, and was the most evangelical Calvinist in the Maine District during the Great Awakening.

An examination of Wise's intellectual sources also casts doubt on his liberalism and modernity. In writing the *Vindication*, he relied on some Puritan divines but apparently drew his principal inspiration—and some *verbatim* passages—from an English translation of Baron von Pufendorf's *De Jure Naturae et Gentium* (1672). The German professor of jurisprudence had not directly focused, in this early work, on church-state relations; but even later when he had perfected his position, his views on church and state were complex and ambiguous, strongly conditioned by the circumstances of Lutheran Europe in the late 17th century, and by the continuing claims of the Catholic Church. The Baron's conception of religious toleration was not, therefore, as modern as that of John Locke. If Wise was the disciple of Pufendorf rather than Locke, one must infer that the Ipswich parson favored duality over synthesis, that he was more concerned with preserving the congregational piety of the church from the corrupt hand of the state, than with the more secular position of freeing the state from religious interference.

There are good reasons accordingly for second thoughts about Wise's presumed secularism. While he was emphatic in defending the congregational polity of the Puritans' Cambridge Platform of 1648 as both scriptural and in accord with reason, he was less definite about the form civil government should take. In fact, he noted that God did not prescribe any one model; this would vary with the climate and the people. He thought all governments ought to secure liberty and yet admitted that great inequalities inevitably arose when man moved from the natural to the civil state. Like so many colonials in the generation after 1688, the Ipswich minister praised Britain as the best exemplar of mixed government. In this he showed some affinity with both the Puritan Founding Fathers and the Real Whigs then emerging in Britain. His political optimism and sharp wit annoyed the Mathers, but he had no organized following. John Wise, an enlightened rationalist for his time and place, was not yet a secular democrat but a precursor of the Spirit of '76, as well as the Age of Reason.

New England's Early Enlightenment

As godliness diminished and the errand into the wilderness encountered difficulties, it was inevitable that some *rapprochement* would occur with segments of British society, mainly middle class Nonconformists, but even with the upper class Anglicans. During the first years of New England settlement, the Puritans had been a transatlantic community, with much traffic back and forth. The settlers in America had seen themselves as merely in exile, awaiting the triumph of their brethren at home. But the Great Migration to New England ended in 1640 and it was apparent soon afterward that the utopia Cromwell and his allies were imposing on England was quite different from the ideal of the American Puritans. The estrangement of the two Puritan communities deepened when the Commonwealth failed and the monarchy was restored; the trade laws of both Cromwell and Charles II threatened the commercial patterns that were already vital to the New England economy.

New Englanders had become isolated and provincial, but by their flagrant smuggling and severe persecution of Quakers and Baptists, they drew attention to their particularism and incurred the disapproval of the Crown. In their own defense, Puritan leaders were forced to concern themselves again with English affairs. The new royal charter, the increased efficiency of new mercantilistic controls and the invasion by missionaries of the Church of England pulled New England closer to the metropolis; and the initial enthusiasm of the colonists for the Glorious Revolution and William and Mary was another centripetal force. In addition, the beginning of the long, intermittent warfare with the French put a military burden on New England, aroused the people against the Papists and savages, and inevitably drew them into closer identification with the Empire.

The Mather faction had only minimal success in developing religious alternatives to replace the oligarchical control of the first generations, and as a consequence the Puritans were vulnerable to new, fashionable ideas from Britain. At this time New England seemed receptive to Newton and the Enlightenment. In fact, the clergy were conscious transmitters of the new reasonable and liberal currents in religion.

Above all, prosperity, particularly in the seaboard towns, brought obvious class divisions and created a "better sort" whose adherence to the Puritan faith was socio-cultural rather than pious; for this group the tug of British upper class standards was growing and many were tempted to shift their allegiance. After the turn of the century, the Brattle Street Church and the Anglican chapels offered such opportunities.

The Mathers and the orthodox party were finally challenged directly in their own citadel, Boston, when some wealthy merchants undertook the founding of Brattle Street Church. The "Undertakers" —John Leverett and the Brattle brothers, William and Thomas— were already the Mathers' foes in the struggle for control of Harvard College. The new church, Boston's Fourth, issued a "Manifesto" proclaiming its departure from the New England Way. The church proposed to baptize any child, and to accept mere visible sanctity for admission to communion. Instead of assent by hand vote, church members' silence would signify the approval of newcomers. Only at the candidate's request would relation of religious experience be heard and then by the pastor alone and not the congregation. The minister would be chosen by all members, not just the males. There were modifications of the liturgy, also. The pastor would give the Lord's Prayer and read aloud from scripture; this change, of course, was decried by orthodox Puritans who called it "dumb reading" and popery.

The Mathers found much to criticize in the organization of this church. The Brattle Street group announced its conformity with the United Brethren, the union of English Presbyterian and Independent dissenters. Mather had at one time endorsed but later backed away from this group. Worse than this, however, was the Undertakers' assertion that the principle of assent in congregational polity came from Nature instead of covenant theology; they shocked the Mathers by finding no warrant for covenants in the word of God!

Leverett and William Brattle induced the merchants to choose Benjamin Colman as pastor of the new church. As ex-tutors at Harvard, they remembered the precocious Colman favorably as a student who had been receptive to rationalism and Anglican authors. At this time, he was preaching in England and they arranged for his ordination by English Presbyterians to avoid running the gauntlet of the Mathers in Massachusetts. Nevertheless, when young Colman settled on Brattle Street, fellowship with Boston's other churches was extended only grudgingly after negotiation. Colman's foreign and non-congregational ordination drew a rebuke from Cotton Mather: "To say that a *Wandering Levite* who has no Flock is a Pastor, is as good sense as to say, that he that has no children is a Father."

In England, Colman had tried to preach in several towns but his delivery was too polite and legalistic to satisfy the folk; he was able, however, to adapt to the taste of Bath, the "wicked" resort community. In his Bath sermons of 1698, he clearly reflected the strong early currents of the Age of Reason.

Colman sought to defend reasonable religion with natural and scientific arguments. Inspired by Newton and Boyle, he aimed to show that science and religion were not incompatible but in complete accord; and because Colman, like these natural philosophers, was close to deism himself, he worried about a further drift—to open materialism and atheism. His knowledge of science was not strong. He was aware of Newton's gravity, the "secret magick" in the center of the earth, and the atoms that "hooked" together to form matter. Yet Colman, when compared with earlier New Englanders, seemed to be sensitive to a wider range of aesthetic stimuli, and he chose to celebrate Nature in general. Like a blind man recovering his sight, he was full of wonder and admiration at God's artistry in making the world.

Colman, as a rationalist, did not invoke prerogatives for Christianity but merely defended it in the manner he would defend any philosophy. He proved God's existence by asserting his own—Descartes' *Cogito Ergo Sum*—and cited Nature, adding revelation only as corroboration.

Thus Colman was a good choice for Boston's "Manifesto Church." He was a pleasant latitudinarian who concentrated on style and method, conveying a "free and catholic spirit" without seeking controversy. Respectable men were drawn to him and very many ladies were enraptured by his musical accents. He was fashionable; he was even able to convince young clerics of the Mather party that the narrow controversialism of the 17th century had become bad form. He substituted Addisonian essays for New England's rigid sermon formula of doctrine, reasons, and uses. While he remained formally within the bounds of Calvinism, he wrote and spoke of the doctrines cheerfully, urging his audience to accept and learn to live with their God-given limitations. In his preference for moderation, decorum, elegance, music and mirth—the smiling side of life—Colman was trying to bridge a culture gap, to bring Boston Puritans closer to the trend of English society.

He proved his catholicity and pliability over the years by staying on good terms with various religious leaders in both England and New England; in the latter case he managed this even during the divisive period of the Great Awakening. His writing helped him as a leader and spokesman; he had ninety titles to his credit, second only to Cotton Mather. When, in 1705, liberals wrested control of Harvard from the Mathers, Colman and Brattle Street Church assumed a commanding influence over the graduates and consequently over religion in eastern Massachusetts and New Hampshire. Given the Colman style and sensibility, it is easy to see this region as the future home of Unitarianism and Transcendentalism.

Yet the line is not perfect; Colman was somewhat more of an aristocrat than his 19th century heirs. Compared to his contemporaries in the hinterlands, he lacked the common touch or an interest in politics. Was this because his parents had not emigrated from England until 1673? Generally, Puritans who survived the Interregnum and were Nonconformists under Charles II, were "burned out," lacking the strong evangelical piety of Puritanism in its ascendancy. In short, Colman was a colonial English gentleman, and not an incipient American.

For those yearning for tradition and not satisfied with Colman's compromise with British culture, there was the Church of England, with missionaries eager to proselytize among the Puritans. The first Anglican church in the region was King's Chapel in Boston, established by Governor Andros in 1686; the populace was alarmed by it and broke a few windows. At this time, the only persons complaining of the lack of Anglican services were royal officials and their families.

The Glorious Revolution and the settlement of William and Mary, however, raised hopes of a reunited British Protestantism, of English Nonconformists and New England congregationalists somehow "comprehended" within an enlarged Church of England. But the old differences in England could not be erased and the "comprehension" bill failed. Instead, the Act of Toleration provided that those who believed in the Trinity but still were unwilling to forget the past and embrace the established church could worship in their own meetinghouses. Even so, it became apparent that Crown and Parliament, inspired by the 1688 Revolution, intended, if they could, to rationalize the Empire, and to homogenize the American colonies both politically and religiously.

New England was the prime target because covenant Calvinism and congregationalism was entrenched there. Although New Englanders, out of expediency, had accepted avowed Anglicans into their churches and colleges, and never treated them harshly as they had the early evangelical Quakers and Baptists, English authorities were well aware of the hostility to the mother church in that region. Congregationalists should not have been surprised that the Society for the Propagation of the Gospel in Foreign Parts, (the S.P.G.) chartered to work among the Indians, Negroes, and frontier whites, also intended to plant the Church of England in the Puritans' rocky soil.

Actually New Englanders retained a naively optimistic view of England's early constitutional monarchs; only when it became overwhelmingly apparent that Queen Anne was going to impose a bishop on America, did they react. With the support of the Bishop of London and the Archbishop of Canterbury, Anne was on the threshold of authorizing the bishop in 1714 when she died suddenly; the episcopal movement subsided but did not disappear and the colonists learned to be watchful.

In 1719 John Checkley, bookseller and apothecary in Boston, published Leslie's *The Religion of Jesus Christ the Only Religion;* the book contained Ignatius' proofs of the existence of bishops in apostolic days. A few months later, he brought forth *Choice Dialogues,* a direct attack on Calvinism and the foundations of New England Congregationalism.

In some ways Checkley was typical of a generation of Bostonians who grew to manhood after the provincial charter. The only son of English-born Puritans, he attended Ezekiel Cheever's Boston Latin School. After study at Oxford, he spent fifteen years as a dilettante in Europe, studying, traveling and collecting paintings. Unlike his well-to-do contemporaries, however, who came back from the Continent enlightened but safe in the ancestral faith, Checkley returned to Boston an avowed Anglican. His wide reading had convinced him of the importance of apostolic succession. When he opened his shop it immediately gained a reputation as a headquarters for seditious Anglicans. Worried authorities passed a law permitting justices to require an oath of allegiance from anyone suspected of disaffection with local government or the king. Of all the persons in Boston, only Checkley was challenged; twice he refused to take the oath to Massachusetts and was fined.

He remained a thorn in the side of the Congregational establishment for more than a decade. His *Modest Proof* (1723) provoked a pamphlet war and he was found guilty of seditious libel, escaping again with a fine. His eloquent defense in this case was published in 1730, perhaps winning a few to his cause. Checkley complained to England of the hardships episcopalians suffered in Massachusetts and finally obtained orders in 1738. Apparently he was so rash and controversial a figure that the Anglican authorities hesitated before giving offense to the Congregationalists by ordaining him.

From Checkley's shop the Anglican infection spread into some less fashionable circles. Prior to the Great Awakening, Anglicans were moderately successful on three different fronts in New England. They established enclaves all along the coast; often this involved merely organizing isolated and inactive Anglicans. Missionaries assisted in the formation of churches from Piscataqua in the Maine District to Stratford in Connecticut; Bristol in the Old Colony was a particular haven. And from their base at Rye, New York, Anglicans infiltrated sparsely settled western Connecticut. In the three counties of the former Plymouth Colony, and in adjacent Rhode Island many of the sons of Baptists and Quakers were growing up in ignorance and inclined to revile all religion. They were vehement against the established orthodoxy of Massachusetts and Connecticut. Churchmen found these dissenters, nominal members of sects characteristically weak in theology and prone to Arminianism, a promising group for missionary work. When the Reverend James Honeyman started services in Providence in 1720, he had to preach outdoors to accommodate the crowds. The stay of Bishop George Berkeley in

Newport—from 1728 to 1731—enhanced the prestige of the Church in Rhode Island.

The S.P.G. moved into these pockets of separatism and apathy, bringing knowledge and books. The missionaries often were well received, not because of any sympathy for prelacy, but because of anti-Puritanism; and also because the Churchmen were subsidized from abroad so that their services were free. Those who disliked the Calvinistic establishments could rally around the banner of their strongest adversary, the Church of England.

The royal governor abetted the cause by inducing Massachusetts to extend limited religious tax exemption to Anglicans in 1727, despite the pro-dissenter bias of the Walpole ministry in England. Churchmen were now free to support their own minister if they lived within five miles of the church, but still might be liable if taxes for the orthodox Congregational minister proved insufficient. In 1735 the Anglicans of Massachusetts received additional concessions that finally put them on a par with the Baptists and the Quakers. Under pressure, Connecticut had enacted its own version of a Toleration Act, but Anglicans there still had cause for complaint.

The most spectacular victory for the Church of England occurred after the Yale College Commencement in 1722. Rector Timothy Cutler used Anglican phraseology in his closing prayer: "and let all people say, amen." The next day in the College library, Cutler and tutors Samuel Johnson and Daniel Brown surprised a board of inquiry by denying the validity of presbyterian ordinations, endorsing the episcopalian mode, and defiantly declaring for the Church of England. Four previously orthodox ministers from neighboring communities joined in "the Great Apostasy." The College trustees immediately "excused" the Rector and tutors and, to prevent any recurrence, required the faculty to subscribe to the Saybrook Confession. Later at a public debate, the four fellow-traveling clergy recanted under pressure, but Cutler, Johnson and Brown were adamant in their new beliefs.

Some weeks later the three apostates sailed to England for Anglican orders. Brown died of smallpox, but Cutler and Johnson returned to plant high church Anglicanism in New England. The S.P.G. gave Cutler the new Christ Church in Boston, and Johnson was assigned to his home town of Stratford, making him the first settled Anglican rector in Connecticut.

According to Johnson, the chief reason for the Yale defections from Congregationalism was the Dummer library gift of 1714. Jeremiah Dummer, Connecticut's agent in London, had persuaded Elihu Yale and other prominent men to contribute books to the young college. A number of scientists—Isaac Newton, Edmund Halley, William Whitson, and John Woodward—responded by sending their works; volumes by Boyle and Locke were also shipped. The majority of donors, including Yale himself, were Anglicans. Dummer's gift of eight hundred titles, although diversified, slighted Nonconformity and leaned toward rationalistic Anglican authors upholding Arminian theology and episcopal polity.

For some time there had been rumors about a "Satan's bookshelf" that threatened Yale with Arminianism. Several orthodox pastors had publicly expressed anxiety about the trouble and confusion such heresy could pose for Connecticut's Standing Order. Dummer's Trojan horse, however, simply accelerated a trend toward scepticism already present among students bored and disgusted by the outworn scholasticism of Yale's curriculum. At Johnson's suggestion Bishop Berkeley gave Yale a large gift of books in 1732; the College accepted it reluctantly, rightly suspecting that this second donation would also subvert collegiate minds. There had been a similar growth of freethinking at Harvard but it was more gradual and less dramatic; tutors Leverett and Brattle had brought an "enlarged spirit" to the College in 1686 and after that students read some Anglican and deistical authors. The benefactions of Thomas Hollis, a wealthy English Baptist, had increased their opportunities.

Even after their apostasy, Cutler and Johnson retained some influence over Yale students. Johnson shrewdly rejected the Arminian label, arguing that the doctrines of Anglicanism antedated Arminius, but he did concede that Churchmen were not Calvinists. Less contentious than Cutler, he was much more persuasive; by 1740 a dozen Yale graduates had followed him into the Church of England. The initial doubt of the converts concerned polity—they viewed those ordained by congregational and presbyterian methods as "usurpers in the house of God"—but this doubt spread to theology as well. Obviously no one who embraced prelacy held to the covenant Calvinism of the New England Way; they all turned to the essentially Arminian faith of England's mother church.

One fact about the Yale defectors has sometimes been overlooked: their low rank in college. (Yale's rankings were frankly more social than Harvard's.) Johnson himself, later a prominent philosopher and educator, placed eighth in a class of nine; five others were near the bottom in their graduating classes. None were in the upper one-third. Curiosity attracted the converts to Anglican works, but they were receptive—perhaps unconsciously—because they wanted to refute or transcend a religio-social system that rated them so low. They probably recognized that their rankings were a handicap within filiopietistic congregationalism, where it would mean settlement in a poor rural church, but made little difference among colonial Anglicans where membership alone conferred some status.

Despite conspicuous Anglican gains, the defenders of New England congregationalism were united and quite effective. All the parties—those of the Mathers, Colman, and Solomon Stoddard in the west—shared a deep and long-standing fear of bishops. Colman and his followers were particularly articulate foes since, in practice, they differed very little in doctrine and mood from the Anglicans. As latitudinarians they found themselves in direct competition with the Churchmen for the urban elite, and an American bishop would have destroyed their middle position.

After Queen Anne died and the prospect of an American bishop diminished, the Congregationalists turned their fire on the S.P.G. men in New England. The Anglicans' high salaries and demands for a bishop made them disruptive; they were attacked as superfluous, their presence was labeled an insult to God-fearing Christians, and they were accused of admitting excommunicated Calvinists to worship.

In his last years Cotton Mather could find no prominent avowed Arminian in New England, but Jonathan Edwards, assessing religious conditions in Northhampton in 1734, wrote: "About this time began the great noise . . . in this part of the country about Arminianism, which seemed to appear with a very threatening aspect. . . . The friends of vital piety trembled for fear of the issue." Were Edwards and others who raised the cry of Arminianism thinking of the sudden gains of the Church of England or the silent percolation of this doctrine into the Congregationalist ranks? If their fear was of the Anglicans, it was exaggerated. The real danger, as Edwards probably suspected, was not from the S.P.G. men but from young Puritans, the graduates of Harvard College, who were transforming the polite and "catholic" Calvinism of Colman into a covert Arminianism.

Before the Great Awakening, the Church's appeal in New England was limited; it tended to draw from opposite ends of the social order. It attracted well-to-do Anglophiles with good British connections and social ambitions, and families who had settled since 1660. At the other end were sailors and fishermen who could not identify with the Puritan middle class. The motives of these people were obviously more social than intellectual; few studied and convinced themselves, as Checkley and the Yale converts did, of the importance of apostolic succession.

Although the Anglicans pushed into New England under the auspices and subsidy of the English authorities, and at a propitious time when oligarchy and piety were in decline, their episcopal polity was a liability that more than offset their other attractions for most people. The Colman faction, unencumbered by bishops, and with its catholic spirit within the formal bounds of Calvinism was a much greater threat than the Church of England to orthodoxy in the coastal area. The crypto-Arminianism of Colman was more palatable to these folk than the overt anti-Calvinism and prelacy of the Church of England. Even to secularized New Englanders, the prospect of an American bishop with an ecclesiastical court was anathema, a real danger to political as well as religious liberty. For Yankees, polity was an early and potent form of patriotism.

Pennsylvania's Holy Experiment

When William Penn and his party landed on the banks of the Delaware to begin the "holy experiment," the evangelical and prophetic phase of Quakerism had already passed. The movement, born at the religious zenith of the English Civil War, was becoming a sect of some respectability. Members revered the founder, George Fox, and valued his advice, but when he reached middle age he was apt to write epistles instead of following God's "openings" to distant places or presenting the Truth to those averse to hearing it. There was a final spasm of persecution at the end of the reign of Charles II, but "sufferings" were declining and quietism developing; and the Toleration Act of 1689 augured a new era among the Friends.

From the beginning, Quakers encouraged receptivity to "openings" of the Spirit—the touch of the Inner Light, the sound of the Inner Voice; for this antinomian notion of direct communication with God the sect was persecuted in the heroic early days. Rejecting a learned ministry of "hirelings," they had encouraged a priest-hood of all believers, people who would itinerate and were willing to suffer and die—if the opposition were stubborn—to spread the message of the Inner Light. The dignified determination of these common folk—women as well as men, usually with no formal educa-tion—was remarkable. Where the authorities explicitly and vehe-mently denied the principle of the Inner Light, as in New England, Quakers found the compulsion to witness irresistible. But even their tormentors learned to appreciate the power of their conviction, their sincerity, and their physical courage.

Many Friends had settled in the colonies, of course, before Penn established his "inward plantation." Although Quaker itinerants of the first generation—known as Publishers of the Truth or "public" Friends—dreamt of long journeys to confront and convince sultans and maharajahs, the natural seedbeds of Quakerism had proved to be the Calvinistic regions of Europe and America. Because the Inner Light attracted largely those reacting against a Calvinistic *milieu*, Quakers were most successful in England, Holland, Ger-many, and the lowlands of Scotland. Colonial Friends were well distributed by the time of the American Revolution, but in the early days, except for the North Carolina settlement, they tended to gather in close proximity to Calvinistic Puritans—in Rhode Island and Plymouth, on the frontier in New Hampshire and Maine, on Long Island, and in the Jerseys.

Penn was aware of the precedents of Massachusetts Bay and his colony was intended to be an improved version of the Puritan Zion. Like the Puritans, the Quakers saw the New World as a special mission, a place where, freed from tradition and decadence, their particular religious perspective could come into full bloom; they too hoped that the colonial experiment, by its example, would win England, Europe and the world to their ideal, the Truth of the Inner Light. But the difference in time of these two utopian ventures was significant. God's Spirit was very evident in the English-speaking world when the Puritans settled Massachusetts Bay, and the Laudian persecution ensured an emigration of educated Puritan leaders for a decade afterward. In contrast, when Penn laid out his colony, God had withdrawn from Restoration England, and the Friends were turning inward to find Him. To the refugees who were rapidly populating Pennsylvania, the pull of good land was stronger than the push of persecution and intolerance. Furthermore many of them were German Pietists who were familiar with the Inner Light but not the English language. During the last decades of the 17th century, alienation from England was not sufficient to attract able political leaders of the Friendly persuasion to Pennsylvania. Because of their ambivalence—not to learning *per se* but to power and politics— Quakers with such talents were in very short supply in any case. For the same reason that those earlier sectarians, the Pilgrims of Plymouth, relied so greatly and so long on a few pioneers—Bradford, Brewster, Winslow, and Standish—the Quakers had to overwork their short list of statesmen and thinkers—George Fox, Robert Barclay, George Keith and William Penn. By 1700 Fox and Barclay were dead, Keith had turned Anglican, and Penn was remaining in England, troubled by creditors and fighting to protect his proprietorship from the Crown. Thus Pennsylvania, founded when imperial commerce was rising, and blessed with a good climate and soil, would forget its errand into the wilderness and succumb to the world in a shorter time than Massachusetts Bay.

As sectarians the Quakers of course stressed the Inner Light and, as a "second rule," the personal interpretation of the Bible; for this reason they at first rejected as Calvinistic any interest in speculative or systematic theology. A generation went by before young Barclay, a Scottish convert from Presbyterianism, provided the Friends with his *Apology* (1676), an attempt to order their beliefs so that they could defend themselves against rationalistic antagonists. On the bookshelves of rural Friends, Barclay's work, with George Fox and the Bible, formed a lonely trilogy.

Instead of theology, we associate with the Quakers a cluster of perfectionist attitudes and behavior patterns that were set in the Cromwellian days of prophecy and persecution, and reached back, no doubt, to the Anabaptists of the 16th century. A Quaker must refuse to swear an oath of truth or responsibility because this act implies a double standard: that these virtues could be observed only on special occasions, whereas a Quaker must be unremittingly truthful and responsible at all times. He must not put on a military uniform to fight and kill because all men are brothers. He must use the familiar second person form, "thee" and "thou" in addressing everyone and keep his hat on in the presence of magistrates and kings, as a token of social equality, to remind the world that God intended a single order of men. A Quaker must confront an unfair ruler face-to-face in the hope of overwhelming him with the sheer power of belief, and with abstractions like Truth and Justice. The first Quakers, of low social station, naive and with little military or political experience, precluded from negotiation or compromise, had to resort to civil disobedience, passive resistance and the Higher Law in trying to alter a society they could affect in no other way. These tactics seemed natural when they were the only weapons of a despised minority, and together with the gray garb, silent meeting and ascetic meetinghouse, set off the Quakers from the worldlings around them.

But what happened to such sectarians when they were no longer oppressed, when their liberty was secure, and they had to assume the major role in a new society being created in America? Cultural shock has usually been the initial reaction of newcomers to America; immigrants have responded by clinging to Old World values despite altered circumstances. For the Quakers, more than the Puritans, this meant retaining the religious values of the lower middle, rather than the middle class. Some have cited the Quakers' lay ministry as an advantage in the New World, because they did not have the task of recruiting educated pastors from abroad like the Reformed churches; but the lay ministry can also be regarded as a reinforcement of sectarianism and consequently as an impediment to accommodation. The Quakers could not adjust their perspective enough to sustain Pennsylvania as a "holy experiment." To change from a sect to a church, from "novelties" to theology, from ruled to rulers was to ask too much of the "plain people."

Most of the Friends in America grew inward but George Keith was the grand exception; he attacked quietism head on. He charged his fellow Quakers with neglect of the historical Christ, and with claiming the sufficiency of the Inner Light, "without anything else." He called for a public profession of faith and assent to it by the faithful, for preaching of the Word, and more attention to the Bible and less to the teachings of George Fox. Although he had been an eloquent advocate of quietism previously, Keith was impelled to make the classic indictment of antinomianism and inwardness, namely that people guided by the Light tended to become lax in discipline and negligent of good works. Keith seemed to be urging the sect in a churchly direction, yet he nonetheless put purity over politics when he condemned officeholding by ministerial Friends in Pennsylvania.

As the only one of the four Quaker leaders to spend any length of time in the colonies, Keith was bound to have had influence; he led his followers, the "Christian Quakers," out from the main body. Keith's excessive contentiousness and pugnacity probably alienated more people than his doctrines, and his invective brought him into court charged with defamation of character. Like Barclay, Keith was a well-educated convert from Scotch Presbyterianism, and seemed to be reverting under the pressures of the New World. In England he was censured by the Yearly Meeting, and afterward defected to the Anglicans.

Why did Keith choose the Church of England after his schism failed to prosper? Perhaps it was his concern for ritual and good works, or perhaps it was revenge. As an S.P.G. missionary, Keith returned to Pennsylvania to renew his attacks on Quaker quietism.

It is historical fact that those who cultivated the Inner Light became immune to Calvinism—even in its evangelical form, the "New Light." Calvinists recognized this and made little effort to proselytize Quakers, preferring to revile and exclude them at every opportunity. Even when the Great Awakening came, Quakers and kindred sectaries, sustained by the Light within, remained unmoved when hearing the Word. Thus George Keith, although his character showed signs of regression to Calvinism, took refuge instead with the Church of England; and in the early 18th century, other Friends drifted into the orbit of the mother church. Quakers and Anglicans had in common a taste for devotional reading and a distaste for Calvinism with its systematic theology and doctrine of predestination. When Quaker peculiarities lost their spontaneity, and prophecy yielded to the small, still Voice within, the reasons for the Friends' separation from the Church were less compelling.

Even for faithful Friends not tempted by the Keithian schism or Anglicanism, connections with Britain remained close. In the 18th century, public Friends from America reciprocated English visits by traveling in the British Isles; communication between the London and Philadelphia Meetings was constant. Quakers of influence in the mother country acted as intermediaries for colonial scientific and philanthropic schemes and aided their New England brethren against the continuing intolerance of the Puritans. Because Pennsylvania was a proprietorship, the Quaker oligarchy in Philadelphia tried, like William Penn, to cope with the complexities of British politics; after his death, this was essential because the rest of the

Penn family was Anglican, and interested in the land revenue, not the religious experiment.

The easy flow of Friendly people and ideas across the ocean has suggested a "transatlantic community" that Quaker historians have praised. In one way, at least, the New World did seem to benefit from the Old: it was the Quaker missionaries—a third of them women—just arrived from England, who witnessed for social justice and against the slave trade before 1740, although they did so in a 17th century manner. But in the crucial area of government and politics, there was little the American Quakers could learn from their English counterparts about coping with a diverse population under frontier conditions. The net effect of the transatlantic community with its great British influence was probably to perpetuate and reinforce sectarianism among the Friends in America. Despite their peculiar habits, the quietistic Quakers looked remarkably like their contemporaries to the North, the New England Puritans who followed Cotton Mather into closet piety and ancestor worship when the oligarchy waned.

Pacifism was a cardinal tenet with the Quakers; it was an inevitable position because the Inner Light fostered a general respect and love for all the creatures to whom God had given His spark of life. To rely on God's intervention instead of arms was a natural tactic that all the pietists shared. The policy was sorely tested in Pennsylvania during the colonial wars; Quaker Assemblymen resorted to subterfuges rather than consent directly to military expenditures for the defense of the colony. Their usual device during Queen Anne's War, one that seemed hypocritical to many, was to vote money "for the Queen's use." In later defense crises, they blinkered their consciences again and voted more funds "for the King's use" and for "other grain" knowing this would be stretched to mean gunpowder. Whereas in England the pacifism of the Quakers resulted only in jail sentences for themselves, in Pennsylvania it contributed to bloodshed and loss of the lives of non-Quakers for whom the Philadelphia government was responsible. Yet the question of defense appropriations was not critical in the earlier years; not until the early 1740s did it seem serious. Pacifism, however, was not the major hindrance of the ruling Friends. Many citizens who were not pietists learned to understand and respect the Quaker reluctance to compromise this tenet, the Quaker interpretation of Christ's teachings. And, no doubt, had Pennsylvania been a republic and not part of the British Empire, pacifism would probably have been successful, since the Quaker "good neighbor" policy toward the Indians seemed to work, and the settlement of rambunctious Scotch-Irishmen on the frontier could have been controlled.

Quaker hegemony in Pennsylvania was more significantly hampered by the Society's aversion to oath-taking. The Friends used both scriptural and rational arguments against the practice. Jesus opposed oaths although the Old Testament sanctioned them. The "So help me God" and the kissing of the Good Book seemed magical or irreverent, and yet did not deter disloyal or dishonest persons. Those who believed that God and Truth dwelt within could not accept the imposition of an outward form on truth-taking. William Penn tried unsuccessfully to substitute his own yea-nay formula that omitted reference to God. The Quakers maintained that, like all Englishmen, they were entitled to their fundamental liberties, and they should not have to swear to the Test Act to get them.

While their position was plausible and rational in theory and under Old World conditions, it proved to be a constant handicap to participation in the affairs of Pennsylvania, and a source of resentment among the non-Quaker settlers. Could Friends, with a reputation for keenness in business, be trusted in transactions when they refused to mention God? Would strict Quakers who could not use the court system overcompensate by becoming excessively legalistic? Could Quakers be relied upon as witnesses and jurors when they affirmed without swearing? Would everyone in Pennsylvania suffer because of the special problems Quaker officials presented to royal authorities? Quakers who affirmed were willing to incur the same penalties for perjury as those who swore, but this only increased suspicion that they were hypocrites and quibblers—just as literal-minded as those who wanted them to swear. Although Parliament legalized a form of affirmation in 1696, strict Quakers still found it too similar to an oath and refused to take it, yet oaths remained important in the functioning of the Empire even after the Glorious Revolution.

Pacifism and oath-taking were major limitations in the Quakers' attempt to govern a whole society. Perhaps, however, the barrier to Quaker effectiveness even more fundamental than these tenets, was the Inner Light principle itself. The more a person turned inward seeking the Light, the more love he felt flowing outward to his fellow men, but it was a general love, a love of Being that while often focusing on the oppressed, seemed to preclude understanding individuals in their natural state. The result was a paradox: the more a person loved and empathized in this way with people, the less effect he had upon them. It was the interplay of theology and piety that made for discernment and adaptation; sectarians like the Quakers, because they lacked theology, could not change their tactics of example and affection when these were ineffective, without losing their identification altogether. They cleaved to their faith and redoubled their duty, obedient to God in anticipation of the afterlife, but oblivious to the many mundane pressures on the people. Non-Quakers called this attitude self-righteousness.

The tone of scholars towards the Friends becomes more favorable after they reverted to their original, sectarian role. Quaker domination of Pennsylvania ended in 1756, when the Quakers dramatically withdrew from the Pennsylvania Assembly and government because their consciences would not permit them to compromise further in consenting to the war measures required when the French and Indians had brought the war to their own frontier.

Afterwards, more of them were free to do as George Fox advised, "mind the Light." Strict Quakers had always tried to do this; inwardness had accelerated following Penn's death in 1718. Friends found that one good way of "keeping in the Light," of reinforcing their powers of introspection, was to keep diaries and read and write confessions and journals. This type of literature proved appropriate and effective for Quakers who had always had an aversion to drama and satire, and a commitment even stronger than the Puritans to "the Plain Style" of rhetoric.

The Meetings encouraged publication for didactic purposes, and after George Fox's *Journal* (1694) came others by prominent Quakers. A *genre* of high uniformity developed immediately. Usually the journals were written late in life from diary entries. To Friends, life itself was a sacrament and so they recounted details impersonally but carefully, interrupting the flow with documents and letters. The writers were public Friends for whom simple, biblical diction was a necessity; only the aristocratic Philadelphians, the "Quaker grandees," were *au courant* with literary models, and they published no journals. The public Friends were the leaders of the faith, and in their extensive travels, served to set common standards of belief and discipline. Their narratives played down ancestry and idiosyncrasies and focused on the religious crises in their lives, particularly descriptions of the submission to the Inner Light. The journals of the American Friends were less mystical and more conventional than those of their British colleagues. They had no sufferings to report in the 18th century and the task of the American Quakers became minding the Light in the midst of colonial prosperity.

Quaker spiritual autobiography reached its apogee with John Woolman's *Journal,* begun in 1756 and published in 1774. His own words reveal him as the pre-eminent Child of Light in America, a veritable saint. Woolman exemplified the Quaker ideal because, in his lifelong struggle to resist the impulses of natural man, he won most of the battles. He submerged his ego in order to transmit in purest form the divine leading; he was careful to examine the origin of each inspiration and tried to remain "easy" and "clear" by never going beyond it. Even as a young child, he had been subject to "gracious visitations"; clearly he had the "gift." His tranquil and docile spirit gave him a peculiar objectivity, the ability to empathize, not only with the oppressed, but with the oppressors. His concern with the most deprived of his fellow men in the colonies—slaves, Indians, and the poor—led him to conclude that desire for gain impeded the Truth, that the system of profit-taking generated a selfishness and luxury not sanctioned by God or the scriptures. Because of these evil influences, he did not expect rulers and magistrates to heed his witness, but believed that if the more otherworldly ordinary folk were convinced by his example and adopted his ascetic standard of living, slavery and poverty would disappear. God did not often intervene to aid his saintly assistant, however, so only a few were convinced, although many admired Woolman's character and simplicity.

By itself the Inner Light could flourish for only a few moments at a time in history, and among a few elements of society. In the 17th century crisis of the Civil War, two quite divergent groups had been drawn to the Truth of George Fox: women, adolescents and poorly educated folk who were confused and frustrated by all the religious controversy; and intellectuals, surfeited by the theological dispute and divisiveness of the time, *e.g.,* Penn, Barclay, and Keith. When the crisis passed, and despite the arduous example of traveling Friends, the power of the Light was much reduced. The Society had to rely on the birth rate of "birthright" Quakers to sustain and transmit the peculiar piety to the next generation. While the Quakers were immune to the New Light of the Great Awakening, they participated in the humanitarianism that eventually followed, and this period coincided also with their withdrawal from politics. The

Quaker role ended in 18th century America as it had begun in 17th century England, with the Friends, not as magistrates or legislators, but as lobbyists for the Lord.

Notes

1. The three classic forms of church polity were the episcopal, the presbyterian, and the congregational. In the first, the power came down from the ruling bishops; in the second, it originated in the presbytery, a mixed body of lay elders and clergy governing a small region; in the third, power lay in the communicating members of the local congregation. Many people came to believe that these church forms were analogous to monarchy, republicanism, and democracy in the secular world.

2. Adherents of Calvinism, the body of doctrines identified with the Genevan Reformer, John Calvin (1509–1564), meant by predestination that God had foreordained a minority of men, the Elect, to be saved, and had "passed over" the others. In its pure form, this implied that God regenerated the Elect, regardless of their wishes or behavior, and that God's grace was irresistible and usually sudden. In this view, Christ's death was a limited atonement, redeeming the sins of the Elect, not those of all men.

3. For many centuries, rulers believed that the security of the government required that all citizens formally adhere to the same religious creed and polity. Those who refused to conform to the church established by the state were persecuted and prosecuted. Finally some states learned to "tolerate" these people, usually termed dissenters or separatists, and permitted them to practice their own religion, but under special legal restraints designed to discourage them from proselytizing.

Chapter 2

The Great Awakening: Revelation and Reason

What role does organized religion play in changing society? Have the churches been, to a great degree, a force for conservatism in American life? In our own time social scientists have publicized widely their adverse findings about the average churchgoer. According to their attitude surveys, he adheres to an outmoded *laissez-faire* economics, is ethnocentric and bigoted, and leans toward authoritarianism rather than creativity. His religious orientation is said to be "orthodox" for the most part rather than "devotional"—more concerned with creed and conformity than faith and spirit. No doubt there is much truth in this portrait, although the specific characteristics would vary markedly by denomination and region. But investigators have not publicized as extensively their discovery of a "saving remnant," a small, pious segment who have internalized the faith but not the dogma, who respond creatively to the devotional life of the church. On the inventory scales, these "true believers," less than 20 percent (some say 10 percent) of the church population, are not only more liberal than their orthodox brethren, but significantly more so than non-churchgoers and non-believers in general. It is natural to ask, however, how effective can 10 to 20 percent of

a group be in the face of a complacent 80 to 90
when the "saving remnant" is further divided
exhorters? Yet the pious minority, including ma:
does have influence exceeding its numbers becaus
discipline and the power of example. This is es~~~~~~~ ~~~ ~~~~
religious excitement has already begun.

During the Glacial Age, the Elect and the Children of Light—the
18th century counterparts of today's true believers—must have been
reduced to a low proportion of churchgoers, despite the efforts of
the Mathers and others. Church leaders, as we have seen, had great
difficulty in keeping "experimental" religion alive in the colonies
until God would provide another "opening." God's people were to
be patient yet ready, when the opening came, to press into the
Kingdom. At such a time, with the ranks of the truly pious temporarily multiplied, major social changes and a great leap forward
toward Christian brotherhood and the millennium could occur. In
the interim, the godly few were to use their ingenuity in a holding
operation, exploiting every new opportunity for recovery. The tactics
of the Calvinists and the Quakers differed, but they both strained to
conserve and extend the dwindling spirit. While an ostensibly inscrutable Almighty created seasons of religious concern, there was
always the hope that man might discover a method for hastening
the Kingdom. If the millennium were to begin in the New World,
the frontier at its western fringe was a likely location. For exhorters
among the true believers, the frontier offered fresh opportunities for
communal piety, once the initial every-man-for-himself stage had
passed.

Stoddard on the Frontier

In western New England, the break with orthodoxy came early.
Soon after Solomon Stoddard settled on the Connecticut River at
Northampton, and persuaded his congregation to accept the Half
Way Covenant he quietly admitted to the Lord's Table not only
those who had testified to saving grace but also those who merely
nourished "hopes." Sometime in the 1670s, without consulting anyone, he ceased to keep a separate list of those baptized but not
converted. When Increase Mather heard this, he objected, saying:
"I wish there be not teachers found in our Israel that have espoused
loose large principles here, designing to bring all persons to the

.ord's Supper . . . though they never had experience of a work of regeneration in their souls." Nevertheless, this heresy spread through the Valley with little controversy and, by 1700, Stoddard was confident enough to defend his innovation against critics on the seaboard. He proceeded to attack orthodoxy as a system that had failed to halt the decline in piety, that seemed to reward only the bold few who were brazen enough to endure the public confession. He knew that many sincere Christians lacked confidence and stayed away from the Supper because although orthodoxy sanctioned attendance, it also condemned persons who partook if they were unsanctified. Facing this uncertainty, only 20 percent of the flock ventured communion. By comparison, Stoddard's plan of admission attracted more to the Table although it was not as "large" as Scotch Presbyterianism, since the New Englander still excluded the notoriously reprobate. Stoddard evidently believed that the churches had been keeping too many people outside, and that discipline could maintain purity even with "open communion."

Stoddard boldly declared the Lord's Supper a converting ordinance; those with reasonable hope should partake. He argued that although grace was a reality, it could be known only by intuition and was not verifiable. In this life, there was no way of distinguishing between saints and hypocrites. He disagreed with the Mathers who saw no reason to abandon the effort to discriminate between Saints and sinners just because it was a difficult task. He was criticized for sacrificing the inward to the outward, for moving toward formalism and popery. According to tradition, Stoddard was converted at the Lord's Table, which goes far to explain his uncommon view of communion.

Yet Stoddard was actually not far in advance of religious tradition in the Valley. The semi-presbyterian views of Thomas Hooker, the beloved founder of Connecticut, had provided ground for the acceptance of the Half Way Covenant. Thus Stoddard, in advocating the halfway plan, found his people receptive and did not have to battle the pews, so that moving beyond it to "open communion" was not the bold innovation it would have been elsewhere in New England. And in his associational organization in the Valley and his calls for a national church, he reflected the Hooker tradition and anticipated the consociationism that Connecticut enacted in the Saybrook Platform.

To thwart any dangerous levelling, Stoddard organized the nearby churches into the Hampshire Association; this was facilitated by the marriage of several of his daughters to neighboring ministers. By dominating his colleagues in the Association and the merchants in the towns along the river—the "River Gods"—he earned the title of "Pope." Stoddard vigorously asserted ministerial power in his own pulpit. He made it clear that the minister "is made the judge by God . . . and it is not the work of the brethren or ruling elders, any ways to intermeddle in that affair or limit him." Moreover, "members of the congregation have a greater fondness for power than the ability to use it."

To his virtually presbyterian attitude toward admissions and church government, the "Pope" added an essential third element: evangelism. Experience in western Massachusetts taught him that God normally brought the light to His people quite suddenly and violently—if the means were right. The proper means were, of course, sermons in the Plain Style, "searching" and extempore. While he preached within the form of the jeremiad, he knew that God did not favor flocks nourished on mere morality or ritual. In working on souls, he preferred the sermon—piercing words spoken to the group—rather than consultation with individuals in the pastoral study. "The Word is as a hammer and we should use it to break the Rocky Hearts of men." His assumption that only God Himself knew the true saints may have permitted some variation in response; but he noted significantly that men usually proceeded slowly through the stages between conviction (a sudden and overwhelming sense of sinfulness) and conversion. The actual conversion, however, must be wrought at once; it must be sudden, " 'in the twinkling of an eye,' otherwise men would be in a period when they were neither alive nor dead." Stoddard kept his church filled by preaching the Terrors of the Law, and he was the envy of his colleagues when special "harvests" of sinners came in 1679, 1684, 1696, 1712, and 1718. These revival successes were hard medicine for the Mathers and their party who had labelled Stoddard an apostate debasing ancestral standards.

To buttress his evangelism, Stoddard stripped away the covenants and postulated a God close to Calvin's original—explicitly sovereign and inscrutable. The covenant was not a rational contract but an absolute fiat; God chose whomever he pleased. Nevertheless, Stoddard created an ethos in the Valley that caused people to prepare extensively and to give attention to the means.

When the Mathers invoked the founding fathers against him,

Stoddard defended his own generation. He believed that each generation should examine the received doctrines and tradition anew; and his findings contradicted the Jeremiahs indicating that New England history did not run downhill from the founding. Stoddard's influence was exerted personally over his colleagues in the Valley, but he also delivered sermons annually in Cambridge at the Harvard commencement. For the pious reader, he provided twenty-five works totalling some 1700 printed pages, including *The Safety of Appearing at the Day of Judgement* (1687), *The Doctrine of Instituted Churches* (1700), and *A Guide to Christ* (1714).

Stoddardeanism bisected New England. The east was subdivided among the Mathers, Colman and his Harvard protégés, and the Anglicans; the vast hinterland of the west, with the Connecticut River as its axis and Yale as its college, belonged to Stoddard and his allies. In terms of people and square miles, the latter influence came to be much greater, reaching across to Long Island, to New York and into the Jerseys, there to modify the Presbyterianism of Scotch-Irish immigrants in the Middle Colonies.

Stoddard found the most satisfactory compromise to the religious dilemma of the time: how to keep the church voluntaristic and pious, yet still large and influential during the religious off-season of the Glacial Age. His formula was to lure people with the Terrors of the Law and open communion—attracting both waverers and the ultra-conscientious—and then hold the recruits with the Plain Style, mixing the fear of the Terrors with the love of the New Birth, and sustaining it all with strict church discipline. He acknowledged that there were seasons of concern, that "piety is not natural to a people, and so they do not hold it long," but he had learned that the right combination of fear and hope made men diligent. While not all those who took communion accepted the obligations of full membership, he was still reasonably successful and carried many churches through the trough and into the Great Awakening.

The other challengers of orthodoxy had omitted the essential ingredient, revivalism. Colman, at Brattle Street Church, was liberal in admissions, but he lacked the Calvinistic technique that induced crises. His professorial and gentlemanly manner was reassuring to men of affairs, and to the ladies, but this style could only sustain itself among the upper classes of the coastal towns, a small fraction of the population in that age, and his young Harvard imitators failed to sell it in the small villages. John Wise called for a return to the original form of congregationalism, the "New England Way," in two clever essays but not, as far as we know, in revival sermons delivered in the countryside. It was "Pope" Stoddard and his followers in the Valley who kept the fires burning, or at least smoldering, until his grandson, Jonathan Edwards, could make them blaze again.

Edwards and the Frontier Revival, 1734–1736

During the first decades of the 18th century the Mathers, father and son, were in their declining years, and prayed regularly for a turn in the religious tide, a return to the piety of the founding fathers. They had tried everything to arrest the secular trend. Cotton even sought the counsel of Professor Francke at Halle, hoping that the Pietism current in Germany could somehow be imported to save "the City on the Hill."

The turn these last Puritans longed for did finally come, but they died without knowing it. By 1721 a reversal had begun in New England and in the Middle Colonies, most notably in the mind of a young Yale graduate, Jonathan Edwards.

Perry Miller has suggested that if we can define Jonathan Edwards, we can define Puritanism; but Edwards had one of the subtlest minds America has produced, so this does not offer any shortcuts. The facts of his family background and early life, however, were surprisingly consistent with the role he was to play in reviving and re-shaping the Puritan impulse in the 18th century.

He was born at East Windsor, Connecticut. The place, a village on the Connecticut River between Hartford and Northampton, lay within the vast western domain of "Pope" Stoddard and the River Gods; the time, 1703, was in the trough of the Glacial Age when mystical piety and rational religion were frequently divorced, and flowing in separate channels.

His father, Timothy Edwards, was a minister. His mother was a daughter of "Pope" Stoddard himself. Clergymen were among Edwards' forebears, although the lines were broken for a generation or two by the hardships of the New World. The first Edwards in America was William, a cooper, who settled in Hartford about 1635. (Tradition indicates a Welsh branch in the family tree, leading one old-fashioned author to speak of Jonathan as a blend of Saxon reason and Celtic imagination.) Jonathan's father was not brilliant, but he was renowned for his learning, and was energetic and successful in stirring his congregation. Although most of New England was religiously stagnant, he made East Windsor, together with Stoddard's Northampton, a conduit of evangelism, linking the piety of the founders with the Great Awakening.

To be the fifth of eleven children was not unusual for the age, but Jonathan was an only son with ten sisters. The family obligation to the ministry must have been strong. His father's calling may have inspired his "playing religion" in the woods, but his meditations were precocious. His temperament inclined to the other world and tutoring by his pious father and sisters reinforced this tendency. By the age of ten he was ready to condemn materialism emphatically. Edwards was born a mystic; his environment made him a theologian with mystical bent.

Young Edwards was indifferent to most of the affairs of this world. Save in religious matters, he was insensitive to the ideas or foibles of the people about him. In college he was a social conformist; he spent his time studying and pulled no pranks. His only real intimate then and later—except for his wife—was his father; fortunately for Jonathan, Timothy lived as long as his son and was never too far away.

Culturally and geographically Yale College and New Haven were about as far away from home as Edwards ever got. He lived out his days in Stoddardean America: at East Windsor, New Haven, Northampton, Stockbridge, and at the end, Princeton. After college he did spend a few months assisting a pastor in New York City, but made only one friend there. Scholars have lamented this insularity and imagined that Edwards' thought might have been quite different had he been exposed, like his contemporary, Franklin, to the greater range of ideas available in Boston, Philadelphia and London. But Edwards learned best from books, not people, and Yale had the Dummer collection. When he discovered Newton and Locke, he privately rejected the scholasticism of the Yale classroom. He studied the New Science and produced a treatise on flying spiders; in his journals he formulated the philosophical questions that were to occupy him for the rest of his life.

These years of relative intellectual independence ended with his conversion in 1721, at age seventeen. Edwards was vague about this but claimed that after reading *Timothy*, 1:17 (his father's namesake!): "Now unto the King eternal, immortal, invisible, the only wise God, be honour and glory for ever and ever," his adolescent resistance to God's sovereignty—never really strong—dissolved and God's justice in the world appeared clear and sweet to him. The verse was prosaic but the time was right; he had a "new sense of things" and wanted to be swallowed up by God. Prior to this infusion of grace, Edwards had experienced wide swings in his spirit, from lassitude to hyperactivity. Some have suspected a conflict between the conscious and the unconscious, and an Oedipal complex that was finally overcome by conversion and reconciliation with his father and his father's creed, Calvinism.

Edwards, when he was later caught up in revivalism, wondered and worried about the genuineness of this conversion. He had not been struck by the Terrors of the Law, overwhelmed by the consciousness of sin, or shaken by "bodily effects." His experience was mild, indefinite, and extended, not the cataclysm that felled the typical unchurched Pilgrim or Scotch-Irishman during a revival. The light had come to him gradually; it was a "freshening," a tearful "renewal," one of the stronger epiphanies in a lifelong series. Tradition has it that the sons of clergymen are rebellious, but there has been a clerical remnant of Saints who accepted their heritage and sustained the pietistic impulse; Edwards was one of those, a veritable prodigy of religiosity.

The stage for New England's Great Awakening was set when Edwards was called to Northampton to assist his grandfather. When the aged Stoddard died two years later, Jonathan fell heir to the pulpit and to the empire Stoddard had built along the River in western New England. But even in Northampton religious deadness had prevailed during the last decade of Stoddard's life, after his "harvest" of 1718, and the town looked to young Edwards to rekindle the spiritual fires.

Edwards was tall and comely. Although he leaned on one elbow as he preached, he retained great dignity and solemnity. The suggestion of fragility in his frame and femininity in his countenance merely added to his power in the pulpit. In a thin but penetrating voice he spoke plainly and methodically as if to children; he was sparing in his imagery. Many different adjectives—languid, earnest, cold, sickly, tragic—have been used to describe him. The personal conviction behind his delivery was immense. In 1731 when Edwards gave the election sermon in Boston, he stressed God's sovereignty, a warning of what was to come from his pulpit. The Northampton folk admired "Mr. Edwards" for his exposition of the sound doctrines of the old Puritans and they understood his words, although they did not understand him.

The dullness of religion continued for some time after Stoddard's death. Families were unable to discipline their youth, and night-walking and tavern-frequenting were common. Edwards preached for at least four years before detecting any change. By the end of 1733 he could report a trend toward decency and flexibility, *i.e.*, some yielding to his advice. A year later he organized the young people into companies that met for "social religion" after the evening lectures. Then a notorious "company-keeper" convinced Edwards that she had felt God's infinite power and was truly broken and sanctified. "And then it was, in the latter part of December, that the Spirit of God began extraordinarily to set in, and wonderfully work amongst us; and there were, very suddenly, one after another, five or six persons, who were ... savingly converted, and some of them wrought upon in a very remarkable manner."

The ensuing "Frontier Revival" lasted from Christmas until May in Northampton. The Spirit of God began to ebb even before Joseph Hawley, a gentleman with a family history of melancholy, cut his throat, tempting others to follow him in departing immediately from this world. The Awakening spread up and down the River until some two dozen communities in western Massachusetts and Connecticut were affected, and lingered for several years in a few villages. The Northampton revival was highly contagious; ministerial observers who came to the River town to see with their own eyes, touched off awakenings when they went home and reported what they had seen. In New England history there had been isolated showers—in a number of churches, not only at Northampton and East Windsor—but never so many at once.

Edwards analyzed this Frontier Revival at length in *A Faithful Narrative of the Surprizing Work of God*. This account, an enlarged version of a letter to Colman, was sent to two English dissenting ministers who wanted to use the specifics of New England's heavenly shower to excite their people. The *Narrative* was published in London in 1737, and in Boston a year later; it became a classic manual on conversion, and went through thirty editions.

Edwards laid the groundwork by describing Northampton's prosperity and compactness, noting especially its religious history—the many "harvests" grandfather Stoddard had reaped there. When he recounted the cases of concern and conversion, he apologized for his youth and inexperience. At many points he mentioned the great variety of temperaments the revival revealed.

Yet Edwards believed that God worked by indirection, that one could learn the secrets of Being by discovering "great analogies." He looked for a pattern and found one. Some folk had sudden transformations, others gradual—he did not indicate the proportions—but he could discern the definite stages called for by Puritan orthodoxy. The first move of the awakened was to cease sinful practices, including backbiting, and to turn to reading, prayer and meditation. They found comfort in the parsonage instead of the tavern. Some were so aroused they could not sleep, and a few harbored irrational fears and were terrified to the very limit of their constitutions (and in the case of Hawley, beyond). Edwards attributed these ill effects to the intrusion of Satan toward the end of the revival, but he could boast fewer cases of melancholy than in Stoddard's time. In general, he noted that the greater the anxiety, the nearer the deliverance.

Whereas at the outset they worried about their sinful behavior, the convicted later came to understand that their greatest sin was inward, namely a selfish and corrupt heart. The signs were obstinacy, a rejection of Christ, and an enmity toward God. They felt envy toward the already converted and privately feared that they were wicked beyond redemption. When in desperation—and with the secret hope of appeasing God—they tried to walk even more strictly, and He did not reciprocate for the good works, they felt more lost than before. This was the difficult path Edwards saw the awakened folk of Northampton taking; there were detours, but it led eventually to a recognition of God's sovereignty and a realization of full dependence on Him. At the last stage before deliverance, the humiliated were ready to concede that salvation was too good for them and were willing to accept damnation. They even relished God's vindictiveness and praised His justice in condemning them.

Sometimes the last stages were protracted; more often God cut the time short by striking quickly and violently. God made his immediate influence known by putting into the mind a particular passage of scripture and these consoling words were usually accompanied by a vision of Christ, in all his excellency and perfection. The result was a powerful longing for communion and union with God. The great joy at the acknowledgement of God's sovereignty gave way to a sweet repose of the soul; a feeling of obligation came later. Because their religious training—even in godly New England—did not prepare them for this ineffable experience, the awakened seldom realized that grace had been infused, and some would not even accept Edwards' confirmation of it.

To anticipate skeptics, Edwards emphasized his objectivity and attention to detail. "I have judged experiences, not people," he said. In dealing with the concerned he was very careful to approve only those experiences which, with only minor variations, followed this classic pattern of conviction, compunction, and humiliation. And because even learned clergy could be fooled by pretenses, the ultimate test had to be deeds, not words. He insisted: "By their fruits shall ye know them."

Jonathan Edwards' effectiveness as a preacher, and his objectivity as an observer of revivalism, owed much to the semantic insights of John Locke. When Edwards read *The Essay on Human Understanding* in 1717, he described himself as like a miser discovering gold; he was among the first colonials to read the work and he saw immediately that it made scholastic theories of the compartmentalized mind obsolete. Locke, of course, was an urbane aristocrat and no friend of Calvinism. Nevertheless, young Edwards found certain aspects of the Englishman's psychology compatible with Puritan views of preaching and conversion. The Puritan rhetorical formula had always been the Plain Style. In past seasons a few pastors had been rewarded with "heavenly downpours" when they pruned classical and literary allusions and gave careful attention to words that triggered all the senses, not merely the understanding. Successful preachers of this style were traditionally called "searching" and their words, "pungent." Grandfather Stoddard had been a pioneer exponent of the Plain Style in the New World. "Don't whisper," he said, "words are hammers." Edwards followed this lead; and Locke's psychology gave him a new philosophical and "scientific" respectability in his calculated use of the Plain Style.

Edwards believed that God brought seasons of deadness and quickening; during the latter, pastors were especially enjoined to move immediately in improving upon the divine opening, and the appointed way was the lively preaching of the Word. In his pulpit efforts, he showed his Puritanism by opting for syntax and fact over metaphor and fiction. He wanted to shock his auditors out of old, stale associations. Locke had said that words should not be mere sounds or noises but should register in the brain as ideas. So Edwards strove to make his ideas clear, and his words true to experience and tangible to the senses. That is to say he used common words, but words peculiarly rich in emotional and religious connotations, and he put them in such good order and delivered them so solemnly as to shock people. In this way he applied Locke's "sensationalism."

Edwards believed the results of the Frontier Revival demonstrated the truth and value of the "sensational" method. Converts had a change of heart; they felt united in love and forgave enemies. Bystanders were strongly affected by the convictions they witnessed, confirming that direct experience and perception were more powerful than proofs or persuasion in bringing abiding changes. That converts could be explicit and precise in language and ideas in relating their experience was proof to Edwards that his diction could give people a new perception, a "new sense of things."

The sovereignty of God, that "blessed" doctrine, had brought "sensational" success; the margin of the victory could even be quantified. Edwards believed that the altered personality and behavior of the converts was a vindication of Calvinism and a clear refutation of Arminianism.

Frelinghuysen and the Dutch Reformed

Stoddard and Edwards were preparing the way in New England, but the revival of piety was also evident at an early date among the Dutch Reformed in the Middle Colonies. The Dutch churches were in an even more dull and formal state than the English. The pattern was to become typical of immigrant churches: *i.e.*, the farmers kept their religion merely to preserve their language and nationality.

Theodore Jacobus Frelinghuysen arrived from Holland in 1720, answering the call of four small churches in New Jersey's Raritan River Valley. The son of a minister, he vowed on shipboard to lead a reformation in the New World. The young domine would find his flocks composed of prosperous but ill-educated farmers. These American-born Dutchmen, reacting to the pressure of English culture in the New York City area, had been moving since the 1690s into the fertile valleys of northern New Jersey. The Raritan Dutch were presumably gratified at the prospect of an orthodox minister sent by the Classis (the presbytery) of Amsterdam to sustain the Dutch Reformed faith.

Yet Frelinghuysen disappointed the lay leaders in his first sermon; he insisted on inwardness rather than external duties. He was reluctant to baptize the infants of, or give communion to, those who asserted good works or in other ways resisted his thoroughgoing Calvinism. He imposed a standard of piety and discipline that even some of the elders could not meet. Opposition developed within the congregations and dissidents sought outside aid from the older domines of New York and from the Classis itself. The critics, well-to-do laymen, charged Frelinghuysen with heterodoxy, highhandedness—and even homosexuality because he kissed a colleague in public. For more than a decade the pastor and the opposers fought for control of the churches. The Classis leaned slightly in Frelinghuysen's favor and in the end he won, although many members of his church withdrew during the struggle. Apparently a large portion of the rank and file supported his regime, although many had not experienced grace. The common folk were probably reassured by this vigorous application of Calvinism by a minister just arrived from the old country, especially in view of the religious confusion in the Jerseys at the time.

Frelinghuysen seems to have been a typical Calvinist evangelical; what the nearby Presbyterians would soon call a New Light. He strove to implant a deep conviction of sin, and expected it to last some time before being succeeded by a sudden and violent conversion. He was explicit in describing the conversion process. His preaching was "searching" rather than terrifying, and he used logic to cut the ground from under the assumptions of the complacent. He conferred privately with the strongly affected. After six years at Raritan, these methods brought some results. In his broad interpretation of the minister's powers and in his requirement of testimony of saving grace, Frelinghuysen may have departed from European Reformed polity and practice, but this adaptation to the American environment was similar to that of his Calvinistic predecessors, the first Puritans at Massachusetts Bay and, particularly, Stoddard at Northampton on the frontier.

Frelinghuysen was a practical man who realized that the Dutch churches in America, operating under the English flag, would have to acquire considerable autonomy. He therefore worked for a Coetus, a local body that could ordain in America. Conservative domines opposed him and split the church, but he carried the majority. Although he did not speak English himself, he perceived that the Dutch language and narrow nationalism would soon perish. He raised five sons to be ministers; they were English-speaking and capable of giving some cooperation to neighboring Scotch-Irish and Puritan New Lights, as well as furthering evangelical principles among the Dutch.

Until recently scholars have followed contemporary Germans and Presbyterians in labelling Frelinghuysen a Pietist. He may have been influenced by German Pietism, but there is no real evidence of it. Although born of German stock in a Westphalian town, he was raised and educated under the Dutch; his intellectual sources were Calvin, Beza, and Dutch Reformed evangelicals. That Dutch Calvinism, although more philosophical and less experimental, could blend with English Puritanism had already been shown in Holland, and events in the Middle Colonies would tend to confirm it. Perhaps the extent of Frelinghuysen's religious successes among the Dutch have been exaggerated; certainly the evidence is thin. He did have considerable influence, however, through young Gilbert Tennent, on the preaching techniques of the Presbyterians settled nearby.

The Scotch-Irish and the New Light

Stoddard's successful formula for sustaining religion on the New England frontier—evangelical Calvinism reinforced by a semi-presbyterian polity—also became the dominant pattern of religious life for Presbyterians in the Middle Colonies. Connecticut Puritans who moved over to Long Island or southward to New York, New Jersey, Pennsylvania and Delaware, carried Stoddardeanism with them. Many of the pioneers were from New Haven, and emigrated to preserve their theocratic piety after that colony was absorbed by her more tolerant neighbor, Connecticut. They turned naturally to Yale College for their clergymen. Scattered at first, they organized on a congregational basis, but as the threat of Anglicanism mounted after the turn of the century, they turned, one by one, to Presbyterianism. They took this course because they knew that the governors in these provinces were under pressure to support Anglicanism and could not permit affiliation with the ecclesiastical establishment of Connecticut. The presbyterian form of church government offered an approximation which moved even closer after Connecticut adopted the Saybrook Platform in 1708. The churches on Long Island remained thoroughly Yankee into the 18th century, but the Puritan-turned-Presbyterian congregations elsewhere were assimilating other Calvinists—Huguenots, Dutch, Welsh, Scotch and Scotch-Irish. The newcomers, while conscious of New England variations in church practices, were generally content with the Presbyterian character of the services and willing to accept pastors from Yale. When the first presbytery was formed from these mixed and cosmopolitan congregations in 1706, it received counsel from Puritans in Connecticut and Presbyterians in London.

And then the Scotch-Irish came in numbers. After 1720 what had been a trickle turned into a stream of immigrants that would continue until the Revolution, occasionally reaching flood-tide proportions. They were called Scotch-Irish because they were descendents of lowland Scottish Presbyterians who had spent a century colonizing Ulster, the six counties of northern Ireland. Threatened from below by Catholic peasants, and imposed upon from above by Anglican landowners and officials, they had fought to preserve their identity and in the process their character and religion had hardened. They reacted to mounting economic and political discrimination by becoming ever more polemical in defending their Scottish version of Calvinism, the badge of their nationality in an inhospitable land.

Yet the harsh conditions in Ulster—and in Scotland itself—produced an exaggerated orthodoxy rather than godliness. The immigrants arrived with virtually no piety and therefore readily succumbed to the hardships and temptations of the frontier. The absence of social restraints in the new country accentuated the latter. The settlers looked to the homeland for leadership and culture, yet very few Scotch-educated clergy joined the exodus to America. Well-educated young clerics do not forsake the motherland unless piety is in the ascendant and God calls them into the vineyard; neither the Scotch-Irish nor the Germans of the Reformed or Lutheran Church were to have the good fortune the Massachusetts Bay Puritans had in bringing their clerical leaders with them.

Given frontier conditions and the absence of state support for Presbyterianism in the colonies, what was the best way to maintain religious standards among the immigrants? The Scotch-Irish leaders, drawing upon the experience of Scotland and Ulster, had an emphatic answer: keep the new churches doctrinally pure by insisting on unqualified orthodoxy from ministerial candidates. They would maintain strict Scottish Calvinism by demanding that neophytes subscribe to the church creed, the Westminster Confession. With no church courts to administer discipline in America, subscription was deemed a necessary protection. The pattern emerging at home seemed to be that those who had refused to sign in such controversies usually joined the Church of England afterward; therefore, to the Scotch-Irish, nonsubscription suggested a drift toward Arminianism and episcopacy. The imposition of such a loyalty oath in Europe had led, however, to dissension and not to a revival of piety. The strength of Papist and Anglican ideas and the ethnic conflict in Ulster might have made subscription plausible there, but in the more fluid and heterogeneous atmosphere of the Middle Colonies, where persecution was non-existent, an expansive rather than a defensive approach would have been more appropriate. The Scotch-Irish, however, were slow to adjust to the altered situation; the few educated pastors, out of an authoritarian tradition and with status anxiety aroused by the diversity of denominations, put their own well-being ahead of the spiritual needs of their people in the New World. Faced with irreligion and immorality, they could think of no other course than to intensify the external requirements, thus crushing any living religion that still remained from a group that had already been drained of its aesthetic qualities in Ulster.

Jonathan Dickinson, the Yale pastor at Elizabethtown, who was the leader of the New England-cosmopolitan faction, marshalled good Puritan arguments against the Scotch-Irish demand for subscription. On important issues, the uninterpreted Bible had to be the sole authority, he said. To rely on extra-biblical authority, even the Westminster Confession, was a step away from the Reformation and toward Anglo-Catholicism and would lead to dull formalism, confusion and schism. There had been no subscription in the primitive church before Constantine, and the New England churches had survived without it. Contemporary experience in Scotland indicated that only ordinary hypocrites were eliminated by the oath; unprincipled heretics were not afraid to subscribe.

The New England party, of course, believed they had a very much more effective alternative for purifying and invigorating Presbyterianism, namely enforcing the provision in the Westminster Directory of Worship that called for a candidate to be examined closely as to his inner state, his experience of saving grace. The New Englanders suggested this remedy when it became apparent to them that many of their Scotch-Irish colleagues were highflyers who believed that correct belief, *i.e.*, adherence to the Westminster creed, gave them assurance of salvation and, consequently, some freedom to relax their moral standards. The Scotch-Irish did not at first oppose a test for "experimental" religion ("experiential" in modern terms) in the candidate, but they did not perceive that their insistence on creedal orthodoxy was conducive to hyper-Calvinism and lax discipline, and became a barrier to evangelism.

The rift between the two factions of Middle Colonies Presbyterianism widened in the 1720s, and was exacerbated by the treatment Scotch-Irishmen were receiving in New England. Because they held the Reformed theology in common with the Puritans, the Scotch-Irish arriving in Boston expected some hospitality; instead they were pushed to the marginal frontier lands to become a buffer against Indian attacks. To Puritans in the New World the Scotch-Irish were a disappointment. Their fellow Calvinists from Ulster had a low standard of living, but beyond that, they were too doctrinaire, too lacking in introspection, too lawless and combative—more homicidal than suicidal—than the staid Puritans could tolerate.

As their numbers grew, the Ulster Scots continued to press hard for subscription. Their dread of doctrinal error, a reflection of their fear and dislike of the culture of England—old and New—was stronger than any fear of schism in Presbyterian ranks. Yet in the synod of 1729, although the Scotch-Irish outnumbered the New England-cosmopolitan faction two to one, Jonathan Dickinson, with some support from Scotch-Irish moderates, was able to push through a compromise that was quite favorable to the Puritan position. He chose the Pacific Act of 1720, Ulster's not very successful formula for a similar controversy, as his model for the Adopting Act; this required the candidate to subscribe to "the system of doctrine," but allowed him to "scruple" non-essential passages, explaining his reservations to the examiners. Defending this flexibility, Dickinson noted that even the Westminster Confession should not be regarded as full revelation but as a "help" in individual study of the scriptures. He reaffirmed the Bible as the sole authority. The synod also decided not to assume legislative power but to allow the existing presbyteries to remain autonomous. This relieved the New England party, since it was in accord with their traditional polity. They controlled only one presbytery to the Scotch-Irish three, and would have been outvoted in a synod government. But this autonomy also made it easier for the Scotch-Irish to violate the new act. In their three presbyteries, they soon denied the right to scruple and demanded unqualified subscription. It appeared that the balance of faith and creed pioneered in the Middle Colonies by the New England Puritans was going to be upset by the arid and defensive hyper-Calvinism of the Scotch-Irish immigrants. If this had resulted, Puritan influence might have dwindled to an enclave in the Jerseys and on Long Island.

The fact that this did not happen, that evangelical Calvinism ultimately prevailed in the Middle Colonies and later in the Southern backcountry, can be attributed to the Scotch-Irish moderates. They allied with the New Englanders to stem the tide of orthodoxy, and work for a general awakening. The moderates got their inspiration largely from one man, William Tennent, through the four sons that he educated himself.

Information about Tennent is rather meager. He was born in Scotland or Ireland and took his M.A. at Edinburgh in 1693. He moved to Ulster and married the daughter of Gilbert Kennedy, a prominent Presbyterian minister. He then inexplicably deserted to the Anglicans in 1704 and served as a chaplain to an Irish gentleman. Yet when he arrived in America he immediately sought affiliation with the Presbyterians again. In applying for a license in 1718, he gave the synod seven reasons for his defection from Anglicanism: in the first six he criticized aspects of episcopacy; in the seventh, he rejected Arminian theology. In his views of conversion and the Christian life he proved to be closer to Dickinson and his party than to his fellow Scotch-Irishmen. What made Tennent religiously different from the other pastors from the old country? From whence came the pietistic impulse that Tennent transmitted to his sons and students, resulting in such consequences for Calvinism and politics in the 18th century? Only conjecture is possible. Was pietism conveyed to him by his father-in-law? Kennedy had spent several years among some of the same Calvinistic evangelicals in Holland who no doubt influenced Frelinghuysen. William Tennent chose his father-in-law's Christian name, Gilbert, for his oldest son who was destined to be the leader of the Presbyterians in the Great Awakening. And the Tennent family spent a decade after their emigration— the formative years for the sons—among the Puritans of New York.

When the Tennents moved to Pennsylvania, William was given fifty acres for a school. He built an eighteen by twenty foot log cabin where he instructed his sons and some others. He was a good classical scholar, and so combined the ancient languages with theology. This little seminary, dubbed the "Log College" by its critics, was just what was needed at this time to democratize and Americanize the Presbyterian pastorate by injecting new blood. At Neshaminy, a small village on the Delaware River, some twenty young men from the countryside gained a sound education without being exposed to the secularism and confusing life styles of London or Edinburgh; even Philadelphia was too far down the river to endanger their pious naiveté. These novices were eager to labor in the vineyard and, upon graduation, to fill the vacant pulpits in frontier communities.

When Francis Alison, the chief and virtually the only intellectual among the Scotch-Irish conservatives, challenged the quality of the Log College and the fitness of its graduates for the ministry, Gilbert Tennent vigorously defended his father. While he conceded that some secular subjects—the sciences and contemporary literature —were neglected, he defended the kind of character-building the College sustained.

Apparently William Tennent did not include revival homiletics in his instruction, however. Young Gilbert was disappointed when his first sermons failed to move his Scotch-Irish congregation in New Brunswick. He decided to consult Frelinghuysen whose reputation as an evangelist was already established. The Dutch domine obviously had faced, some years earlier, essentially the same problem Tennent now confronted: how to arouse stolid Calvinists who had reacted to the New World and the encroachment of British mores by turning their faith into cultural religion. Frelinghuysen showed the young man how to be powerful in the pulpit, and Tennent, combining this with his father's theology, became the Middle Colonies' pre-eminent Son of Thunder.

Thus the Tennent faction, together with the New England party— less than 40 percent of the Presbyterians—were able, through revivalism and superior statesmanship, to check and largely offset the Scotch-Irish subscriptionists. A large beachhead for Stoddardeanism was made in the Middle Colonies, and perhaps the Americanization of some Calvinistic immigrants was hastened. The evangelical victory, however, was not assured until George Whitefield arrived, and did not become overwhelming until some time later, after a schism had occurred.

George Whitefield and the Great Awakening

The separate and sporadic stirrings of religion fostered by Edwards, Frelinghuysen, the Tennent brothers, and their respective followers were finally consolidated into the Great Awakening when George Whitefield came from England to tour the Middle Colonies and New England in 1739 and 1740.

In appearance Whitefield, the Great Awakener, was not unattractive; his complexion was fair and his countenance manly. His eyes were dark blue, and one of them was askew, presumably from measles in childhood. Because of this, London actors, who came to regard him as a rival, applied the epithet, "Dr. Squintum."

The ultimate source of Whitefield's astonishing power over the multitudes was the great timbre and sonority of his "magical voice." He could thunder and he could whisper; and his cadence was exceptional. Franklin estimated that the Great Awakener could be heard, without shouting, by 30,000 at one time. David Garrick, the actor, noticed that Whitefield could convulse an audience merely by pronouncing the word "Mesopotamia"; actually he could get this effect with other less exotic words, too. Dr. Samuel Johnson denigrated Whitefield's power by attributing it to a "peculiarity of manner—he would be followed by a crowd were he to wear a night-cap in the pulpit or preach from a tree."

Whitefield did have talents as a mimic and raconteur. Without notes, he looked steadily at his audiences, and he was at his best acting out anecdotes, parables and history. He began flights of fancy frequently with the phrase, "Me-thinks I see. . ." and favored surprise endings. He reinforced his pictorial language with a mobile face and active fingers. His taste was vulgar but his wit was ready. When a clergyman in Boston Common told him, "I'm sorry to see you here," he replied, "so is the Devil."

When he raised emotions to a high pitch, Whitefield was usually a casualty himself, weeping more or less openly as he preached. Yet crowds had a strong tonic effect on him, giving at least temporary relief from his chronic intestinal and respiratory disorders.

For Whitefield the starting point and theme of his life was his own conversion. After a year of anxiety and distress, it came suddenly in the spring of 1735 when he was twenty years old and a student at Oxford. At the University, he had gravitated toward "the

Holy Club," a small group inspired by German Pietism, who culti-vated their piety and were therefore ostracized by their worldly fellows.

Whitefield's friends convinced some Church officers that God had called him for great things, and he was ordained at the tender age of twenty-one. He subscribed to the thirty-nine articles of the creed but immediately departed from many Anglican practices: he de-picted hell more vividly than heaven, emphasized the New Birth and, confounding himself with Jesus, reminded his listeners that he was born in an inn. He abandoned all notes and preferred to preach to the unchurched in the open fields. Yet, despite this developing confessional style, the "boy parson" respected the Inner Light he had seen at the Holy Club and among the Moravians, and this antinomian sympathy continued during his first sojourn in America at Oglethorpe's colony in Georgia.

But, when Whitefield on his second visit to America in 1739 landed in the Middle Colonies, the Log College men won him over to their brand of Calvinism. By supporting predestination, he broke with the Wesley brothers, his colleagues in the Holy Club, and from that time revivalists in England divided into two factions, the Calvinistic Evangelicals and the Arminian Methodists. Whitefield then backed away from pietistic associates and was careful during the rest of his life not to make statements that could be used by antinomians. He was constantly accused of sacrificing reason to faith, but at least Whitefield's citations from scripture increased with his Calvinism; beyond the Bible, he said, were only illusions.

Earlier, Whitefield had been exposed to explicit Calvinism when David Erskine's Associated Presbyterians invited him to Scotland, but he found their application too doctrinaire and partisan. He saw that identifying himself with this splinter group would limit his appeal to the Scotch people, whereas by 1739, in America's Middle Colonies, the New Light—of New Englanders, Welsh, English, Scotch-Irish, Dutch and a few Germans—appeared to rest on a broad popular base. The Great Awakener sensed that, by using their doctrines to buttress his sermons, his effectiveness might be in-creased. Yet he must have retained some of his Arminian attitude because, compared to the American-educated New Lights, he was gentler, preaching more of other parts of the gospel and less of the Terrors of the Law. Whitefield's biographer has concluded that "he professed Calvinism, lived by an Arminian faith and preached them both."

It was not surprising that Whitefield's actions were Arminian. To evangelize effectively, even Calvinists had to treat large audiences as if they were all potentially of the Elect. In practice the Awakener treated men as if they could of their own volition come to God. Whitefield, in fact, itinerated all his life in the belief that he was putting those who heard his message under a definite obligation to respond. He never let his theology destroy his optimism. For Whitefield, as for most 18th century revivalists, Calvinism was a technique as well as a creed; the results of the technique constantly verified and justified the creed.

Whatever the precise technique, Whitefield's appeal was wide. In England he liked to scold the gentry for their sins, yet his obsequiousness in their presence suggested that the innkeeper's son might be yearning for status. All the same, the Great Awakener enjoyed open field preaching to the untutored, sought out prisoners as well as colliers and sailors, and relished even the martyrdom that came from being insulted by the ignorant and profane.

In the colonies Whitefield was most successful among the Calvinistic folk north of Maryland, especially in the towns where dissenter meetinghouses were being challenged by new Anglican chapels. Like a modern revivalist, Whitefield tried to plan his campaign and had an advance man who planted newspaper stories that would heighten interest. Before his arrival, the colonists knew that his Church superiors in England had labeled him an "enthusiast" and denied him pulpits because of his preaching style and emphasis on the New Birth. In America, the "dissenter priest" gained further publicity in public battles with the Anglican commissaries in Charleston, Philadelphia, and New York. New Englanders were flattered by Whitefield's constant praise of their principles and institutions. In Philadelphia, even Quakers and German sectarians who were immune to revivalistic emotion could enjoy the discomfiture of their political enemies when Whitefield needled English society and the Church of England. Only in Virginia and Maryland, where there was no Anglican-dissenter tension, did the Awakener fail to awaken; in these places he drew only polite attention. Confronted with this coolness, Whitefield rationalized, "I fear Deism has spread much in these parts."

Closer examination suggests that Whitefield did not affect all classes in the north the same way. In the large seaport towns, a genteel minority was much more responsive than their counterparts in southern planter country, but these people seldom fainted or fell down. Well-to-do churchgoers were "renewed," "quickened," or "melted down" but not convulsed by his pungent delivery. In the early stages of the revival in New England, Colman and his party furnished sympathizers. Whitefield's rejection of the Anglican style was reassuring to the "nice" people who were by tradition against popery but were tempted by the social status of the chapel.

For the majority of Whitefield's listeners, his message of the New Birth was paramount, not his gibes at the Church of England. Farmers who traveled many miles to see and hear him were not disappointed. These unsophisticated folk found themselves drawn into the vortex of religious concern and conversion was sometimes the result. More often Whitefield was effective indirectly. Preachers inspired by his New Light did the follow-up counseling in the wake of the Awakener or carried God's sovereignty and the New Birth into the hinterlands. Whitefield himself came to recognize that there were others in the emerging New Light ranks who were more searching as preachers than himself; that is why he persuaded Gilbert Tennent, the outstanding Son of Thunder, to follow after him in New England in 1740, consolidating the gains he had made.

Inevitably Whitefield has been compared to the other great evangelist of the 18th century, John Wesley, an orderly and systematic gentleman who preferred to instruct, patiently and lovingly, his social inferiors. The founder of the Methodists stressed ethics over doctrine, and his printed sermons were well wrought. While he preached often to the working classes with occasional disorder ensuing, many historians believe that the Wesleyan movement dampened and diverted lower class discontents during the industrialization of Britain.

Whitefield was less rationalistic and more sentimental. His style was more impetuous, but his content was more orthodox, observing the festivals of the year and dwelling on Old Testament doctrines. Yet scholars have found him to be less competent than Wesley in speculative theology. In extenuation, however, Whitefield left only seventy-five printed sermons, all dating from early in his career when he was new in his Calvinism. The conclusion must be that, even more than most evangelicals, the Great Awakener was better in the flesh than in print; the medium was essential to the message.

Although Whitefield's emotional tours created moments of ecumenical bliss among the concerned, disorder and divisions followed inexorably in his wake. Opposers of the revival blamed Whitefield himself for inspiring the most spectacular example of enthusiasm in the Awakening: the case of Reverend James Davenport of Southold, Long Island. Davenport was a descendant of the ultra-pious John Davenport, founder of New Haven Colony. He was the son of a minister, and at fifteen, a Yale graduate; his background and his early saintliness identify him, like Edwards, as a member of the clerical elite. His fanaticism was set off by a meeting with Whitefield and Gilbert Tennent in 1740. Davenport tried to imitate them in his itinerations, praying and preaching in a confused manner wherever a crowd could be gathered. His behavior soon revealed the classic stigmata of enthusiasm: extravagant gestures, the rending of his clothes, indecent familiarity with Christ, pretense to immediate inspiration, millennialism, invective, and rash judging of the inward state of others, especially clergy for whom the New Light shone less brightly. When he addressed a crowd on Boston Common, the reaction was mixed; some laughed, some melted, and some swooned. Leaving the Common with a mob at his heels, he strode through the streets with his hands extended, head thrown back, and eyes on heaven. Davenport was singing in his own peculiar manner—the "holy whine"—and the group looked more like "a Company of Bacchanalians after a mad frolick than sober Christians worshipping God."

New Englanders—even ardent New Lights—could not help but associate Davenport with Anne Hutchinson and George Fox, the antinomians who had portended anarchy to the founding fathers and provoked them to undertake severe persecutions in the 17th century. In the 18th century, Davenport got off more lightly: he was transported out of Connecticut, admonished for enthusiasm in Massachusetts and jailed for slander in Boston, the court judging him *non compos mentis* and therefore not guilty. Before his friends finally restrained him, he was to imitate the Florentine friar, Savonarola. At New London, Davenport instructed his young followers to go house-to-house collecting worldly objects that induced idolatry—rings, necklaces, wigs, cloaks and gowns—and put them in a heap for burning. He took off his plush breeches and put them on top, then added a pile of unsafe religious books from a catalogue he had prepared. Singing "Glory to God" and "Hallelujah," his disciples made a bonfire on a wharf and watched the flames lick the pages of the "heretical" works. At the last moment the clothes were saved, but the books were burned; among the authors were Flavel, Colman, Sewall and Increase Mather. To most Yankees, who respected learning and the printed word, the bonfire was shocking antinomian enthusiasm. The next year Davenport apologized publicly and at length for his "false spirit" and the "blemishes" he added to the work of God.

Edwards and the Old Lights

At the height of the Awakening and before the extreme excesses, Jonathan Edwards was invited to give the Yale commencement sermon. His collegiate audience was presumably concerned about revival ephemera and ready for scholarly analysis. When he delived his sermon on *The Distinguishing Marks of a Work of the Spirit* (1741), he spoke as the author of the *Narrative*, with an authority no one else in New England had. As the pre-eminent apologist for evangelical Calvinism, he was nevertheless discriminating, even at this moment when New Lights predominated and the critics were biding their time.

The Whitefieldian excitement had given Edwards the opportunity to add to his sample of conversion cases. After close observation of these new instances, he affirmed that they conformed to the signs indicated by the apostle John, that they were similar to those of Stoddard in his "harvests" at Northampton, and they were a more distinct—a purer—version of the Frontier Revival he had examined in 1735. Although some persons did not volunteer their experiences, interrogation revealed that these conversions, too, fell within the historic pattern. Few were stirred by "vain shadows or notions." For most individuals the light and comfort was greater and came more readily than in the Frontier Revival, even though there were always a few "false blossoms" who suffered conviction but gained no deliverance. Edwards believed that hearts hardened with exposure and age; he noticed that those convicted but not converted in 1735, repeated the cycle of anxiety in 1741 and failed again.

Edwards' explanation of bodily effects, the most criticized byproduct of the revival, was reasonable. Humans differed widely in temperament; the strong emotions needed to move the great majority might prove too much for a melancholic few. Adolescents, a group vulnerable to a second birth, were by nature unstable and liable to extremes. After many years of religious deadness, the preaching of the Word would evoke extreme reactions from some of the unchurched. He suggested that some of the disorder could be attributed to indifferent pastors who offered little guidance to their people and let them wander into the arms of the exhorters. Such a powerful movement could not avoid great manifestations and interruptions "any more than if a company should meet on the field to pray for rain, and should be broken off from their exercise by a plentiful shower." He advised pastors to treat souls and leave the physical symptoms to the physicians. Bodily agitation was correlated with temperament, not godliness.

Edwards' wife, the lovely Sarah Pierrepont Edwards, was the daughter of a very respectable minister and was (appropriately) subject to periodic renewals; these experiences were mystical transports, yet they were usually accompanied by marked physical symptoms. Scholars have speculated that this circumstance was the reason for Edwards' charitableness in evaluating such behavior.

Nevertheless, Edwards met the opposers halfway by conceding the major shortcomings of the New Lights. He found them often guilty of spiritual pride, rash judgment of others, and errors in belief, especially of an antinomian tendency to put individual promptings over the teachings of scripture. He reminded his New Light colleagues to be on guard against stereotypic and counterfeit accounts of a second birth. Slight departures from the general formula might be good evidence of genuineness since, as he knew from experience in his own family, temperaments varied so widely.

Finally, Edwards called upon the skeptical to put aside individual cases and incidental errors and consider the revival "in the lump." He expected them, as reasonable men, to agree with him that "if this is not in general the work of God, then we must throw away our Bibles, and give up revealed religion."

Even as Whitefield and Tennent were touring New England in the fall of 1740, opposition was emerging. It grew rapidly, and when Whitefield returned to the region in 1745, he found it badly divided, with many who had earlier sympathized with him having turned against him.

The "opposers" put their case skillfully in the Boston newspapers and won over to their side many of "the better sort." Their chief spokesman was Charles Chauncy, pastor of Boston's First Church. At the very beginning Chauncy was critical only in his private correspondence, but by 1742 he came to believe that the excesses of the New Lights were so blatant as to be vulnerable to rationalistic attack.

In his *Seasonable Thoughts on the State of Religion* Chauncy undertook to answer Edwards, and assembled all the evidence against the Great Awakening that he could uncover in eastern Massachusetts. The subscription list for the book proved to be a reliable roster of opposers, and Chauncy made a comprehensive case for their side. He relied on scripture and tradition as well as reason, and his criticisms were to become familiar to Americans who witnessed later cycles of religious excitement.

The foremost complaint was against the itineracy that formed such a large part of "the great Work." Pastors aglow with the New Light, trying to emulate the successes of Whitefield and Tennent, took to the road, intruding on neighboring parishes without the permission of the settled minister. Chauncy saw this as a violation of the Cambridge Platform, and of New England Congregationalist tradition where each minister is ordained into a particular church. The Bible was no precedent because in those early days itinerants spread the Gospel only where it was not being heard, and not into godly communities like New England. Exploiting Puritan prejudices, he compared the itinerant to an Anglican pluralist in England. He publicly wondered how a traveling evangelist could neglect his own people so long. In the case of Whitefield, were not those orphans in Georgia starving from neglect? Bolder opposers were ready to suggest that there were no orphans, that the Awakener was indeed pocketing the considerable funds he collected for this charity.

What made the intruding pastor so obnoxious to the opposers was his New Light. They saw him as bursting with certainty of his own Election, and strongly tempted to pass judgment on the spiritual state of those around him, especially any ministerial colleague who was aloof or equivocal. Obviously, after an itinerant rashly judged the local minister unsaved, it was hard for the latter to hold his flock together; parties, divisions, and in some cases, separations were the result. Itineracy also meant frequent preaching on week days; it kept people away from their callings and families and often led to disorder and tumult.

Worse than itinerant pastors were lay exhorters; young converts, usually with little education, trying to spread the "good news." The danger that these persons would mistake their own impressions for divine suggestions was great. The opposers saw this as a recurrence of Anne Hutchinson's antinomianism, and professed to fear political as well as religious anarchy. Most of the exhorters were white males; they were accused of excessive familiarity in references to God and in behavior with women, particularly at night meetings. A few of these novices were Negroes or women, and Chauncy noted that church canon was explicit in denying women the right to speak in church. Exhorters usually harangued people in the streets but sometimes attempted to outshout a parson in the meetinghouse. Their style—extemporaneously invoking the Terrors of the Law, and denigrating book learning—convinced critics that the New Light in general was anti-intellectual.

Chauncy's major objection to the Awakening which he dwelt on at length was its tendency to produce "bodily effects." He probably exaggerated the hair-tearing, swooning and falling; to him this was the animal passions and not God at work. He was annoyed by the ostentatious joy of the saved; their kissing and laughter sometimes suggested a euphoria bordering on madness. "Excessive heat" was a sign of the ungodly, not the godly. He claimed that women, children, Negroes and Indians were more susceptible to these excesses, presumably because their nervous systems were weaker. How unfortunate that the New Lights chose to exploit young children in their revivals! In all this they were forgetting that reason is the Candle of the Lord. He tried to link the New Lights with the Camisards, the French Prophets who spoke in the tongues and murdered priests; these "enthusiasts," when they came across the channel at the turn of the century, had shocked the reasonable English. Chauncy had another objection to the revival that received less publicity. He was much disturbed by the censoriousness of the New Lights towards their unawakened colleagues. He realized that he personally was too rational and cold in the pulpit to arouse emotions. Because he lacked a sufficiently mystical temperament, he resented the New Light implication that only people with it could enter at the Strait Gate.

Effects of the Revival

The very characteristics of the Great Awakening that the Old Lights found distasteful had a profound and as yet unmeasured effect on

American intellectual and political life. In most places, the Calvinistic emphasis on Terrors of the Law was important in attracting male converts. It appealed to the "middle aged" men who had a rising concern for life after death and had not heard before—during the barren period of the early 18th century—the full exposition of Calvinistic federal theology. The conundrums of Calvinism were also a challenge to young men dealing with an abstract system for the first time. While fear for their souls dominated both groups, there were those analytical and skeptical enough to be more angry than afraid. These particular "children of wrath" were angry that God could be so unjust, so unreasonable and inhuman as to impute Adam's sin to all mankind and predestine the vast majority to hell. This anger heightened the suggestibility of many stable men who were not neurotic, exceptionally intelligent, or easily scared.

Gilbert Tennent was the epitome of the New Light in his ability to arouse fear and anger and bring on sudden convictions. Like Jonathan Edwards—who could be as effective on occasion—Tennent relied heavily on direct address and made no agreeable gestures to diffuse the impression of his words. The relentless manner of such preachers in presenting astringent doctrines affected not only those of choleric and melancholic temperament, who were more easily stirred, but often reached the sanguine and phlegmatic men as well. And when the latter were "re-born," they were not likely to fall away.

The initial power of evangelical Calvinism came from stressing God's sovereignty and the Terrors of the Law, without exploring certain implications. Presented in the right way, the authoritarian idea of God's sovereignty could appear equalitarian. All men were worms dependent on God's mercy, incapable of understanding life's higher meaning. Even the Saints might be fooling themselves, and further introspection might reveal hypocrisy. The proud and the complacent as well as the overtly sinful were in danger. No one was secure. God's sovereignty could be a reminder to the *nouveaux riches,* the upwardly mobile who were forgetting Him, and this aspect could gain approval from pious and less self-confident common folk. At the same time, it could comfort members of old families of the Elect who felt their status threatened by impious climbers.

Beginning a sermon with the Terrors was a prerequisite for evangelical pastors. Aroused by fear and anger, listeners were made ready for the "good news." Of course the clergy alternated it with other themes and adjusted the severity to the audience. Jonathan Edwards was unusually terrifying when he preached "Sinners in the Hands of an Angry God" at Enfield in 1741 because he knew the congregation there had become loose and indolent. A delicate proportion was involved; the Terrors had to last long enough to stir the most secure, but not so long as to bring mass insanity or suicide. Ministers who moved too soon from this theme to God's mercy failed to reach many souls. Edwards seldom made this mistake. Of all God's doctrines he believed sovereignty the most blessed. He wrote: "But the most awful truths of God's word ought not to be withheld from public congregations, because it may happen that some melancholic persons in Christendom exceedingly abuse the awful things contained in the scripture, to their own wounding."

Preaching that was merely an emotional assault on the brain was not enough; the preacher also had to provide an escape from the induced stress. Hellfire was presented solely as the result of rejecting the offer of eternal salvation won by faith. Emotionally disrupted by this threat, then rescued from everlasting torment by a total change of heart, the convert was now in a state to be helped by emphasizing the complementary gospel of love. The punishment for backsliding from a state of grace was always kept in mind; but once conversion had taken place, love rather than further fear could be used to consolidate the gain. John Wesley described the right method as beginning with the preaching of the law "in the strongest, the closest, the most searching manner possible. After more and more persons are convinced of sin, we may mix more and more of the gospel, in order to beget faith, to raise into the spiritual life those whom the law has slain."

Today sects that believe in retribution and an imminent holocaust attract more males than other religious groups. Two small bodies that have these tenets are exceptions to the rule that sects enroll three women for every man. The anti-Christian Black Muslims, preaching the early collapse of the white man's rule in the world, have attracted many more men than women and the converts take an active part in the administration of the sect. Clean-cut young men in dark suits form the Fruit of Islam, a para-military unit that provides not only security, but also acts firmly in matters of church discipline, especially in cases of sexual misconduct. The Jehovah's Witnesses, emphasizing the millennium and the small number to be saved, also have somewhat the same appeal. Poorly educated people—men particularly—have been attracted by the ideological intransigence and a certain relish for the violence to come. Authoritarianism is the magnet as it was for the New Lights and Separates.

There would seem to be a definite relationship between males, Terrors of the Law, and sudden experiences. A psychologist in his study of college and seminary students in the 1920s, distinguished 143 instances of sudden conviction; he labelled them "Definite Crisis" cases. Of these, three-fourths were men, although in his general sample, only a third were male. He also demonstrated a strong link between type of theology and Definite Crisis experiences. Those who had heard "stern theology," namely preaching of the Terrors of the Law, were *more than five times* as likely to have a Definite Crisis as those who had heard only "moderate theology." This suggests that the New Light emphasis on the Terrors was apt to "convict" more men than women and to do it more suddenly.

Is a Definite Crisis to be preferred to the gradual or temporary emotional stimulus experiences because it leads to a more profound and permanent change? Does it have greater political and social consequences than the others? Modern scholars disagree but evangelists have always said yes. Jehovah's Witnesses, among the most involved in this field today, have learned to expect—like other direct salesmen—an early decision to "close with Jesus" or no decision at all. Eighteenth century awakeners explicitly favored the crises although professing sympathy for those who suffered prolonged anxiety and indecision. Jonathan Edwards believed that the immediacy of spoken words and not the memory of them were most likely to prick the heart and that great terrors led to sudden light and joy. Samuel Buell thought that the more powerful the conviction, the sooner the relief. After a lifetime of evangelism, John Wesley affirmed that sudden effects seemed to be the most enduring. Early in this century, America's most distinguished psychologist of religion reached the same conclusion. In his *Varieties of Religious Experience,* William James wrote, "As a matter of fact, all the more striking instances of conversion, . . . *have* been permanent."

The emphasis on "the Word," spoken and written, provided some check on mysticism and promoted literacy and rationality. Edwards liked converts who had "seen" passages from scripture and felt joy afterward. Whitefield said he clung to the scriptures because beyond them were only illusions.

Modern religious educators, offended by the aggressive and vulgar tactics of many Fundamentalist revivalists, have deplored Definite Crisis cases. They have associated such phenomena with religious illiteracy, backwoods ignorance, and susceptibility to hysteria. These educators admit that crises are apt to occur among the unchurched after puberty and urge the early Christian training of children as insurance against such emotional excesses. Their disapproval is rationalistic and aesthetic, but it also rests on the belief that crisis conversions in our own time are superficial and impermanent.

The British psychiatrist, William Sargant, provides strong endorsement of Definite Crisis experiences, however. He emphasizes the therapeutic value of total collapse and argues that the potential for reformation is greatest among those who have been completely overcome. When the cerebral apparatus short-circuits to save itself from unbearable stress and the victim slumps into a comatose state, a *tabula rasa* condition follows. It may be three or four months before the patient's pre-collapse habits and thoughts are fully restored. If, in the interim, the patient is systematically reconditioned, he may well be transformed for life; he may be "born again." On this ground Sargant admires Jonathan Edwards' techniques and praises as psychologically sound the elaborate follow-up system of John Wesley and the Methodists, particularly their stress on "classes" and self-criticism to maintain morale and discipline among the converts and weed out hypocrites in the crucial retraining period.

There were many physical and mental collapses in the Great Awakening. Charles Chauncy referred frequently and deprecatingly to the "swooning" and the "struck." Jonathan Parsons of Lyme saw several stout men fall "as if a cannon ball had been discharged." David Hall of Sutton, a sympathizer, believed that the New Lights were encouraging too much crying and falling down.

It should be remembered at this point that the New Lights were not seeking sudden conversions alone, but sudden convictions followed at appropriate intervals by definite, datable conversion experiences. The interval between conviction and conversion could vary considerably, depending upon the temperament of the individual. Two weeks was too short; two years was too long; two months was an optimum. It would be a misrepresentation of the New Lights not to emphasize this, because the period of anxiety was important. The minister could use the signs, stages and behavior of this interim to corroborate the testimony offered by the convert later; and the pastors were cautious, in the 18th century, resisting pressure to telescope these days of concern and trial. In the revivals of the 19th century, when conversion followed conviction closely, the cases of abiding change seem to have been fewer.

The impact of the Great Awakening on learning was profound although it is still not fully understood; only some of the immediate aspects will be indicated here. When the joy and relief of sudden conversion subsided, most converts felt a strong sense of obligation, at first to God and then to the community at large. They were receptive and educable; young male converts were eager to become ministers and begin proselytizing. Respectable New Light clergy offered their pastoral studies as "schools of the prophets" to train these neophytes. The young men hungered for instruction, not only by hearing the Word in extra lectures, but also by reading good books. In addition to the scriptures, they sought out the solid works of Puritanism: Ames, Baxter, Flavel, Hooker, Shepard, Cotton, Willard, Mather and Stoddard. The majority of the authors were colonial divines of the 17th century; studying their works was more effective than the jeremiad had ever been in reinforcing ideas of special destiny and separation from Europe, and in fostering incipient nationalism.

In Britain, many of the converts of Whitefield and Wesley were motivated to learn to read and write, but in the northern colonies where people were already literate—except for the Indians and Negroes—the energies and discipline released by the New Light were the inspiration needed to master abstract religious material. In comprehending theological as well as devotional printed matter, the emotions aided the development of cognitive skills. The novices in focusing on the stages of conversion were studying a process analogous to the still mysterious secular sequence of gathering data, altering hypotheses, and somehow relying upon intuition to synthesize the conclusions. This type of thinking would have a more general utility later. The Great Awakening induced a grass roots intellectualism that ultimately spread in every direction, from belief in God's sovereignty all the way to agnosticism.

There is ample testimony that community morals improved markedly after large-scale conversion. Reformations were common and religious talk was everywhere. The saved even displayed affection for people they had formerly hated. There is no way to measure how long such effects lasted, but the revivalists, of course, believed that their ministers, like Jonathan Edwards, were so careful in admitting newcomers to communion that few backslid. New Lights describe the awakened as animated by a new principle, pursuing their daily life with a new confidence, satisfaction, and purpose.

At the same time, the Church of England received refugees from the emotionalism of the revival. Rectors boasted of the high quality of families joining their flocks and the general Anglican immunity to the New Light.

The Awakening accentuated divisions and produced schisms in the Reformed churches. In New England the opposers were dubbed Old Lights. In the Middle Colonies, both the Dutch Reformed and the Presbyterians split into Old Sides and New Sides. The factions created earlier by Frelinghuysen and the Tennents were thus confirmed and revealed openly. In the ensuing competition for churches and believers, the evangelical New Siders proved to have a big advantage in youth and numbers.

Separation was one inevitable result of the revival. In cases where a conservative minister failed to respond to his awakened parishioners, they sometimes seceded, gathering the true believers into a new congregation. The separatists justified themselves by asserting the Cambridge Platform and trying to operate independently and democratically. In Connecticut, because of the religious establishment created by the Saybrook Platform, they ran into legal trouble. The separated churches could not get tax revenues and had to support themselves at the same time their members were still compelled to contribute taxes to the established churches. The Connecticut laws had the effect of reinforcing a natural tendency of many separatists to organize as Baptists in order to take advantage of the legal toleration afforded that sect in the colony. Separatism was marked in sparsely settled eastern Connecticut and in Plymouth Colony.

The Great Awakening may have added as many as fifty thousand church members and 150 new churches to New England; and the composition of the flocks was altered significantly. In the quiet era before the revival the churches had catered to women and to men of affairs. The Awakening brought into the churches a variety of new men—rural, youthful, middle-aged, phlegmatic, unchurched, Indian, Negro—and some of Pilgrim stock. In churches following the halfway plan, many became communicants and some "owned the covenant." This influx of males guided by the New Light resulted in increased power of the church in the community since in virtually all the congregations, only men could vote.

The majority of the clerical elite found the New Light satisfying and incidentally useful in regaining some of the clerical power that had ebbed away. Many of ministerial lineage, although quakerish in their own piety, identified with the New Light party, and encouraged or sympathized with the strong responses of the unchurched and the backsliders. This respected group aided the Awakening, believing that it was, by and large, in the tradition of mid-17th century Puritanism and the founding fathers. It accepted as allies the many converts who became New Light pastors. The newcomers were activists ready to work among the unchurched and on the frontier. They were different from the elite in at least two ways: they were not the sons of clergymen and they had graduated from college in their twenties, not in their teens. Yet these evangelical parvenus complemented the older, genteel ministers. Together, the two elements in the New Light ministry consolidated the newly pious among the Calvinistic population in the northern colonies.

The Great Awakening, after its initial phase, divided the colonies along rather sharp lines. To assert, however, that the upper classes of the towns were anti-revival, and the yeomen of the countryside were eager for the "good news" is an oversimplification. It is perhaps more accurate to agree with Jonathan Edwards that the inclination toward the New Light was a matter of "sensibility," a quality unevenly distributed in the community. The old stock of clerical lineage and the yeomen evidently had more of it than the rationalistic men in-between who had come to town to make their fortunes.

Chapter 3

Indians and Negroes: the Heathen in America

How different were pagan peoples from Christians? Were they men? Of the same species? Did God create only one human race or were there many special creations, a hierarchy of races? By the 18th century, the English colonists were becoming aware of the scope of these questions that had troubled European intellectuals from the time of Columbus. English slave traders were flooding the plantation colonies with Negroes, while at the same time, most of the surviving Indians, having been pushed back across the Appalachians, were allied with the French in the vast imperial struggle for North America. There was ample incentive for colonial thinkers to ponder the nature of man, focusing specifically on the strangers in their midst and on their borders.

What were the destinies of the Indians and the Negroes in North America? Were they Satan's minions, doomed to eternal opposition and eventual extinction; or would they gradually accept Christ and European civilization and assimilate into the predominantly English culture of the colonies?

If there were indeed sheep of the Lord among the heathen wolves, what was the best way to reach them? In the case of the Indians, was it better to preach and teach in their difficult languages, or to insist on greater acculturation, *i.e.*, some competence in English? In the case of the Negroes, could pidgin English convey the complex ideas of the Christian faith? Must conversion come only after some exposure to Christian civilization, or could it precede and perhaps facilitate the latter? Many noted the paradox that the more the Indians imbibed of the English version of Christian culture, the more demoralized and degraded they became. Christianity sapped native vitality and seemed to have disastrous effects on simple people. Moreover, preliterate people measured words carefully against actions; could Indians and Negroes be only "hothouse" Christians, segregated from their co-religionists for fear of bad examples?

In Europe the long-standing interest in native peoples was flowering into a cult of the Noble Savage. Intellectuals, in criticizing European society and mores, found the "erudite" tribesman an even more clever and effective literary device than the world traveler. They continued to liken Indian ways to those of the revered Greeks and Romans, and contrast them with those of decadent contemporary Europeans. The attributes they found lacking in Europe, they were apt to find among the peoples of other continents, particularly the Indians of the Americas.

The French—Jesuits and freethinkers—were the leaders of this school of thought and Rousseau's *The Noble Savage* (1762) marked the apogee. These men, protected by geography or classical education and sensibility from the full apprehension of barbarism, were exhilarated by the freedom and spontaneity they perceived in savage life; but their real interest was in Europe and they saw only what they wanted to see in the aborigine.

In the English colonies of North America, the Noble Savage impulse was much weaker and subsided earlier than in Europe. Colonial Protestantism was a barrier because of its Calvinist cast; the very notion of an Elect militated against the heathen, however learned. This attitude weakened only when Calvinists were evangelized during the Great Awakening. More importantly, the agonizing colonial wars with the French and Indians, stretching from 1689 to 1760, served to stifle some of the nobler sentiments about the red man, particularly if the source was France. The colonists were simply too close to war and the frontier and too isolated from Continental thought to reflect very much primitivism; although there were traces in the southern colonies before they became engulfed in war in the 1740s, and some suggestions of it at the time of the Revolution.

The Red Man and the Missionary

Columbus proudly showed King Ferdinand and Queen Isabella six natives he had brought back to Europe from the New World. They looked different from the Africans and proved that he had sailed into uncharted seas. Exhibiting the painted red men was the most he could do since no gold or silver was discovered on his first voyage. The explorer was capitalizing on a growing curiosity in Europe based on the medieval tradition of an earthly Paradise or Arcadia, the land of Prester John, the Orient of Marco Polo, and some newly printed travel accounts that had added to the atmosphere of expectancy. European interest in the inhabitants of the New World was high in 1492 and persisted for a very long time afterward.

Columbus called the natives "Indians," of course, because he believed he had landed on an archipelago off the Asian continent; that he had actually reached the fabulous Indies by sailing westward around the world. The first facts reported about the Indians were the obvious and popular attributes: physical characteristics, sex habits, and dress and manners. To the Europeans, the faces of the Indians were handsome and their anatomies—they seldom wore clothes—were large and well proportioned. From the beginning, artists were tempted to bestow the classical features of the Greeks and Romans on the statuesque aborigines. In 1512 the Pope had affirmed that the American natives were descended from the single pair, Adam and Eve. It was therefore assumed that the natives were Asians who had made a long trek, leading to speculation that they were Phoenicians or Tartars or—among the more pious—members of the ten Lost Tribes of Israel. Discerning no religious creed, the explorers readily believed that their greatest gift to the heathen was destined to be Christianity.

The English came into direct contact with the Indians during the settlement of North America in the 17th century; until then they had known of them chiefly through Spanish accounts. The naive Old World belief that the mere example of order and morality in Christian civilization would evoke immediate emulation was soon dispelled, except, perhaps, among the Quakers. The few Virginia

Anglicans catechizing the savages had their hopes dashed by the 1622 massacre when one quarter of the colony's English settlers were slaughtered. The presumption had been that the Indians were men endowed with natural rights, but this bloody lapse—and another one in 1644—led many colonials to reconsider. With public opinion very adverse, Churchmen in the Old Dominion never recovered their rather limited missionary zeal.

The record of the New England Puritans in "Indian Work" was not very much better. The Calvinistic conviction that the savages were the Devil's agents proved inhibiting, and counsels were therefore divided on the procedure for Indian conversion. A minority believed, citing *Revelation,* that the awakening of the heathen had to wait on the conversion of the Jews and the destruction of the Anti-Christ. If, however, the Indians were of the Lost Tribes and therefore Jewish, it might be proper to proselytize. A majority evidently conceded that there might be some of God's Elect among the heathen in the forest but, needless to say, they were spread very thin compared to those covenanted together in the meetinghouse.

All the New Englanders seem to have been repelled by the savage life. Roger Williams, the "anthropologist," and John Eliot, "Apostle to the Indians"—each in his own way—gained exceptional rapport with the Indians, but even these men shared some of this revulsion. Although Eliot considered the natives to be members of the Lost Tribes, he said they were "the dregs of mankinde and the saddest spectacles of misery." Earlier he had estimated that it would take forty years to teach them English, and a hundred years to make them Englishmen; later he admitted they were a long way from "common civility, almost from humanity itselfe." The "Apostle" was discouraged when the Indian chief, King Philip, said he cared no more for Christianity than for the buttons on Eliot's coat. When King Philip's War broke out in 1675, settlers burned the villages Eliot had worked so hard to foster and murdered many of his Praying Indians. The war took many lives, red and white, and was the counterpart of Virginia's massacres; the meager Puritan missionary effort was virtually destroyed. On his deathbed in 1690, Eliot questioned the utility of his missionary labors with the red men. War, disease, and liquor were taking a heavy toll; New England's Indians were internalizing defeat. Realizing that they were a dying race, they described themselves as, "melting away like snow in the midday sun."

After Eliot's death, his method of using the Indians' language to inculcate Christianity was challenged. Many doubted that the native tongue adequately conveyed the subtle, abstract truths of the Protestant religion. Did Eliot's Praying Indians really understand his Indian Library, his translation of the Bible into Algonquian? The Puritan leaders came to distrust the profundity of precocious Indian boy converts who could recite "prettily" in English and Latin. Cotton Mather and other leaders argued that a contemplated third edition of Eliot's Indian Bible would be too costly and that not all Indians could read it, because of variations in dialect. Instead, at the insistence of Judge Sewall, a number of short edifying pamphlets by Cotton Mather in Algonquian were run off; but they went unread. Practicality prevailed; for a generation after 1710, if Indians were to learn Christianity, they would learn from standard English Bibles and primers. For both races, the language barrier became an excuse for lack of progress.

Other Puritan schemes to civilize the red men also failed. Indian parents were reluctant to send their children to school or apprentice them if it meant separation from the family. Journeymen did not want Indian apprentices and refused to instruct them. Cotton Mather's prizes for good behavior did no good. The few Indians who did show some academic promise and facility in English invariably were taken by "the hand of God" before finishing their studies. Puritans found it financially burdensome to assign clergy fulltime to the red men or provide adequate incentive for pious young men to master the Algonquian language. Although intermittent warfare with the French began in 1689, even patriotic appeals to save the aborigines from the sly Jesuits evoked little response.

After the destruction of Eliot's Indian villages, the few New Englanders still drawn to Indian Work focused their attention on Cape Cod and the offshore islands of Nantucket and Martha's Vineyard. King Philip's War had bypassed this region, and many of the remaining Praying Indians lived there. The Indians in these parts had been less bellicose from the beginning, and some prominent white families were establishing a tradition of Indian Work, producing a son or two in every generation who would dedicate themselves to the cause and learn to cope with the dialect. The most famous was the Mayhew family, proprietors of Nantucket until 1659 and of Martha's Vineyard from 1642 to the Revolution. For five generations Mayhews learned the language, treated the sachems as virtual princes, and dispensed paternal Christianity to the natives. But when the white population of the Vineyard came to exceed the Indian early in the 18th century, the Mayhews were charged by white newcomers with nepotism and favoritism toward the aborigines.

Before this happened, however, Eliot's methods received a full test on Martha's Vineyard. By the time Experience, the fourth generation Mayhew, began his labors in the Vineyard in 1694, the Indians had lost their tribal connections with the mainland and were free from intertribal warfare. Many of the women engaged in agriculture and many of the men fished. Mayhew encouraged settling in villages and used the various books of Eliot's Indian Library to spread Christianity. But Experience decided he disapproved of Whitefield's methods when the Great Awakening threatened to come over the water from Connecticut, so the revival had very little impact on the island. After that, missionary effort seemed to decline markedly. The Indians were intermarrying with Negro servants and becoming "people of color," thereby increasing the social distance between reds and whites. The colonists approved of this development in the belief that Negro "industry" and "docility" would temper Indian idleness and wildness. Their mixed blood, too, made the dwindling Indians more vulnerable in land title disputes with the expanding white community. Experience Mayhew became quite discouraged in his old age.

In seeking support from the New England Company, Experience had made much of the fact that over 95 percent of the island Indian population was Christian. Some Eliot Bibles may have appeared worn, but the adherence of the Indians was nominal and most of them could read the dialect only haltingly. In his preaching, Experience was flat and dull; his lack of a liberal arts education may have caused him to wander off from orthodoxy. He had to simplify the doctrines for his native charges, and this together with his humane impulses seemed to have resulted in a de-emphasis of sin, a crypto-Arminianism that may have been transmitted to his famous son, the Boston minister, Jonathan Mayhew. Before 1700, both islands had been probed by a few men with Baptist leanings. By mid-18th century, the Baptists had openly broken the Mayhew monopoly of Congregationalism, and—turning Calvinistic in belated response to the Awakening—were getting a good response to their evangelical labors. The dignified Old Light Calvinism of the proprietors was receding. The last Mayhew missionary, Zachariah, accomplished very little. The Mayhews had been able to retard, but not to halt, the decline of the Indian Work.

The Quaker missionary efforts were different but their results were equally discouraging. William Penn, gentleman, statesman and philosopher, set a high standard for Indian relations. Even before he arrived with his settlers to take up his grant in Pennsylvania, he had written to the Indians explaining his land policy. Following the best colonial precedents, he purchased land from the Indian chiefs. He dealt with them as sovereign to sovereign and assumed they had the right to sell—but it is doubtful that he believed, as Roger Williams did, that Indian titles to the land were absolute.

Penn expected the Indians to assimilate into the white community rather than to continue to live separately. In Penn's charter, one purpose was "to reduce the Savage Natives by gentle and just manners to the love of civil society and Christian religion." He also had confidence in Indian judgment. In addition to banning the importation of Indian slaves in 1706, the enlightened criminal code of Pennsylvania provided the same penalties for white men and red men; Penn proposed a mixed jury of six each to settle disputes between the races. This was the Quaker ideal of equality before the law.

Beneath these characteristically Quaker policies lay a substratum of paternalism. Somewhere—perhaps from George Fox who had toured America—Penn acquired tactics for winning over the aborigines. He impressed them when he walked alone and unarmed into the woods, and when he entered and won a leaping contest for braves. He found their words "sweet" but in his replies he was grave, perceiving that the Indians did not like to be "smiled upon." He was generous with gifts and tried hard to license trade and control the liquor traffic. He did not react moralistically to their religion or culture, or suggest that he intended to reform them. For these things the Indians praised him; they called him "Onas," their word for pen.

Despite this auspicious beginning, Quakerism nevertheless failed to take hold among the Indians. It might seem that the Quakers' beliefs—brotherhood, simplicity and the Inner Light that glowed in all men—gave them advantages over other Protestants in missionary work. But these very attitudes made the Quakers oblivious to the cultural collision that was destroying the red men. The Indians did ultimately acknowledge a special affinity with the Quakers and learn to distinguish them from other Englishmen. They did respect the Friends for living peacefully among them, but they were not "convinced" by such examples to adopt white civilization; this was too hard to do. Perhaps the Indians needed more than an ethical code; they needed a dramatic and emotional religion to facilitate acculturation.

Meanwhile, in 1701, Anglican humanitarians in England had founded the Venerable Society, also known as the Society for the Propagation of the Gospel in Foreign Parts. Its chief concern in America was supposed to be among the heathen, since Protestants had accomplished so little with them in the 17th century. But nationalism was also involved. The first missionaries of the society were sent to the New York frontier where the French were intriguing with the Iroquois, traditional allies of the English. Despite the pious hopes of their benefactors at home, the clergymen in the field, like their predecessors in Virginia and New England were quickly discouraged by direct contact. Indian males were so often drunk that the Churchmen concentrated their efforts on the women and children. Indians might seem to venerate the Anglican liturgy and even tremble at the Litany, but when, if ever, were they ready for baptism? Although they preferred to learn in their own language, the scriptures sounded odd in Indian tongues and many translated works were long and cumbersome. The clergymen complained that Indian culture was so alien that work among unchurched frontiersmen or even Negro slaves would be more worthwhile. Anglican gentlemen remained optimistic but there was fatalism among the clerics. One missionary concluded that the decline of the Indians was God's decree; there was no other way to account for the dying off, unless it be "the liquor we have given them or the distempers we brought with us."

In the parade of missionaries to the Indians, the Moravians, a Hussite sect, were the last in time but the first in results; at least this is the conventional judgment. One of their most renowned missionaries was David Zeisberger. In the best sectarian tradition he refused to be a "hireling" by accepting a salary and worked among the red men for half a century merely for his keep. He knew the Indians well and presumably loved them but, his editor said, "was not misled by romantic notions of Indian character." Undoubtedly his pessimism increased with white expansion and accelerated disintegration of the Indians during the Revolution. "Virtue one must not seek among the savages," Zeisberger opined, but "the grace of God is able to accomplish wonders among them."

The Moravians, like the Jesuits, put conversion before civilization. The converts they made proved faithful under the trying circumstances of persecution, migration and war. It may be that they had no choice, for the Moravian Indians were despised by pagan tribesmen and distrusted by frontier whites. But when the Revolution came, Moravians could not protect their Indian settlements from the disruptions. They accepted this failure stoically nonetheless. These pious folk were motivated by the love of God in Christ rather than by God's glory and thus it was sufficient to sustain the right attitude and behavior and leave the actual conversions or lack of them to God's will.

The Great Awakening revived and altered the Calvinistic missionary efforts. New Light preachers, with their Terrors of the Law and Plain Style, affected many hitherto impassive Indians deeply. Stern theological messages were appropriate for a warrior society. Itinerants were in a more favorable position than resident missionaries to give this kind of delivery and bring on convictions. Those who lived among the Indians too long or too intimately were apt, through charity and pity, to soften the description of man's inherited sinfulness. This was apparently the case with Experience Mayhew on Martha's Vineyard and David Brainerd in New Jersey. An emotional preacher of a harsh style, rather than a piteous one— a Tennent rather than a Whitefield—got the best results. For reasons explained in a previous chapter, males were particularly vulnerable and the sudden convictions led to permanent conversions in very many cases.

Indian Work was a natural outlet for emotions aroused by the revival. To the New Lights of the Awakening, the Indians were unfinished business left by the earlier Saints; an angry God was making them the scourge of the frontier. The New Birth gave some young converts the energy and determination, that was lacking earlier, to master the Algonquian tongue again. To New Divinity men, work with the Indians was ideal for displaying disinterested benevolence. Thus a distinguished group returned to the vineyard of John Eliot: Brainerd, John Sergeant, Eleazar Wheelock, Samuel Hopkins, Gideon Hawley, James Davenport, Samuel Buell, and Jonathan Edwards after his dismissal from Northampton. Among the aborigines, the missionaries could feel appropriately ascetic and altruistic;

by teaching in the forests they could preserve their piety better than by arguing with Arminians in the towns.

In their missionary work, the New Lights gained an advantage over their rivals by the use of song; for them hymns were an important adjunct to the Word. Some years before the Great Awakening, the "Old Way" of singing—"lining out" the psalms—had been challenged, and progressive young clerics had persuaded many flocks to follow the English dissenters into the practice of singing in unison, by notes and parts. Some of the older Congregationalists—who shared the views of Quakers, Baptists, and Pilgrims—vehemently opposed this change on the ground that hymns were human adaptations and that performing in unison was not spontaneous and sincere expression but ritualistic popery. The Awakening, however, was accompanied by much singing, and the New Lights discovered it was very effective with the unlettered, especially the heathen. Davenport supplemented his holy whine and spontaneous songs with hymns of his own composition and they became popular; his collection was reprinted three times in the 18th century. He had great success with New England Indians. His famous convert, Samson Occum, became an ordained minister and a celebrated author of hymns; the Indian had a pleasant voice and could preach well in both Algonquian and English, but relied heavily on music in working with his own people. Edwards, who loved melody, used singing to stir the affections of the Indians at his Stockbridge mission. Samuel Davies, the New Light Presbyterian had a Welshman's talent for hymns. He was impressed by the warm response to singing among the Virginia slaves; they have "a natural musical ear," he said. Isaac Watts' hymnody was even more popular among them than among Anglo-American evangelicals in general.

Although not a great deal of the Christian faith was transmitted across cultural barriers to the red and black men, much of what did pass was undoubtedly facilitated by hymn-singing; music was a catalyst. While the sentiments of the Quakers and German sectarians toward the heathen were quite similar to those of the New Lights, the greater success of the latter can in large part be attributed to their appeal to the oral tradition. In becoming Christians of the Quaker, Old Light, or even Anglican variety, the Indians and the blacks had to suppress their heathen ways, to turn inward, and became puritanical in conduct. In converting to the New Light, they could still release some of their pre-Christian spontaneity in song. Thus, while the content of the hymns reinforced the patterns of the new faith they were trying to absorb, the change came with a little less difficulty.

The Awakening demonstrated to the Calvinistic missionaries that they may have been too rigid earlier; strong religious experience could precede civilization—at least a minority of the Indians could be redirected by the New Light. Even Edwards—whom most historians have faulted for lack of sociological insight—was convinced by his mission at Stockbridge that education should be practical and interesting to the Indian, not pretentious and academic. Thus, the Calvinists moved in the direction of their more successful rivals, the Moravians and the Papists, opportunely during the generation of the French and Indian War. But this change should not be exaggerated; the Calvinists continued to make the Indians wait a long time—sometimes indefinitely—before admission to communion. It was actually conviction, not conversion, that the New Lights induced with little preparation; the period afterward, between conviction and conversion, they found conducive to civilizing, and the weeks or months of this interim were suffused with more urgency, certainly than the period following the Catholic baptism of an Indian. The motives for the Indian Work probably remained much the same from Eliot to Hopkins; as Cotton Mather ranked them they were: God's glory, pity, and combating Catholicism.

Colonial popular literature did much to reinforce the Calvinistic view of the Indians. After King Philip's War, captives of the red men began to print narratives of their harrowing experiences. The pious Christian colonists, suspicious of English novels and raised on jeremiads, were ripe for adventure stories that made heroes and heroines of their pioneer forebears. These "poignant recollections" fell easily into a literary form—capture, trek, ordeal, and return. A definite *genre* developed, the vogue for this escape literature becoming strong in the 18th century and lingering into the next one. Some have suggested that captivity tales were the first indigenous American literature. The prevailing tone of these narratives was fear, which the captives in the late 17th century countered with piety. Spiritual captivity to them was worse than physical; they particularly dreaded exposure to the Catholicism of the Indians' French allies. Mary Rowlandson was offended by Indian violations of the Sabbath but found comfort in the Bible she brought with her. The captives were surprisingly successful in suppressing death wishes, and clinging to hope of return to the settlements.

Cotton Mather, in depicting the ingenious tortures the Indians used on women and children, claimed he would bring tears to his readers' eyes. And he probably did, with his emphasis on atrocities —babies forced to eat hot coals or bashed or drowned because they cried, and pregnant women with ripped-open abdomens. The Spartan code of the Indians, who disapproved of displays of emotion, especially whining and lamentation, ran completely counter to Mather's disposition. At this time the Puritan leader was trying to deepen the channels of personal and family piety, to capture some of the pietistic spirit at work in Germany. His disgust at the red man's lack of familial affection was heightened by the knowledge that some young Puritan offspring, captured early in life, would be Indianized or Catholicized and thus be lost to civilization and heaven. Historians critical of the Puritans have claimed that Cotton Mather was preoccupied with sex. He and the other ministers did expatiate upon the lust of red men for white women. (Female captives may have been relieved to find that the Indians wanted them to make bread, not love.) Even for his time and place, Mather was sentimental; native treatment of captive women and children was particularly offensive to him, and influenced his attitude toward the Indians in general.

Given the acquisitiveness of the white Protestants pushing westward for land, it probably made little actual difference how the missionaries taught Christianity to the Indians—whether they met them halfway and used the Indian languages or attempted to impart European languages and civilization. Instructed in their own language and kept apart, as in the case of the Moravian Indians, they remained vulnerable when outside forces, either advancing whites or hostile tribesmen, broke in on them. If, alternatively, the red men were required to meet the rigorous Puritan standard of language and understanding that prevailed after Eliot, or even lesser standards of other Protestants, only a very few could be "saved." And these poor souls were deracinated and devitalized, at once contemptuous of their savage kinsmen and too painfully Christian to be acceptable to the middling and meaner sorts of the white settlements. Acculturation was to be slow and partial.

The Noble Savage

The Jesuits of New France were among the important forces up-holding the Indian way of life—and sometimes romanticizing it—in the early 18th century. These clerics contributed to the image of the Noble Savage. A few decades later anticlerical deists and primi-tivists would delight in quoting them out of context to undermine religious belief.

Several reasons lay behind the Jesuits' praise of the Indians of New France. The promotion of lay contributions was one factor. Also, their classical education and emulation of the Greeks and Romans encouraged a detached view of barbarism. Beyond that, as Christians they expected to find virtue in an unpretentious setting, and above all, to combat French atheists they had to insist that the red men had a natural sense of the divine.

The influence of Molina, the Spanish Jesuit who challenged origi-nal sin with a hypothesis of a state of "pure nature" contributed to softening the Jesuit picture of the savages. Thus the heathen were gradually shifted from a "fallen" state to one of "pure nature." Al-though the pagans were not entitled to eternal life, they were de-serving of dignity as men. Man was not as depraved as the imputa-tion of Adam's sin implied. But the priests' favorable accounts were outnumbered by many more adverse observations, since they were convinced that savage life was miserable. Actually they reserved their best flights of description—those of a Noble Savage quality—for the Indians already converted to Catholic Christianity.

One of the major reasons why the Jesuits made more converts than the English was because they sought conversion before civiliza-tion rather than afterward. They assumed that humanity and theism existed as universal qualities, even in savages. The Indians did not therefore have to be "Frenchified" and could be segregated from luxury, diseases, liquor, and the general bad examples of *coureurs de bois* roistering at the trading stations.

This generous view of savage nature made it easier for Jesuits to accommodate to Indian religion and customs. Protestants (and even other Catholic orders) often criticized their concessions to heathen ways, but Jesuits explained that such compromises were immaterial and provided points of contact with native culture, and places to begin the conversion process.

Father Lafitau found the religious traditions of the ancient Greeks and Hebrews, the Chinese, and the American Indians to be similar and made the claim that true religion had existed before Moses. Fables, of course, had varied in form in the different cultures but underneath it all was a fundamental identity. The Jesuits often used "Figurism," an allegorical interpretation of the Old Testament, to buttress their comparative approach. The Indians gained status by being linked with the acknowledged pagan cultures of the world. The Jesuits so intensified their comparative approach to the heathen that finally, in 1742, the Catholic hierarchy condemned their latitudinarianism.

In the English-speaking colonies, only the gentlemen of the tidewater South seemed susceptible, after 1700, to the romantic French view of the Indians. This was reinforced by intellectual currents in England. During Queen Anne's reign, Addison and Steele and other British *literati* lionized the various Indian "kings" who came to London for a visit.

Robert Beverley, who wrote the first complete account of the Indians, reflected this moderate romanticism. A native-born planter promoting his beloved colony, Beverley devoted seventy-five pages in his *History of Virginia* (1705) to the aborigines. He steered between the pessimism of Recollect Father Hennepin and the extravagant romanticism of Baron Lahontan; specifically he aimed at correcting the many errors of the popular British historian, John Oldmixon. He wanted to be truthful and up-to-date but he had a weakness for classical parallels and the additional motive of attracting French Huguenots to the Old Dominion.

Although Beverley was a tolerant Anglican, he still felt the major drawback of Indian culture was the religious aspect. "No bigotted Pilgrim appears more zealous ... than these believing Indians do, in their idolatrous Adorations." By plying an Indian with cider, Beverley got him to admit that the tribesmen worshipped an "insensible log" in their longhouse; with some embarrassment the red man blamed the Indian priests for this superstition. But Beverley could nonetheless conclude that these harmless people were "Happy, I think, in their State of Nature, and in their enjoyment of Plenty, without the curse of Labour. They seem as possessing nothing, and yet enjoying all things."

In his description of Indian "damsels" Beverley obviously succumbed to the mingled impulses of romance, chivalry, morality and Virginia patriotism. The women he depicted were "generally beautiful" with "uncommon delicacy of shape and features, wanting no charm but a fair complexion." Suspicious Englishmen might assume promiscuity simply because of the girls' good humor and free conversation, but he found no prostitution or illegitimacy. He endorsed, however, their customary treatment of a distinguished visitor: "a brace of young beautiful Virgins are chosen, to wait upon that night, for his particular refreshment. . . . They deem it a breach of hospitality, not to submit to everything he desires of them. After this manner perhaps many Heroes were begotten in old time, who boasted to be the sons of some Way-faring God."

As he reviewed the history of Virginia, Beverley regretted that the precedent of John Rolfe's marriage to the beautiful Indian princess, Pocahontas, had not been followed. From the beginning the Indians themselves had urged intermarriage and had come to distrust the English as friends when the latter refused to permit it. Had their advice been taken, native jealousy and the consequent murder and rapine could have been averted. Many of the Indians would have been converted to Christianity, while retaining their numbers instead of dwindling away. "Success and prosperity" instead of so many "Frights and Terrors" would have come to the Old Dominion.

Beverley was not alone in this regret; other southerners were suggesting intermarriage. Colonel William Byrd, Beverley's father-in-law, approved the more permissive French policy. He believed that a white lover was the best missionary to an Indian maiden. The Indians were really not much greater heathens than the first English adventurers anyway, he claimed. If the original settlers had emulated John Rolfe and the French, "the shade of skin would not be any reproach at this day." If a Moor could be "washed" in three generations, an Indian might be blanched in two. James Oglethorpe, the founder of Georgia, also favored intermarriage. Later, Peter Fountaine observed that the children of such unions were "born as white as the Spanish and Portuguese." Besides, he added, the taking of Indian wives might somehow compensate for the taking of Indian lands; the latter could be considered dowries.

In 1709, John Lawson, the surveyor-naturalist of Carolina, offered the most advanced suggestions on this subject. He tempered his romantic allusions with realistic details in a way that adumbrated the relativistic view that was to come after 1750. Lawson noted that Indian women smoked and pilfered and, compared to their men, were vigorous and impatient in love-making. Yet they were not as "uncouth as we suppose." He approved of their anatomies and praised their submissiveness. Taking one as a bedfellow was the best way of learning their language. His solution to the "Indian problem" was the English government offering land grants to low-ranking Englishmen who would marry Indian girls. As the Indians became one people with the English, mixed groups would move westward, bringing Christianity and civilization to the Indians on the frontier. In this way too, the English could reverse the drain of potential Christians into the heathen forest that occurred when Indian mothers were left to raise the children of white fathers. Lawson claimed his plan would be more effective than indentured servitude in the English settlements and was far better than the Spanish method of superficial conversion or bloody warfare. There was at least one faint echo of this scheme: after the Revolution, Patrick Henry proposed that the new government pay a bounty of ten pounds for each child born of a white man and an Indian woman; nothing came of this proposal, however.

The advocacy of intermarriage reached its peak early in the 18th century, and was never very popular. Beverley omitted his endorsement as well as some flattering phrases from the second edition of his *History* in 1722. Sir William Johnson, the Superintendent of the Indians, was one of the few white men who was faithful to an Indian wife. The usual situation, so much lamented by the missionaries, was one of "licentious miscegenation," where traders and soldiers took temporary wives, leaving them and their offspring behind when they moved on.

Why did the English fail to intermarry with the Indians like their rivals in the New World, the French and the Spanish? It has been assumed that the Northern Europeans—Anglo-Saxon Protestants in particular—were simply too race-conscious and moralistic. A newer explanation emphasizes sex ratios. Single adventurers accumulated in great numbers in the French and Spanish territories and miscegenation was common; in the absence of European women, many unions were legalized. When some French and Spanish women did eventually come to the New World, the tradition was already established and was generally accepted (for the same reason, intermarriage came to be accepted in Protestant Hawaii in the 19th century). In the English colonies, by comparison, settlement was largely by families—especially in New England—and there were enough white women present to create a *milieu* adverse to out-marriages. Emigration by family units may have added morality and stability to the English communities, but it also reinforced ethnocentrism and thereby increased Indian enmity.

Whereas the Puritans in examining Indian life stressed moral conduct, religion and sex, the southern gentlemen seemed to reverse that order. And certainly, the attitudes of the latter on sex and religion were more secular. The incipient nationalism of the Virginians led them back to the Elizabethan tales of Captain John Smith, Pocahontas, and her powerful father, "Emperor" Powhatan. The Indian confederations of Virginia—and New York—were much more impressive to the adjacent white men than were their counterparts in New England. Tidewater Virginia, having suffered considerably from Nathaniel Bacon's Rebellion in 1676, was inclined, in retrospect, to find the Indians more tractable than the more numerous and prickly farmers of the piedmont. Colonial warfare did not directly threaten the southern colonies until the 1740s, so that planters could continue to show some affinity and sympathy for French thought for a longer period. Lacking the intense psychological fear of Papists harbored by Calvinists to the north, these men were freer to admire the French arrangements with the Indians and to indulge the Noble Savage impulse that was so compatible with an agrarian and gentlemanly style of life.

The Indians and Natural History

The influence of the Scottish philosophers, important to colonial thinking in several respects, was particularly relevant to the status of the Indian. Climate alone as an explanation for the contrasting modes of life of different continents and peoples was clearly not enough, satisfying as it was to be in the case of the Negro. The American colonists became sensitive and defensive on this score anyway; they either denied the claim of greater humidity than Europe or argued that it would lessen when the forested areas were reduced. The Scottish school offered a welcome alternative: *i.e.,* it was not climate but types of economic organization that dictated stages of civilization. Four broad types were discerned—primitive, pastoral, agrarian, and commercial. A stage of civilization theory could explain the red man's status without denying the single creation theory of Christianity. It could, moreover, account for the decline of the Indian population and culture, despite missionary efforts to Christianize and civilize. This was so because, as the word "stage" suggested, there was a developmental sequence, from low to high, simple to complex, primitive to commercial; one succeeded the other. Progress was evolutionary and God-ordained. The philosophers were able to substitute—in the minds of many Scotch Calvinists, and later their American co-religionists—progress toward a heavenly city on earth for God's promise of a millennium.

By mid-18th century thoughtful colonists were abandoning the idea that the Indians would be assimilated into white civilization. They were ready to conclude that the cultural gap was too wide to be bridged, and the Scottish theory rationalized this belief. The red men with their nomadic, traditional society represented an earlier stage destined to be supplanted by Christianity, private property and progress. It was foolish to dwell, as Calvinistic clergy and captives had, on merely invidious distinctions, on the tortures, strange cuisine, or lack of abstract ability among the natives. No longer should the aborigines be regarded simply as defective Europeans; they had to be measured on a different scale. Their virtues and vices were to be related to their stage of development and not compared directly to European standards.

In explicating their theories, the Scottish philosophers revealed strong anthropological and sociological, as well as legal, interests. The analysis of social structure appealed to them more than the emphasis on individual men and events; they were drawn to facts that could be fitted into a thoroughly systematic exposition. They were philosophical, empirical and comparative, but they also held that man was an active creature, and despite the stages, was capable of improvement.

Benjamin Franklin's apparent adoption of the stages theory may account for his detached and "philosophical" attitude toward the red man in most of his writings. As a budding philosopher-statesman, Franklin subscribed early to the stages of civilization concept. In his enthusiasm for America's population growth, it seemed clear he expected the Indians to give way to an agrarian order of white farmers. Their doom was inevitable.

Franklin's long sojourns in London, after 1757, undoubtedly modified his view of the American red men further. There he was vulnerable to an even more "philosophical" outlook. No longer the *arriviste* printer challenging the hegemony of the Quakers and the Penn family, Franklin was by now a renowned scholar and scientist; it was appropriate that his opinions of the aborigines became more ambivalent, overlaid by sympathy, humor and knowledge as well as Scottish and French influence.

Nevertheless, even in the wake of the American Revolution, Franklin showed little patriotic concern for the Indian *per se*. He was content to collect and reissue his earlier observations on the Indians—*Concerning the Savages of North America* (1784). He acknowledged the virtues of Indians within their culture, but used them chiefly for the purpose of criticizing European civilization. He was skillful in making his Indians, when confronted by European traditionalism, sound properly philosophical and deistical. Franklin was almost a Continental *philosophe* in his satire and anticlericalism, but the usual Noble Savage overtones were missing. He did not espouse the pantheism of the *philosophe,* and therefore was not so concerned about the origins of the Indians or their exact position in the cosmos. Nor did he need to prove that the red men, as inhabitants of the New World, were degenerate. He knew better; he had been there. Franklin did not typify even the enlightened of America but he did reflect the full impact of the Enlightenment on this country's attitude toward the red men.

Franklin used the red men in the typical Enlightenment manner to criticize civilized life. He struck the right tone of cultural relativity when he said, "savages we call them, because their manners differ from ours, which we think the perfection of civilization: they think the same of theirs." He indicated the futility of higher education and the acceptance of savagism when he reported the words of an Indian chief in 1744 rejecting a white offer: "we must let you know we love our children too well to send them so great a Way, and the *Indians* are not inclined to give their children learning. We allow it to be good, and we thank you for your invitation; but our customs differing from yours, you will be so kind as to excuse us." He put his imagination to work and pictured Indian youths returning to the forest from college and finding that they were incapable of killing deer, catching beaver, or surprising an enemy. He did defend peaceful red men on occasion; an example was his famous rebuke of the Paxton boys of Pennsylvania for murdering the Conestoga Indians without cause. But this was offset somewhat by his earlier endorsement of bloodhounds to hunt down unfriendly Indians. This "canine solution" put him in the company of Cotton Mather, Solomon Stoddard and the Spaniards.

In the Revolutionary generation at least two prominent Americans provided enlightened descriptions of the Indians: James Adair and Thomas Jefferson. Their accounts, like Franklin's, demonstrate in varying degree the Enlightenment tendency to be erudite, anticlerical, satirical, systematic and still humane. They were not sensational; their evolutionary stance was intermediate between the realism of the missionaries and the parochial exoticism and promotionalism of the gentlemen scholars, yet they were not as detached as Franklin.

James Adair was a Scotchman who spent most of his life on the Carolina frontier as a trader among the Indians. In *The History of the American Indians* (1774) he adhered doggedly to the thesis that the red men were descendants of the ten Lost Tribes, who had migrated from Asia to North America. By this time, the Hebrew, as opposed to the Tartar theory, was distinctly a minority view. He was with the great majority, however, in reaffirming that all men shared a common descent from Adam; and in refuting Lord Kames, the Scottish philosopher, and Bernard Romans, the Dutch engineer, who had resurrected the idea of separate creations and races. Adair called the colors of men "accidental," deriving from climate and different styles of life, but he put ultimate blame on God for permitting these changes. How much jealousy and bloodshed had resulted! He referred to "ignorant and wicked clergymen" who served as missionaries. He preferred chieftains to "despotic" kings, and *laissez-faire* to mercantilism. It was the poor who suffered when there were too many laws. At this time he was reflecting the frontier American's impatience with King George, his Churchmen, his trade laws and his minions along the seaboard.

In Adair's work, frontier realism, savagism, and the Noble Savage were thoroughly mingled. In the early pages he was conventionally realistic as a frontier trader when he noted the Choctaws had "no human attributes except shape and language." He conceded that the Indians could not accommodate to European civilization. Yet some Noble Savage sentiment lingered because Adair was sensitive to the dangers of overcivilization; he wanted to rehabilitate the aborigines, not incarcerate them. Traders like Adair had to push rather hard for their very limited Noble Savage effects because they were practical, not literary, men who knew all too well the details of Indian life.

Thomas Jefferson's fullest reflections on Indian nature appeared in his *Notes on the State of Virginia*. He wrote these during the Revolution in response to a questionnaire from the French government. He was Governor of Virginia during the Revolution and saw this inquiry as an opportunity to correct the many misconceptions Europeans still held about the New World. His reply was aimed particularly at the skeptical naturalists DePauw, Buffon, and Raynal. Jefferson was scholarly and courteous and he managed to praise Buffon, the most influential of these men, for a few of his insights. But his total analysis of these naturalists was devastating; he destroyed thirty-one different premises they had made about natural history in America. Jefferson had a great distaste for theories not buttressed with facts and experience. He said he would not speak of South America, but only of Virginia—"on what I have seen of men, white, red, and black. A patient pursuit of facts, and cautious combination and compilation of them, is the drudgery to which man is subjected by his Maker if he wished to attain sure knowledge." He was careful to abide by this dictum.

Jefferson derided Buffon's description of the Indians on several counts. The French naturalist claimed that the Indians were moved only by hunger or thirst and were otherwise lethargic. The absence of overt family affection and low birth rate were explained by their lack of sexual ardor. The sparseness of body hair on the red man was for Buffon, as for most Europeans, a clear indication of low sex drive. Jefferson rejected this association, and reported that the Indians were averse to body hair on aesthetic grounds and so plucked it out; the natives believed body hair appropriate only for hogs. As a clincher, the Virginian observed that while Negroes had little body hair, they had a reputation for being very ardent. If Indian squaws had fewer children, it was probably because of the nomadic way of life; when Indian women married white traders and settled in one place, they were as fertile as white women.

The peculiar gravity and eloquence of Indian oratory had strongly impressed white men since the days of Columbus. Deistical thinkers of the 18th century, inclined to rate the ancients above the Christian fathers, were even more admiring than the missionaries. Jefferson claimed that the address of Logan, the Mingo chief, to Lord Dunmore, the Governor of Virginia, was a classic ranking with the best efforts of Demosthenes and Cicero. Many observers described the speech of the red men as concise, precise, artful, and, on occasion, vehement. The Indians, too, were masters of evasive parables when they needed them. Their metaphors were good but there were not enough of them. Their solemn oratory in council was especially dramatic and, unlike Europeans, they never interrupted one another. The men were never garrulous; they did not, for example, boast of their intrigues with women.

In later years, as head of the Philosophical Society, and President of the United States, Jefferson retained his interest in the Indians. Although he was disappointed at Indian agricultural failures and white encroachments, he kept an open mind on Indian origins and nature. Daniel Boorstin, the historian, has suggested that Jefferson could do this more readily in the case of the Indian than in the case of the Negro, because the Indians had maintained their own society, such as it was, and self-sufficiency of a people in the environment was an important value in 18th-century America.

The Black Man and the Missionary

The Portuguese who sailed down the west coast of Africa in the 15th century were devoutly Christian and very credulous. They were seeking not only a passage to the fabulous Indies but also the distant empire of Prester John. Influenced also by classical authorities, these explorers expected to see chaos, barbarism, bestiality and monstrosity beyond the Mediterranean world. The Moors, Berbers and Egyptians were known, but not the Africans south of the Sahara.

When they reached the teeming coast of West Africa the explorers were not disappointed. By European standards, the black men and their manner of life were very different. The white adventurers perceived no civilization and social regulation, and in their accounts tended to emphasize aspects that offended their sensibilities or excited their desires. Ship captains, slave traders and mercenary writers provided sensational travel narratives for several centuries. In the 18th century, slavers, in defending their activities, still cited these lurid works.

The image of the Africans these adventurers offered the European public was quite unflattering. Supposedly innate character defects were stressed. The Negroes were charged with being lazy, careless, crafty, and cruel. Undoubtedly these observers were reflecting their

own interests as well as those of their readers when they reported on
adultery, polygamy, and the details of wedding night rites. Mariners
and bourgeois alike enjoyed tales of women so amorous that penalties could not keep them from European men.

To Europeans, and later to American colonists, the most important feature of the West Africans was skin color—so dissimilar to
European men, especially to the British and Dutch. Medieval
thinkers had associated skin color with the Greek humors, namely
temperament; this may have led to the notion that the Negro was
different internally as well as externally. Unfortunately, the color
black already carried evil connotations. The word was defined as
foul, wicked, sinister and deadly long before contact with black
Africa. In Elizabethan England, fair skin was the ideal of beauty.
White was compatible with red—the lily and the rose, John Rolfe
and Pocahontas—but black was not. Shakespeare—notably in *Othello,*
but also in *Twelfth Night* and the sonnets—had indicated that black
should not be mixed with white. This superstition was so strong that
the perception that non-European peoples might find beauty in
other hues was a relative judgment that only a very few Europeans
were capable of making.

Ethnocentrism and religious concern disposed the Europeans to
find a single explanation for the Negro's blackness. Since they believed that the normal skin color was white and that the Bible was
definite in indicating that all men derived from a single pair, how
did the Negro become black? Ptolemy had blamed the sun and assumed that men in different latitudes varied in skin color. But the
Indians of America in the same latitude with West Africa were
not black, but "tawney." By the beginning of the 17th century there
were several generations to disprove the earlier theory that Negroes
would "whiten" after residence in Europe or, conversely, that Europeans would darken in Africa. Jeremiah had anticipated this in
his query: "Can the Ethiopian change his skin or the leopard his
spots?"

Reformation thought in the 16th and 17th centuries with its strong
religious tone shifted the explanation of Negro color from climate to
the curse of Ham. When Ham looked upon his father's "nakedness,"
God punished him by making his progeny dark slaves; the Negroes
were Ham's descendants. This view found favor among some bibli-
cists and was perpetuated later by Joseph Smith and the Mormons.

From the outset the effect of Christian ideas in Africa was quite mixed. The concept of the unity of single creation and the implied equality among the saved in the next life were offset by the connotations of heathen status, allowing many convenient rationalizations. The Calvinistic Protestants, of course, made the additional assumption that God's Elect were not evenly distributed among the races or over the globe. Only a few of the Lord's sheep mingled with the heathen who had not heard the Word. It might be morally acceptable to enslave non-Christians in order to tame the old Adam and bring them to Christ; it might even excuse drastic measures in West Africa—kidnapping and the march to the sea in chains. Tribal warfare made this kind of conquest relatively easy, and planted the idea of Negro inferiority in European minds. Because they did not intend to colonize with their families and tame the Dark Continent, these sojourners could be casual, complacent, and indifferent. They were not sufficiently analytical to examine how Africans treated each other and thereby gain insight into the social structure; instead they focused on how Africans reacted to outsiders. Suffused with Christianity, but not true piety, and lacking even the comparative methods of the *philosophes* and Scottish philosophers that would emerge in the 18th century, these Europeans felt free to pass moral judgments. Protestant attitudes in the American colonies, and the sudden nature of British contact with Africa accentuated this tendency, when compared with Spanish and Portuguese reaction. Evangelical Christians in the colonies, insecure about their own degree of gentility, tended to emphasize the heathen "before" and the Christian "after" that would reinforce the already excessive distinction between civilized and uncivilized. Despite some laudable motives, the early result of Christianity for the Africans was to intensify and intellectualize differences and prejudices.

The Negro did not benefit as much as the Indian from the Noble Savage myth. No traveler of Marco Polo's fame publicized African civilization; when the locus of Prester John's empire moved in the 14th century from the Indies to Abyssinia, it somehow lost much of its exotic appeal. Moreover, the Africans themselves had excluded white men from the hinterlands of the Dark Continent, so that the nature of life in the relatively complex African states did not receive sufficient exposure in Europe. The result was that the Africans were considered interesting but not as instructive to the civilization-conscious Europeans as the Asians, Incas, Aztecs, or Red Indians in general. Although the first Noble Savage drama performed in England—*Oroonoko* (1688)—featured a Negro rather than an Indian, this was the exception, not the rule. In Europe the Negro got some favorable literary attention, but in early 18th century America he carried the stigma of the "ignoble savage."

At first the British were more inclined to view the Negro as a factor in production than as a literary figure. Mercantilists were persuaded that African slaves were the answer to the labor problems of overseas plantations. Their numbers added to the imperial population without subtracting from the metropolis, their maintenance was cheap and, if not docile already, they could be made obedient. Extremists could even argue that transportation of the Africans would justify a large navy and that although slaves would provide a demand for cheap textiles for clothing, they would require little else and so would not subtract from the commodities available for export.

As mercantilistic thought became more sophisticated, however, the disadvantages of the Negro slave came to outweigh the benefits. If it was a productive population that made a nation strong, rather than absolute numbers, the sick, the old, the idle and the unskilled were of slight utility. The ideal immigrant or colonist was not an unskilled African laborer, but a white Protestant craftsman or farmer. Another drawback was the alleged non-assimilability of the Negro. In peacetime he could not be integrated into church or society; in wartime he might be a subversive threat.

This change in mercantilistic attitude was reflected in the colonies. In 1698 South Carolina moved to encourage the immigration of white workmen, and imposed occupational restrictions and import taxes on slaves. Oglethorpe in his plans for Georgia excluded both enslaved and free Negroes as a military precaution since anarchic Spanish Florida was at the border. Despite tax barriers, the importation of African slaves increased in the southern colonies, and Georgia, affected by the mores of the Carolina low country to the north, reversed itself and permitted slavery. By 1710 the supply of white indentured servants from Europe had been exhausted, and since transported felons were too few, blacks seemed to be the only choice for plantation labor.

Slavery based upon color as well as upon pagan condition seems to have existed in all the colonies from an early date. The Dutch sold the first Negroes to the colonists in 1619; by 1640 there was strong social discrimination against the Negro. But there were so few blacks in the first years, the arrangements were not yet formalized. The term "servant," taken from English law, was used generally in the 17th century to refer to the bound working class—white, red, and black. The Indian and Negro servants, however, were always treated somewhat differently from the whites. They were less likely to be allowed arms and more likely, when punished, to have their terms of servitude extended, not merely for a few years, but for life. Indian and Negro female servants—unlike white—worked in the fields and were counted as tithables for tax purposes. Although white indentured servants were preferred because they had more aptitudes, the prices were as much as three times as high for Negro servants; the obvious explanation is that the purchaser expected a longer period of service from the latter. With the mounting influx of Africans after 1680, the colonists felt the need to legalize, codify and extend restrictions that were already customary and Negro "servants" became "slaves." The result was the "peculiar institution" of North American slavery. The system grew out of experience in the tobacco colonies, was strongly affected by conditions in the West Indies, but was still *sui generis,* having no real counterpart farther south, nor, of course, in England itself.

Until the mid-18th century, however, it was religion and the church, more than law or literature, that best defined the Negro's status in the colonial world, and even later the religious aspect remained important.

The Puritans, in their estimate of Negro character, were less negative and more ambivalent than they were toward the Indians. The Negroes, after all, had never been a threat to New England's expansion. In 1675 there were less than one hundred Africans in New England; the number rose to about 3 percent of the population in the 18th century. Most Negroes were domestic servants, but some were on plantations in the Narragansett district of Rhode Island. After the defeat of the Pequots in 1637, many of the captured Indians were exchanged for Negro slaves from the Caribbean, and in the 1640s some West Indies whites migrated to New England. These developments, plus increasing maritime contacts with the West Indies, gave the "peculiar institution" a foothold in New England although there was no pressing economic need for slavery there.

Puritan literature on the Negro was not large in this period; the chief authors were Judge Sewall who wrote *The Selling of Joseph*

(1700), the merchant John Saffin who answered him, and the ubiquitous Cotton Mather. Sewall could not believe that the Old Testament, so important to the Puritans, sanctioned slavery; he wanted to end the trade. He believed that "all men, as they are the Sons of Adam, are Co-heirs, and have equal Right unto Liberty," and a title to property could not result from manstealing. Saffin, in the only openly anti-Negro publication in colonial times, denied Sewall's thesis. There was the weight of tradition behind his claim that God "hath ordained different degrees and orders of men, some to be High and Honourable, some to be Low and Despicable." "If there were a mere parity of men," then the course of Divine Providence in the World would be wrong and unjust—an unthinkable view—and all the "sacred Rules, Precepts and Commands of the Almighty which He hath given the Son of Men to observe and keep in their respective Places, Orders, and Degrees, would be to no purpose." The Negroes were accursed and as a consequence cowardly and cruel, unlike Joseph who was one of the Chosen.

Mather was on Sewall's side, believing that all men were brothers, that God did not judge men by their complexions, and that some Negroes could be among the Elect. But they were a "different nation," and were presumably incapable of freedom and assimilation. Of course he expected that good Puritans would do their duty by their black brothers and encourage piety among them. He reiterated John Eliot's charge that New England masters were harsh and negligent; but he was oblivious to the culture and language barrier, declaring, "the greater their stupidity, the greater must be our Application." Mather had learned about inoculation for smallpox from a slave, and he did suggest that the white men could learn about nature's wonders from Africans as well as Indians. William Douglass, a Scottish physician who was Mather's chief adversary in the inoculation controversy countered that the Negroes were so notorious as liars that nothing instructive could be gleaned from them. The clergy were more sympathetic to Negroes than the laity, and evidently Mather was regarded as an apologist. A navy lieutenant, in derision, named his slave "Cotton Mather."

The Quakers were on record very early as opposed to slavery. George Fox had pronounced against it on his tour of the West Indies in 1671. Penn had suggested manumission in fourteen years; Father Pastorius had condemned the "traffic in menbody." George Keith, the schismatic, denied that the scriptures sanctioned slavery. English and German Friends in Pennsylvania indicated their disapproval at the 1688 Meetings. Moravians and other pietist sects felt the same way, regarding slavery as a breach of the Golden Rule; they asserted that Negroes also were in the image of God, part of the vast world population as yet ungathered. As in the case of the Indian, Quaker views and the accompanying behavior earned the respect of Negroes but not their adherence.

For Quakers, particularly, the slave trade and manumission were sensitive issues in the first half of the 18th century. Everywhere, from Rhode Island to the West Indies, Quaker slaveowners were less brutal, more humane and more conscientious than others about bringing their Negroes to the meeting, but they nevertheless did have reservations about Negro character. Despite pressure, many of them had become complacent as the impetus of the Holy Experiment diminished. It was the arriving Friends, rather than the already settled American-born, who kept alive the Fox-Penn anti-slavery position. Slaves appear to have been unprofitable in most of Pennsylvania and New Jersey, but there were some field hands and house servants.

The Quaker position may have had some small, delayed effect on Ben Franklin. In 1729, at some risk, he published the pioneer Quaker anti-slave pamphlet, and later printed others. Yet during this period of his life, he and his wife owned slaves; and he also wished that the country were composed solely of whites, without tawneys or blacks. When Pennsylvania passed anti-slave laws later, Franklin was in England and had no connection with them. At the time of the Revolution, Franklin in his more humanitarian phase, did charge the British with foisting slavery on her colonies—a nationalistic but not a very accurate claim.

In the Middle Colonies, the Anglican clergy were somewhat more pro-Negro than their Puritan counterparts in New England and noticeably more humane and less rigid than their Dutch predecessors in this region. The S.P.G. missionaries concentrated on the liturgy and doctrines; they hired local catechists and encouraged memorization. Without evangelism, they tended to attract the more docile women and children who were shy about pronouncing English words but accepted books as rewards for their adherence. Attendance varied considerably with the seasons of the year; actual conversions were rare.

Historians of the Anglican Church have been proudest of their work with the Negro in New York. The young missionaries assured the planters that baptism did not imply freedom and that Christianity actually made the Negroes less willful and more law-abiding. The Society supported a law that specified that conversion did not require manumission by an owner. The clergy offered only bland homiletics; although they did not attack the slave system, they did not attempt to give it religious sanction, either. Yet the planters worried; the proximity of Baptists, Quakers, formerly free Spanish Negroes, and cosmopolitan New York City heightened their anxiety. The City's population was nearly 15 percent black and laws were promulgated forbidding slaves to congregate unless they were attending church where whites were present. The first major slave insurrection hit Manhattan in 1712 and—although the rebels were non-Christians—the S.P.G. afterward had to push a bit uphill against the laity and the general population. Nevertheless, the young Anglicans in New York were zealous, and their educational efforts—classes in reading, writing, arithmetic—continued to have limited success.

South of Pennsylvania, however, Anglican efforts were much weaker. In Maryland and Virginia, although the Church was established, the clergy was dependent on the local goodwill of the vestry and the planter class, and that group was indifferent or hostile to the conversion of the slaves. Apparently the masters did not fear for their own souls and were less concerned about the souls of their bondsmen. Conservative slaveowners believed that baptism and a Christian life would take time away from plantation labor, promote equalitarianism and threaten insurrection. In the tidewater of South Carolina, where blacks heavily outnumbered whites, this feeling was particularly strong.

During the first wave of importations from Africa from the 1690s to 1740, the missionaries were hindered by the general belief that the "Guinea" slave adults were unteachable. While there was no conspicuous assumption of intellectual inferiority, the consensus was that the slaves' knowledge of the English language was so poor and they had so much "rudeness in manners" as to be beyond redemption. The clergy therefore concentrated on the young native-born slaves growing up in America.

In colonial days the planters did not claim that their bondsmen were content or happy; that rationalization was part of the Old South mythology that came later. Instead it was conceded that the imported slaves were perverse, obstinate, sullen and wild.

Reverend Hugh Jones, an Anglican, noted that "those that have been slaves in their own country, are the best Servants for those that have been Kings and great Men there are generally lazy, haughty and obstinate; whereas the others are sharper, better humoured, and more laborious." William Byrd fretted that Virginia was becoming "New Guinea"; the clergy might postulate spiritual equality, but Byrd and some other planters were ready to believe that the Negroes were cursed by God as the descendants of Ham.

Before 1740 the Negroes had very few articulate champions in America. These few were European-born and with a religious orientation, either pantheistic Quaker radicals or philanthropic Anglican educators.

Linnaeus, Jefferson and the Negro

The Great Awakening and Linnaeus' ingenious system of classifying flora and fauna occurred at about the same time and tended to polarize colonial thought. After 1740, two rather distinct groups—the scientists and the evangelicals—discussed the condition of the Negro.

The "scientific" group took its cue from Montesquieu, Buffon, and some of the Scottish philosophers, and focused on climate, the anatomical differences between white and black, and the role of slavery in the economy. Among those who rejected organized religion, climate was revived as a major factor in explaining racial differences. Montesquieu's *On the Spirit of Laws* (1748) gave the classic idea new currency. David Hume, the Scottish sceptic, was ready to assume that no real civilization could exist except in the temperate zone, and as a consequence polar and tropical peoples were inferior. Because the Negro race was concentrated around the equator, the climate was always seen as more important in accounting for the Negro than the Indian. It was presumed that because his skin was black and he sweated profusely, the Negro could more easily endure a humid climate than could a white European. His African origin also suggested that he was more resistent to malaria and any skin diseases affected by the sunshine. Thus God and Nature intended that, in the tropics, the black man should work in the field under the hot sun and the white man should supervise, wearing a hat. Of course, white men could and did work in the fields and swamps on occasion, and these places were not very healthful for either race.

Yet climate remained a major rationalization for Negro slavery until the Civil War.

But because climate came to be a rationalization, it should not on that account be dismissed as "unscientific" or irrelevant; it was—and is—in various ways a significant factor in race relations. It was obvious, for example, that English colonials in the tropical plantation country were doubtful of the Negroes' abilities. As a Virginian and a scientist, Jefferson struggled, not very successfully, to keep his mind open on this question, but further south in Carolina and the West Indies, sharper lines were drawn; in the districts of big plantations and big work gangs, notions of innate Negro inferiority naturally found favor, and linger to this day. In this way climate and a low estimate of Negro ability were related.

Linnaeus' new method of classifying plants and animals, and the venerable Great Chain of Being—the belief that God had forged a chain of many gradations of life and no missing links— both hinged on differences. Linnaeus had confirmed what the majority of Christians already believed, that all mankind came from one species. He did allow, however, for "varieties" of men, accidental differences attributed to the environment. Since the species division was given by God, scientific speculation centered on the environmental varieties. While Linnaeus himself was innocent of ranking, it was inevitable that others, habituated to hierarchy in society and still influenced by the Great Chain, would use the varieties to rank different colors of men. The early effect of the Linnaean system was therefore divisive of mankind; investigators were encouraged to search out and measure any anatomical, biological, or mental variations they could find. And the *philosophes* naturally looked to America to provide much of the data, to classify the Negro as they had previously classified the various exotic plants and animals of the New World.

In the case of Man, the greatest, most obvious difference was skin color. But the naturalists were not interested in red skin. They did not even feel the need to hypothesize that red men were the result of a black and white blend, perhaps because evidences of Indian culture—languages and utensils—were obvious. Negro slaves by contrast, showed few vestiges of African culture. Eighteenth century curiosity about origins, therefore, did not focus, in the case of the Negro, on Africa, but on how his skin got to be that color. Although of diminishing influence, the descendant of Ham theory would incline investigators in the same direction.

To Dr. Benjamin Rush of Philadelphia went the credit for advancing the most novel explanation of the Negro's color. The physician suggested that the Negro race was originally white but had contracted leprosy. This disease not only blackened the skin, but accounted for certain facial characteristics and traits as well. Rush believed that, although the disease was inherited, it was no longer contagious; as a good Presbyterian and abolitionist, he looked forward to the day when the Negroes could be cured and assume their places in white society, free from prejudice.

It was Virginia, the oldest plantation colony, however, that first supplied Europe with detailed and "scientific" observations about the Negro's skin color and his other attributes. Dr. John Mitchell published his *Essay on the Causes of the Different Colours of Peoples in Different Climates* in 1746. After studying at the University of Edinburgh, Mitchell had spent about twenty years as a physician in Virginia. He corresponded with Linnaeus, Collinson, Colden, Kalm and Bartram. Turning aside from his botanical and zoological work to consider this matter, the naturalist decided that Negro skin was only quantitatively different from white. He claimed that the environment had made it thicker and more opaque and that black skin resulted from the absence of whiteness. Implicit in the thinking of Mitchell, Rush and other investigators of that period, was the idea—derived no doubt from the scriptures—that these men had degenerated, by means of a bad environment and through acquired characteristics, from a primordial type, probably the white man of the Caspian region, who had been in a state of primitive perfection. (In the last stage of this degeneration, dark people turned white again; this explained those curious people, the white Indians and Negroes, that were being discovered in remote places.) Thus even the secular and anticlerical theorists of the time retained some religious assumptions. Their "scientific" theory was a close cousin of the descent from Ham; bad environment had merely been substituted for God's curse to explain the fall from whiteness.

At the time of the Revolution, Thomas Jefferson was the most renowned expert on the Negro in the mainland colonies. He had built his science on the Linnaean system of one species with some varieties. But with respect to the Negro, Jefferson found it difficult to follow Linnaeus consistently. Negro differences loomed so large in his mind that he was often to treat them as more than environmental. Jefferson sometimes sounded as if the Negro were a different species after all, not simply another variety.

In his discussion of color, Jefferson made his own preference specific; in this he was obviously more of a Virginian than a *philosophe*. He echoed 17th century Englishmen as well as Beverley and Byrd when he found red and white "the expressions of every passion by greater or less suffusions of color in the one, preferable to that eternal monotony . . . that immovable veil of black which covers the emotions of the other race." Negroes themselves thought whites more attractive, he claimed. "The circumstance of superior beauty, is thought worthy of attention in the propagation of our horses, dogs, and other domestic animals; why not in that of man?"

In this age of equalitarianism Jefferson's tone remained very rational. He thought it was time to look at the Negroes and Indians scientifically: "though for a century and a half we have had under our eyes the races of black and red men, they have never yet been viewed by us as subjects of natural history. I advance it, therefore, as a suspicion only, that the blacks, whether originally a distinct race, or made distinct by time and circumstances, are inferior to the whites in the endowments of both body and mind. It is not against experience to suppose that different species of the same genus, or varieties of the same species, may possess different qualifications. Will not a lover of natural history then, one who views the gradations in all the races of animals with the eye of philosophy, excuse an effort to keep those in the department of man as distinct as nature formed them. This unfortunate difference in color, and perhaps faculty, is a powerful obstacle to the emancipation of these people." He did hazard his opinion with great diffidence because the conclusion might "degrade a whole race of men from the rank in the scale of beings which their Creator may perhaps have given them." Although it breached the Linnaean system, this was Jefferson's position on the Negro. Throughout his life he gathered data on Negro talents and abilities, but he never shook off his suspicion.

The fact that Thomas Jefferson, author of the Declaration of Independence, was as tentative, inconsistent and even negative as he was about Negro potentiality, while useful to a few segregationists, has been disquieting to most latter-day Americans. There are several interesting lines of speculation that may help to explain, if not excuse, Jefferson on this score. One approach uses the concept of cultural shock to explain the personalities of the field hands of those days. Acording to this controversial theory, Negroes who had not been slaves were suddenly wrenched from West African life by kidnap or capture, marched to the coast in chains, inspected, branded, and crushed into a few square feet of a vessel bound for the West Indies. Of the many Negroes imported to America this way, only about one-third survived this ordeal and the subsequent "seasoning" in the West Indies, and ultimately reached the mainland colonies. The assumption, then, is that these survivors were the victims of cultural shock; their psychic states could be likened to those of Jewish prisoners in Hitler's concentration camps. All along the way, and for some time after arrival, the vigorous and rebellious were maimed or killed for their obstinacy; many committed suicide in futile resistance, believing that if their bodies were intact, they would return to the African homeland. With these firebrands gradually eliminated, and with new restrictive laws on the books to weaken their personalities further by treating them as chattels, psychologically "numbed" field hands became numerous after 1750 on the big plantations. The African heritage, rich and diverse, was virtually drained out; for these unfortunates the real world had narrowed down to the fields of tobacco, rice, and indigo. According to interpersonal theory, every developing personality needs to have some psychic security, which is built up by observing and emulating the behavior patterns of "significant others," *i.e.*, those in proximity who have status. In the closed society of the tidewater South—so the argument runs—young Negroes had very few "significant others" to emulate—only the slaveowner and overseer. Thus these American-born slaves growing up—cut off from the past, with no town life, and working in large field gangs—tended to assimilate the attitudes and styles of their white masters. For their psychic security, the slaves tried to picture the white bosses as good fathers; the result was a sort of perverted patriarchy. They internalized their dependency and inferiority, adjusting to the intolerable by regression. The desire to run away or commit suicide diminished.

The slave personality that emerged was maimed. The slave was a child who never grew up, a perpetual minor, hedonistic, lackadaisical, superstitious, loyal and lovable in his place. He had a child's indifference toward death. He was the classic Sambo; his fantasies were limited to catfish and watermelon. He was mentally even more devitalized and deracinated than New England's Praying Indian. But Sambo and the Praying Indian must be viewed as the casualties of a severe cultural collision, and their extreme cases revealed little of what was innate or potential. John Woolman, the Christ-like Quaker, in promoting empathy for the slaves, quoted *Ecclesiastes*, VII:7, "Surely oppression makes the wise man foolish."

The cultural shock theory has been criticized on the ground that it is unnecessary; there is no need to assume that field hands unconsciously internalized in this way. The older idea of role-playing is still viable; if slaves did fit the Sambo stereotype, it was because, living in an oppressive atmosphere, Negroes consciously learned to play a role, to behave in an overtly servile but covertly mocking manner. Such a façade would conceal Negro abilities from the planters' eyes. The frequent whippings and the revolts, moreover, would tend to contradict any hypothesis of slave docility. Nonetheless the shock theory is a possible insight in interpreting the detailed testimony of contemporary southerners, even those like Jefferson who tried to speak the language of natural history.

In his *Notes on Virginia,* Jefferson compared the slaves of Augustan Rome to those in the Old Dominion. He noted that the Roman slaves were sexually segregated, and sometimes sold or exposed when old or diseased. Evidence of crime was extracted from a slave by torture; when a master was murdered, all the slaves in the house were condemned to death. Despite these deplorable conditions, Roman slaves displayed talents as artists, scientists, and tutors. Virginia was more humane on all these counts, he believed, yet he found "no black that had uttered a thought above the level of plain narration; never saw even an elementary trait of painting or sculpture." The Roman slaves excelled in poetry, a good vehicle for the oppressed, but Jefferson found no talent in Virginia. The efforts of Phyllis Wheatley, the black girl who wrote an ode to George Washington, were without merit. He scored the lack of imagination of the slaves, compared not only to the Roman slaves, but also to the Indians; the red men with their carving knives and crayons were more creative. He conceded that Ignatius Sancho, a Negro writer, wrote gracefully but charged him with an imagination that was wild and extravagant, as incoherent and eccentric "as is the course of a meteor through the sky." Sancho substituted sentiment for discipline and demonstration. Evidently Jefferson was seeking, among the Virginia slaves, imaginations that were properly attuned to the Age of Reason.

Another recent line of inquiry gives some general support to the shock idea, and also puts a different perspective on Jefferson's comparison of slave talents. Scholars of this school stress the difference between slavery in Protestant America and the same institution in Catholic America. The Protestants were thorough, efficient and doctrinaire in maintaining a rigid caste line in this period. To the south, what began as a caste system in the Catholic colonies turned into an open class society. To explain this difference, this school enumerates several factors operating in Castile and Portugal that affected development in the Catholic colonies: the heritage of Roman law and experience, the extended contact with the non-white Moors, the power retained over the colonies by the bureaucratic governments on the Iberian peninsula, and, above all, the strong alliance of Church and state.

These scholars would therefore challenge Jefferson's conclusions in comparing Roman and Virginian slaves. They would argue that the Roman slaves, despite some harsh treatment, were more clearly recognized as people, as having personalities, than were slaves under Virginia law. While the Virginians were ambiguous and inconsistent, they did tend to regard the slaves as chattels—as things or cattle. The Roman slave, as Jefferson himself noted, was not separated by caste and could mingle with the population after manumission. Even as a slave he had many rights as a person. If this were the case, the comparison Jefferson made was unfair; the Roman slaves were not as oppressed psychologically and could be expected to perform better in creative assignments.

In Latin America the role of the Catholic Church in race relations was vital. Instead of acting as Defender of the Faith as in Europe, the Church in America adapted to very different conditions. It reverted to an earlier medieval role and acted as the sympathetic guardian of the Indians and Negroes, restraining the conquistadores and Creoles. The Church, reinforced by the state, acted as an intermediary between master and slave, encouraged manumission and marriage, and kept families together. To be married, slaves had to be baptized; under normal conditions this might mean three months of instruction in Church doctrines. Slaveowners were required to send their bondsmen to church.

A syncretization of Catholicism with African folk religion was quite successful, at least socially. Negroes gathered on Sundays and holidays in separate houses that constituted clubs. The clubs were organized to represent the various regions of West African immigration. The members sang, danced and fraternized. While the Church only tolerated and did not condone some of the exuberance, it did make these groups part of its system of religious brotherhoods. The clubs were given their own virgins to worship. African costume, ceremony, music and mythology found outlets; the clubs marched as units in religious processions on special days. Thus the Negro population kept a sense of identity, and at the same time learned to take part in community affairs. The retention of some of Africa seemed to make assimilation to Latin America easier.

In North America even the religio-politically oriented friends of the Negro were reluctant to acknowledge African antecedents or probe the African background; they apparently feared evidence that might be derogatory to the Negro and to the promotion of the rights of man. Jefferson, the *philosophe,* could have taken this risk but he was apparently not interested. In fact, he said that in order to be "fair," he would not consider them. He had promised not to speak of South America but only of Virginia and "what I have seen of men, white, red, and black"; yet with his Roman comparisons he strained this rule. In his lack of curiosity about Africa or South America, Jefferson was certainly in agreement with the white Protestant majority. But in retrospect, this failure of even the enlightened colonial to detect or acknowledge black culture—or to consider the contemporary forms of Roman slavery flourishing elsewhere in the New World—demonstrated how difficult it would be for the black man to find his identity and thus mitigate life in the hostile white world of the new United States.

The status of the free colored group has been taken as a good indicator of the racial attitudes of the two societies—the English colonies and Latin America. In Cuba, for example, the free colored were a major element in the population—40 percent in 1774—and received commensurate status. The Church had encouraged manumission, and in this way energetic slaves were fed into the free population constantly. Life was substantially urban and the freedmen occupied many positions among the skilled artisans. Church schools were open to all. Since freedmen could bear arms and Spain relied heavily on the local militia to repel invaders, the military was an important avenue upward for Negroes. Some black officers even managed to buy their sons into the racially exclusive professions of law, medicine and religion. "Passing" was facilitated by fees; in most circles, if one were wealthy enough, one's skin color was overlooked. As might be expected, color was still operative; the mulattoes outnumbered the blacks in the free population two to one. Nevertheless, the caste system declined and was supplanted by an open class system. When independence finally came, Cuba already had a racially mixed middle class.

In Virginia, on the other hand—in the absence of a British imperial policy—the position of the freedmen, like that of the slaves, was defined legally by the Burgesses and the county courts. These bodies reflected local prejudice and consequently the free Negroes in the 18th century were a small and despised group. Between 1691 and 1782, manumission was granted by the Governor's Council for merit and was rare, so that the number of freedmen grew only by natural increase to a mere 4 percent of the population. Free Negroes were denied the right to bear witness, bear arms, vote, hold public office or intermarry with whites. They were confined by residence laws and barred from many occupations. They had no separate, independent organizations and no leaders; they lacked group consciousness and remained rural, relatively unskilled, and surrounded and isolated by the whites. A thorough caste system prevailed.

Yet even in 1781, when Jefferson was writing his *Notes on Virginia* and the Americans were about to win their independence, he offered no alternative but exportation for any freed slaves. Many of the colonists were euphoric over the example of freedom the new republic would set the world; they thought the Revolution was the preliminary to a worldwide movement for human rights and against autocracy. But the man who had contributed much to that optimism, including the stirring passages of the Declaration of Independence, did not envision the freedmen sharing in the experiment. Ignoring the Catholic American experience and thinking only of ancient Rome, he observed that, "Among the Romans emancipation required but one effort. The slave when made free, might mix with, without staining the blood of his master. But with us a second is necessary, unknown to history. When freed, he is to be removed beyond reach of mixture."

When a man of Jefferson's standing and enlightenment could write in this vein, there was little hope that Negroes, slave or free, could improve their status to any significant extent in the plantation states. His opinion demonstrated to southerners that one could advocate liberty and equality for most men, yet for "scientific" reasons, deny them to others. The Revolution did lead, of course, to gradual emancipation in the northern states where slaves were not numerous. Even in the South, the spirit of the Revolution brought liberalized manumission, but restrictive laws reappeared after the invention of the cotton gin and the slave revolution in Santo Domingo. Colonization was not economically feasible on a large scale, although Negro colonists established the Republic of Liberia in 1822.

Outside the plantation South, libertarian writers could accept the prospects of emancipation more calmly. Even the conservative Alexander Hamilton of New York called for the use of Negroes as combat troops rather than as "pioneers" (auxiliaries) in Washington's army; it was good preparation for emancipation, he said. Franklin, with his Philadelphia perspective, had come to be critical of slavery, offering the full panoply of ethical and economic arguments against it. In Europe, Buffon opposed the system on moral grounds, and Adam Smith largely for economic reasons. Yet Baron Chastellux, Jefferson's correspondent, sympathized with the Virginian's aversion to miscegenation. While almost all prominent secular writers believed that man should be free and that the Negro was a man, they were much less sure of his native endowment and capacity for civilization. On the last point, Jefferson's report from Virginia was not reassuring.

Finally, in fairness to Jefferson, it must be conceded that he did assert that the Negroes' talents were no measure of their rights. This logical position was, nevertheless, psychologically vulnerable, and would perpetuate paternalism. Still, he was more liberal than other public men of the South—George Washington, James Madison, George Mason—and more aware of the moral as distinct from the social and economic evils of the slave trade and slavery.

The evangelicals or New Lights constituted the other major stream stemming from the watershed of the Great Awakening in the 1740s. These thinkers were motivated by a shifting blend of religious and political concern. A few maintained their religious orientation down through the Revolution but many more found their otherworldly impulses transformed into a desire to bring about the Kingdom on earth immediately and politically by leaving the British Empire. Applied to the slaves, this meant that manumission became a more important goal than conversion.

The Great Awakening in its early stages gave no indication of concern for the Negro, slave or free, comparable to the revived missionary zeal directed toward the Indians. Although George Whitefield was regarded as dangerously "enthusiastical" by some of his Anglican colleagues in America, he was orthodox on slavery; he held slaves at his Georgia orphanage; they were essential in a hot country, he rationalized. The Awakener assured the planters that conversion would only make slaves more obedient. The revivalism of the 1740s did, however, touch Negroes in the Middle Colonies and New England more deeply than previous Christian efforts, and a fair number were baptized. Generally the pastors were skeptical of Negro emotions and there were long delays before such persons were admitted to the first communion, many never reaching that status and remaining in a kind of halfway relation.

Later, in the 1750s, when the Awakening took hold in the southern backcountry, its potential for Negro freedom increased. The tidewater had been uneasily aware of the backcountry ever since Bacon's Rebellion; the planters were coming to fear the equalitarianism of the Baptists, Quakers and German sectarians who were settling there in the 18th century. The aggressiveness of the awakened Baptists confirmed this fear. They sent their semi-literate preachers to harangue gangs of slaves under the trees and away from the masters' scrutiny. The planters retaliated by invoking the law; the preachers were often whipped or jailed for disturbing the peace, and some Baptists even became martyrs for preaching the Word to the illiterate field hands of Carolina. Both the evangelical style of the Baptists and their emphasis on the equality of all men proved subversive to the *status quo* in the slave country. The preachers aroused emotions, promoted some literacy, and accentuated the discontent of the youthful Negro males.

The Quakers, losing political power because the colonial war was intensifying, turned to humanitarianism and philanthropy. Uninhibited by the doctrine of the Elect, they could insist that all men were free and equal; that even the Negroes were eligible for salvation. But the Friends segregated their meetings and buried their Negroes in a separate place. Anthony Benezet, John Woolman, and Tom Paine, more liberal than the rank and file, were environmentalists who believed that freedom and education would reveal a normal spectrum of talents in the Negro. These men rejected the idea that the Negro was a foreigner who should be shipped back to Africa, or that his condition could be attributed to vestiges of African culture. Woolman traced white prejudice to pride and ignorance.

A small number of religious men—some Arminians but especially Calvinists—shared these views. A list of sympathetic clergy would include Ezra Stiles, Samuel Davies, William Gordon, Benjamin Coleman, Levi P. Hart, Samuel Hopkins, and Jonathan Edwards, Jr. Frequently these religious leaders took the same high ground that the patriots were taking against Britain, namely that the equality of the Negroes with white men was self-evident, a truth written in the hearts of men. They did not need the kind of evidence Jefferson and other natural historians were seeking. They even interpreted the French and Indian War and the Revolution in the Puritan manner—God was displeased that sinful slavery was being allowed in his Chosen Land.

The effect of the Great Awakening on the Revolutionary generation—discussed in a later chapter—in most cases was manifested indirectly through the rising demand for liberty and natural rights. There was one major figure, however, whose ideas about the Negro could be traced directly to the Awakening and the teachings of Jonathan Edwards. Samuel Hopkins, an Edwards disciple, was the most insistent advocate of equality for the Negro. Hopkins followed his mentor in stressing the affections and their demonstration in service to God and all beings. After Edwards' death, Hopkins seemed to modify Edwards' thought and adjust to the secular ethos by shifting the emphasis from God to all beings. He championed the Negro because, to him, slavery was the ultimate example in America of man's inhumanity to man, the greatest opportunity for selflessness, for disinterested benevolence. When the Revolution came, the New England pastor accused the patriots of being hypocrites for not extending freedom to the slaves. He also invoked the Puritan concept of the covenant. The Revolution was a renewal of the covenant with God, but the ensuing Confederation era was a "critical period," a crisis in the young republic, because the white people of America had not honored their implied promise to God and continued to maintain the sinful institution of slavery. Although the New England pastor spoke, at the last, in the accents of a Federalist partisan, he was a fervid millennialist. He wanted to send the Negroes back to Africa, not to avoid miscegenation but to evangelize the natives of the Dark Continent before the Second Coming. But Hopkins' special emphasis on the Negro was extreme and not typical of the New Lights generally.

In the North where the Negroes were mostly servants or artisans

—slave and freed—the religio-political crusade for freedom and equality drew strong response. The black men themselves used the language of natural rights successfully to insist that they had been committed to bondage without their consent, that all men are born free. Crispus Attucks, part Negro and part Indian, has received the most attention because he was killed in the "Boston Massacre," when beleagured redcoats fired into the unarmed "mob" of patriots. The five casualties of that night in 1770 were actually the first in the long struggle for Independence that did not officially begin until 1776. There were, however, a number of other politically-conscious Negroes who identified with the patriot cause, and by contributing to the military effort, hastened their own advancement to freedom. In the North the Revolution benefited the Negro and brought gradual abolition.

But in retrospect, the assumption that a republic based upon the principle of natural rights and self-government would set an example of the equality of all men was naive. The Negroes and the Indians were not meant to share in the benefits, and in the 19th century were positively excluded from sharing in the American prototype of democracy.

In the generation of the Revolution, energies became concentrated in the political sector. A by-product of the intense concern with political principles and self-government was pity for those in the autocratic countries of the world who were without these principles and were denied the right to govern themselves. But there was also some contempt on the part of a prickly middle class for those who, having been exposed to these excellent principles and institutions, were slow to perceive their value and to adopt them. While most of the animus was directed upward toward British officials and home-grown tories, some was also directed, from the non-religious folk, toward those who were neutral and apolitical, and even to those isolated by culture from the mainstream of colonial society. Citizens of a newborn republic felt threatened not only by gentry and plutocrats, but by peasants.

While probably a majority of the Americans favored an end to the slave trade and even slavery itself, and hoped that the Negroes and remaining Indians could become sedentary, industrious and republican, it was against their *laissez-faire* and republican principles to aid the transition of these peoples. When the British—and the Anglican missionaries—withdrew, even the very limited benefits of imperial paternalism were removed. The Indians and the freedmen, left to fend for themselves, were surrounded or soon engulfed by the bumptious ex-colonials who, although they were in an optimistic and expansive mood when considering their own prospects, were definitely restrictive in their attitudes toward the red men and the black men around them. In New York the Acadians of Long Island —the French Catholics transplanted from Canada—showed the most friendliness to the slaves; significantly, the natural allies of the red and black men were pantheistic groups or religious libertarians— those who were marginal and politically impotent themselves.

We have been slow to recognize a paradox, namely that an equalitarian, capitalistic middle class society is apt to be much more conspicuously racist than is a predominantly traditional society. Its equalitarian ideology is so appealing and universalist, its benefits to the majority seem so great, and the development of this society in certain parts of the world seem so inevitable, that this shortcoming has been overlooked; it is natural to assume that the benefits will reach everyone. But if we make the comparison between North and South America that Jefferson avoided (even conceding that 18th century Cuba was the best and not the typical example of race relations in Latin America), it would still appear that our kind of middle class society must plan with more deliberation and care than a traditional one to offset the racism generated within it.

Chapter 4

Ben Franklin and the Spirit of "A Rising People"

Mercantilism is the word that describes the shifting combination of economic ideas that accompanied the rise of European nation states from 1500 to 1800. The mercantilists attacked both localism and universalism, and thereby reinforced the nationalism that was manifested in the Protestant Reformation and in the replacement of Latin by the vernacular languages. Theirs was a narrow and suspicious world of international rivalry, concentrated on specific goals and restricted problems. Their ideas were neither as coherent as those of the medieval thinkers that preceded nor of Adam Smith and the classical *laissez-faire* school that followed. Production rather than consumption received the primary emphasis. The more a country produced, the more favorable its balance of trade and the more bullion accumulated. The greater the production, the less dependence on others, especially in wartime—and wars were inevitable. With bullion a nation could always protect itself by hiring soldiers and ships. The assumption that the world had fixed and limited resources —one country's gain was another's loss—intensified the Machiavellian and antagonistic atmosphere.

On the Continent, the thinkers were bureaucrats who devised and recommended mercantilistic controls to presumably benevolent monarchs. Their views were those of statesmen, rather than merchants or philosophers, but the actual results were limited. Colbert, Louis XIV's minister of finance, had found that his minute regulations were successful for a portion of France only; in Germany and Italy—where nation states had not yet been formed—little of the mercantilistic program took hold.

British mercantilism was quite different in style. Advice came not from bureaucrats in whole programs, but from men of affairs in letters and pamphlets on specific issues. The motives of the writers were not always clear; they might be patriots with good ideas or corrupt special pleaders. The American colonies inherited this *ad hoc* style of treating each important question as it arose. The British version of mercantilism, although eclectic, was called the "Old Colonial System" and prevailed from the Restoration until the American Revolution. Trade abroad was the complement of production at home. The desire for raw materials led eventually to colonies, to an Empire, and ultimately to a "reactive nationalism" among subject peoples.

The British ideal of empire was a large self-contained commercial unit, with complementary sub-units. At first the British thought of the colonies as suppliers of raw materials but by the 18th century many mentioned America also as a market for finished goods. Either way, the colonies were an economic convenience. In the view of British mercantilists, the Empire was not a confederation of English nations; the colonies were possessions, not extensions of the mother country. The Crown did permit some autonomy and political freedom where economic interests were not affected, but the colonist was regarded as a producer or a consumer, not a fellow citizen.

There were never more than a few English-born men who suggested otherwise. James Oglethorpe, founder of the Georgia colony, did assert the equality of parts of the Empire in 1732, but with no discernible effect. Later, in 1768, Thomas Pownall, a royal governor and colonial official, perceived the possibility that the center of the Empire might shift from the British Isles. But no Briton had clear blueprints for the relationships in a new Empire.

In colonial America, Benjamin Franklin was the chief funnel for European economic ideas. He borrowed very heavily from Sir William Petty, and this was a wise choice. Petty was a self-made man of middle class origins, one of the most enlightened theorists of the

Restoration, and a forerunner of the Adam Smith liberals of the late 18th century. The colonists found his works congenial. Franklin, of course, enlarged upon Petty's conceptions in adapting them to the American situation. Although Franklin's ideas were as scattered as those of his British counterparts, they drew attention on both sides of the Atlantic during his lifetime and long afterward. Adam Smith, Thomas Malthus, Karl Marx, and Max Weber were among the most prominent theorists acknowledging the contributions of the Philadelphia Sage.

Three aspects of Franklin's influence on economics stand out. First is his Protestant Ethic, the source of his philosophy of success and wealth. The maxims of *Poor Richard* have been held to be typically American and bourgeois, and Franklin and his America continue to be the locus for arguments about Weber's thesis that there was a particular affinity between Calvinistic Protestantism and the rise of capitalism. Second are greenbackism and Physiocracy, which illustrate Franklin's idealism and his streak of agrarian divergence from British mercantilism. Third is population growth, a subject that was central to mercantilism. Franklin was shifting from entrepreneur to statesman; his findings were quite original and surprisingly nationalistic and had a considerable impact on the Continent as well as in Great Britain.

The Protestant Ethic

When the German sociologist Max Weber returned from his sojourn in the United States in 1905, he completed his controversial essay, *The Protestant Ethic and the Spirit of Capitalism.* For him as for his contemporary, Werner Sombart, the United States was the quintessence of capitalism. Although less familiar with America than Europe, he wanted to illustrate his thesis from this country. But which American would best personify the Protestant Ethic? Jay Gould? John D. Rockefeller? Since Weber was trying to demonstrate, as a modification of Marx, that ideas could give rise to, as well as derive from, economic arrangements, he needed an example from early American history. In this way he could show that the "Spirit of Capitalism" had preceded industrialization and was not a consequence of it. This led him to choose as his "ideal-type" Benjamin Franklin, who had been reared in Puritan Boston, made his fortune in Quaker Philadelphia, and wrote the maxims of *Poor Richard.*

In his choice of colonial America and Franklin as case studies in the link between Calvinism-Pietism and the capitalistic spirit, Weber appeared to have been more fashionable than wise. Quantitatively, there was little, for example, in the teachings of the early 17th century American Puritans—Winthrop, Cotton, Shepard, Hooker—that suggested that they were lenient toward usury or that in their view an individual's wealth was a sign of God's grace. In fact, in the pioneer stage, almost the reverse was true. The Americans, like their Calvinistic counterparts in Europe, were more determined and rigorous in their condemnation of economic individualism than the Catholics. Various American colonies tried to regulate wages, prices, interest and other economic activities in the beginning, but the Puritan oligarchy tried harder because their ideal, "the city on the hill," was a modified form of the medieval welfare state. Although such regulation did not survive the first generation even at Massachusetts Bay, Puritan distrust of selfish wealth was reiterated throughout the 17th century. Nevertheless, the tension between God and Mammon grew. While the potentialities for a spirit of capitalism lurked in the behavior patterns of the Saints, they were submerged under traditional anti-capitalist pronouncements.

Weber also labored to distinguish his kind of capitalism, chiefly the result of the Protestant Ethic, from the "adventure capitalism" that he claimed had existed from antiquity and continued to flourish in Catholic Europe and in other traditional societies. Protestant capitalism, he insisted, was rational, systematic, methodical and legal. In contrast, the adventurers were irrational, irregular, speculative and often connected with illegal enterprises or dependent on state monopoly. Usually land was involved, and capital was thus diverted from industrial development. Florence was the center of the earlier type, but Boston and Philadelphia emerged as the *foci* of its successor, he believed.

Again, the facts of colonial American history did not seem to give Weber clearcut support. Because New England had so few products Britain wanted, the colonials were compelled to trade elsewhere to accumulate the capital necessary to maintain themselves as Englishmen by purchasing English goods. After 1660 some merchants found they had to trade in violation of the Trade and Navigation

Acts; they had to live with monopolies and the uncertainties of shipping and consignments. Some smuggled and bribed Crown officials, and made fortunes trading with the enemy French during the colonial wars. This behavior could be considered more akin to the traditional adventure capitalism than the new Protestant kind Weber was trying to define. In any case, was the hypothesis of two kinds of capitalism absolutely essential to the argument linking religion and capitalism? R. H. Tawney, in his *Religion and the Rise of Capitalism* (1926), suggested that perhaps Weber had gone too far in postulating the emergence of a new kind of capitalism directly attributable to the Protestant teachings; it may have been enough to suppose that the Protestant Ethic supplied a "tonic" to the old, familiar capitalism that enabled it to expand more readily in modern times.

Some historians have also contended that it was not the Calvinists but their antagonists who opened the door to capitalism. As the oligarchy grew weaker, ambitious men asserted themselves, taking advantage of New World circumstances. In this view there was a class cleavage, the clergy and magistrates versus the rising merchants. When the latter eventually won, economic individualism was on its way, despite Puritan theology. Yet critics point out that these two privileged groups were not mutually exclusive and became less so as the 17th century wore on. There was a great deal of intermarriage between the families of merchants, magistrates and clergy, and they moved in the same social orbit. Since the tension between the individual and the community was especially strong in Puritan theology, perhaps the conflicts are best described as being primarily within individuals, rather than between classes.

In his analysis, Weber made much of what Martin Luther had termed "the calling." He believed that this doctrine led good Protestants to serve God, not by withdrawing from mundane temptation to a life of contemplation behind monastery walls, but by adopting monk-like discipline in pursuing secular careers. Protestants were enjoined to look upon the world with "weaned affections," to be in the world but not of it. Weber was convinced that the calling, as interpreted by the theological successors of Calvin, contributed heavily to a Spirit of Capitalism, a reinforcement of attitudes and habits that were conducive and even necessary to the rise of a capitalistic order. Before considering the impact of the idea of the calling on Franklin, it is necessary to examine briefly the evolution of this concept from Luther's day to the 18th century.

Calvin developed the duality of the calling: the general and the particular or personal. The general calling was a sign of Election, the resulting obligation, stemming from a subjective experience, to do good works for God and the community. God also required that everyone have a particular or personal calling. With the proper attitude, no job was sordid, but it ought to be honest and lawful. To avoid covetousness, one should choose an occupation on the basis of public need. Calvin, more than Luther, stressed activism, performing the duty to God strenuously and persistently. Both callings should be followed in this manner, but the general calling was supreme; in case of conflict, the personal had to give way.

Seventeenth century ethical thinkers, notably William Perkins and Richard Baxter in old England and John Winthrop, John Cotton and Samuel Willard in New England, made further refinements on the concept of the calling. While they all condemned covetousness forcefully, there was a subtle trend toward permissiveness on the temporal side, allowing the individual more latitude in his personal calling without incurring moral taint. Perkins approved of aspiring to a higher position if the motive was duty to God and man; under proper conditions a man might engage in two trades at one time. A bondsman, if offered his freedom, ought to accept it. God had made distinctions between man and man in every society, but there were some men fit for many callings, and they had the religious obligation to choose the one that best served the family, the church and the community.

Across the Atlantic, the collective ideal was strong among the pioneer Puritans and Winthrop and Cotton labored to reinforce it; the personal calling remained distinctly subordinate to the larger goals of the Wilderness Zion. Yet Winthrop, suspicious as he was of individual wealth, recognized how necessary it was as an inheritance to a family or to the community in a crisis. Cotton upheld the price controls attempted by the founders, but claimed that a pious man, given an "inclination" from God for right judgment, could be left to follow his general calling in advancing the Gospel and his personal calling in maintaining his family. By stressing inclination, or worthy motive, as the criterion for judging men's duties, Cotton left the door ajar a bit for the individualism which was to come. Later in the century, the pious Willard could urge men to seize all opportunities, guided by intuition from God; "Hearken to its voice, and you shall never go astray." Yet he feared the flesh and Man's irrationality; to combat these dangers, a man should pursue the Truth with his whole soul. Riches were a test of man's ability to conquer the flesh; wealth, which he saw as a probable consequence of election, was not something to be given to the whole community. Willard reflected Puritanism on the defensive when he suggested that the pious individual could be right, as against the community, populated by the unregenerate and wicked who had forgotten the "Errand of their Fathers."

The trend to economic individualism among Calvinistic thinkers in England was not consistent in the 17th century. Although Baxter was ambivalent during the Restoration, when Nonconformists were barely tolerated, Weber claimed him as a harbinger of capitalism; but Baxter sometimes thought prosperity too great a threat to piety and fell back on traditionalism. Among Puritans in America, however, the tendency was somewhat more consistent. After the strong communalism of the first generation, individualism gradually crept in with the religious indifference towards the end of the century. The psychological barrier posed by the waning oligarchy was probably not as great as that caused by government persecution in England, so the shift could be more natural, hastened by the physical circumstances of the New World.

Cotton Mather, one of the last Puritans, skillfully used the personal calling to revitalize the general calling. Out of power and living in a time of religious trough between the peaks of Cromwell and Whitefield and Wesley, Mather must have felt the increased tension between this world and the next. On one hand was the temptation to reject the world, proclaim the traditional creed to a faithful remnant and wait for the millennium, inveighing against sensuality and materialism. The other course was to yield to secular pressures, to put aside systematic theology and jeremiads, to bring religion closer to the wavering and the lost. Mather felt tugs both ways, but moved somewhat in the latter direction. This meant reassessing the role of preparation and good works, and reaching out for those who might regard Puritan precepts as merely useful rather than "saving." In his reduced position, he could not dictate reform but only plead for it. In his economic writings he seemed to go so far as to suggest, not that religion was the cause of prosperity, but that it was the handmaiden of the upwardly mobile, that it could hasten one's advancement. He assured his following that even without exceptional native acumen, a godly and methodical man might achieve success because God, acting through the Invisible Hand, would help him. While prosperity was normal for the godly, sometimes God did test one's faith with affliction; it had to be accepted and such a trial should awaken the impulse to do good. Mather was more tolerant than his predecessors had been of diligent, wealthy individuals. He viewed them hopefully as God's instruments for reform. While earlier writers had urged that all superfluous wealth be donated to the church, Mather praised generous Christians but was ready to settle for the scriptural tithe. He was not as patient with those not eager for work—the "unwilling" poor—they were sensual and wicked. Worried about idleness, he was ready to elevate good works in relation to faith. "Faith without works is dead," but profane work, when done with a pious heart, was sacred.

With the community beyond his control, Mather sought other sources of renewal. He stressed family piety and since New England families were largely nuclear rather than extended, it was up to parents to raise godly progeny. And he borrowed from Nonconformist England another defensive device that had possibilities—the reform society. He urged membership in these societies in order to do one's duty to others, to become sensitized to sin, and to save one's self by doing good. Although he clung to 17th century notions of hierarchy in society, his tone and language indicated how much, during the long season of religious apathy, he was relying on well-to-do individuals, parents, and reform societies, rather than the whole community, to restore piety and moral order.

But Cotton Mather had not yielded the supremacy of the general calling to the personal; he had not given the latter autonomy or succumbed to economic individualism. His supplications to God were constant and sincere. He vacillated in his emphasis, but in moments of particular despair and with advancing age, he tended to be more otherworldly, and the general obligation to God took clear precedence. Nevertheless, he did discuss in more detail than others had previously, the techniques for doing good in specific occupations and in civic endeavors. One result of this approach was to raise the personal calling relative to the general calling, but this has been overemphasized. More important was the extent Mather wanted to utilize the attitudes and habits held by the pious in the private sector, in families and especially personal callings, to revive and make effective godly efforts in the public sector, in order to regain moral direction of the community. Mather's essential message was that persons must become businesslike in their civic enterprises. Doing good in the community must be rationalized.

Cotton Mather spent his whole life doing good, and most of the more than 450 printed titles attributed to him offered ingenious advice on this theme. The most famous and influential of these was *Bonifacius: An Essay . . . to do Good* (1710), written when he was forty-six years old. In its pages, the Puritan interpretation of the calling reached its climax.

It was this little book that had such an impact on Franklin and—eventually, and indirectly—on Max Weber. Young Ben was aware of the *Essays* early, because when he began his popular advice column in the *New England Courant* in 1722, he chose the pseudonym, "Silence Dogood." Was the "Silence" prefix a jibe at Mather for the verbosity in his good works? Much later, however, when Franklin, the creator of *Poor Richard* and reigning philosopher of the *bourgeoisie*, was writing his *Autobiography*, he was careful to acknowledge his intellectual debt to Cotton Mather. And he went even further; in 1784 he wrote Samuel Mather, Cotton's son: "When I was a boy, I met with a book entitled 'Essays to do Good'. . . that gave me such a turn of thinking, as to have an influence on my conduct throughout life; for I have always set a greater value on the character of a *doer of good*, than on any other kind of reputation."

From the foregoing, it should be clear that Cotton Mather and other Puritans, despite their social conservatism, understood more by the calling than simply faithfulness to one occupation in a lifetime; or mere private accumulation, even if lawful. Weber recognized this. He saw that the mark of true faith was an abundance of good actions in both callings; carriers of the Ethic must persist in "intense worldly activity," in a certain manner, right up to the edge of the grave.

What was that certain manner? The *Essays* provide some suggestions. Perhaps Mather's section on advice to rich men is pertinent here since Franklin withdrew from active participation in his printing business in 1748 when he was only forty-two years old. In that section the Puritan pastor stressed the stewardship the rich man owed the community. He must not die with his treasure or merely give it away to charity; nor was tithing alone adequate. He should become involved by endowing schools, colleges, and hospitals. He should publish Bibles and other pious works. Better yet, he should write a pious book himself; a gentlemen should share his talents and learning. Ask a minister to be your advisor; he will think of additional ways to do good, Mather suggested. "Idle gentlemen and idle beggars are the pests of the Commonwealth." "Be up and doing."

By themselves, these ideas did not fully indicate the certain manner. A gentleman who was not a Calvinistic Christian could follow them. The Calvinistic flavor was revealed in Mather's specific recommendations. For example, reforming societies should bring pressure on landlords to put clauses in their leases requiring tenants to keep Bibles rather than dogs or hawks in their homes. In return for gifts of good books to the poor, the donors should extract from them promises of good behavior. The certain manner was evidently organizational, contractual, and impersonal, *i.e.*, businesslike rather than paternal. Persons were to be guided by the printed word—not the scriptures directly—but by elaborate rules, that were accompanied by "inspirational" messages or admonitions from contemporaries with status in the community. What looked like a social gospel among Mather and his followers, was actually close to the gospel of wealth that Americans would come to know later.

The Calvinistic teachings did bring out tendencies that were conducive not only to skilled labor but to science and administration, either private or public. The emphasis on the sudden conversion, rather than growing in the faith, led not merely to introspection and diary-keeping, but to other moment-by-moment analyses, to a general urgency about time; the millennial hopes aroused by evangelism reinforced this feeling of time fleeting. With so little time on earth and so many good deeds to perform, the Puritans felt pressed. They learned to hold a distant goal in mind, while gaining intermediate satisfaction by small, discrete, sequential steps towards it. Poor Richard's version was pithy: "Little Strokes, Fell great Oaks." The Calvinists' consistent rejection of idolatry, pantheism and spontaneity freed them from many institutional distractions, and made them objective—their enemies thought "cold"—and energetic in dissecting economic and social phenomena. While they tried to screen sentimentality out of their workaday world, some like Cotton Mather let it spill over, especially in prayers to God, admonitions to wrongdoers, and on to the pages of diaries, sermons and histories.

When Weber read Franklin's *Autobiography* he was convinced that he had found the archetype of the secularized Puritan, the perfect exemplar of the Protestant Ethic. Franklin had done an amazing amount of good in Philadelphia. He had "rationalized"—Weber's pet word for structured—the militia, the fire and police departments, the post office, and even intellectual life by founding the Junto that led in turn to the subscription library and the American Philosophical Society. Weber was duly impressed: "Rational organization for the provision of humanity with material goods has . . . always appealed to representatives of the capitalistic spirit as one of the most important purposes of life work." He surmised that Franklin derived great satisfaction in providing employment and keeping statistics on progress in his "home town." In this passage Weber confirmed that the hallmark of the Ethic or Spirit was not personal fortune *per se* but organizational activity in the larger community. In this Protestant scheme, innovative Rotarians, not affluent magnates or paternal nabobs, would be the most welcome at the Strait Gate.

The Puritan rationalism of Franklin seems quite evident in his educational ideas. He found self-education and the informal methods of tutors too uneven and haphazard for such a vigorous society, and made some proposals for increasing order and efficiency. He would begin by establishing a model academy for boys, eight to sixteen years old, in Pennsylvania. Because he lacked formal education and hoped his ideas would be considered by the "educational establishment" in Philadelphia, Franklin titled his suggestions "Hints" but they were characteristically detailed and thoughtful. His recommendations were specific but his goals were general. He suggested a curricular sequence of History, Geography, Chronology, and ancient customs. Subjects that were useful in colonial society—agriculture, accounting—might also be encouraged. Physical education was endorsed because a weak body could not hold strong ideas, and natural history was added for general utility. It would improve conversation and the contents of letters.

Franklin knew that his curriculum challenged academic custom so he quoted selectively from respected authors—Locke, Rollin, Milton—to lend support to what were essentially his own pedagogical plans. He wanted the emphasis shifted from classical education for the few to liberal education for the many, stressing the use of English, rather than the dead languages in writing and speaking. Because "Art is long, and their Time is short," all students should not be required to study the classical languages; only those with leisure and inclination need pursue them. He thought it ridiculous and wasteful that all some boys got from their schooling was Greek and Latin enough to recite in a monotone, without real understanding. He described these languages as the *chapeaux bras* of learning, hats carried under the arm by European gentlemen for the sake of appearance, but never put on the head.

At his proposed academy the boys were to proceed by discrete increments in their studies and to receive small rewards and encouragements, weekly and monthly, along the way. Franklin wanted public debates because they "warm imaginations, whet industry, and strengthen natural abilities." The best time to introduce the principles of logic, he suggested, was when the boys were preparing for a debate. Thus the good doctor sanctioned competition in learning. At the same time, however, he hoped that the trustees would regard the students as their children, and feel equal concern for them all when they graduated.

Franklin intended that his school provide skills for a variety of personal callings open to young men in the New World; it was not vocational education in any narrow sense. From his own experience, Franklin knew that communication was primary for upward mobility; hence his stress on the Plain Style in writing and speaking: "That is best wrote which is adapted for obtaining the end of the writer." and "If a Man would . . . have an effect on the Generality of Readers . . . he would use no Word in his Works that was not well understood by his Cook-maid." From their concentration on history and customs, he expected the students to discover that true merit lay in applying the mind to solving problems for "Mankind, country, friends and family." This was how a man served God. The general calling then was not something one turned to after material success, but rather an obligation one should feel from the outset. Was he explicitly rejecting the New Light when he observed that "general virtue is more probably to be expected and obtained from the *education* of youth, than from the *exhortation* of adult persons; bad habits and vices of the mind, being, like diseases of the body, more easily prevented than cured."?

Franklin's educational beliefs reflected the American environment; he had acquired a confidence in the rational ability of the average man that the *philosophes* could not muster. They hypothesized such talent in society's lower orders, but Franklin knew from experience. He was ready to presume—like the Puritans who believed that everyone, even unregenerate children, could profit from a theological sermon—that most boys could put their materials in order and abstract ideas from them.

Franklin's religious history, as it relates to the Ethic, needs some explication. As a youth he could not rationally accept Original Sin and throughout life he retained a strong aversion to metaphysical speculation and sectarian dogma. He could be described as a freethinker or deist who secularized the practical divinity of Cotton Mather and made it his own. When George Whitefield evangelized Philadelphia, Franklin was among his admirers. Like so many others, he was amazed by Whitefield's pulpit style, but he was also attracted by the Awakener's non-sectarian approach, and the power that was evident in the preaching of the New Birth. The Sage, of course, never had a conversion experience himself, unless we count the occasion when he was overwhelmed by Whitefield's preaching and gave all the coins in his pockets for Whitefield's Georgia orphanage. After this, he could support non-denominational, Calvinistic evangelism for the populace, if not for himself, because he sensed that it could bring tangible, utilitarian changes in attitudes and behavior. He anticipated what Weber and others noticed later; that this type of religion made men susceptible to change, made it easier to inculcate the bourgeois virtues and to spread education and efficiency among large bodies of men, both workers and freeholders. At the time, Franklin, as well as the evangelists and mercantilists, identified the vulnerable segment of the population as those people in proximity to the lower class–lower middle class borderline. These "rising strata" were the major targets of mercantilist "success literature," in England and of Franklin in America when he published the maxims of *Poor Richard*.

Some scholars have seen Franklin's aversion to theology and inclination toward freethinking as demonstrating a weakness in Weber's theory. If Calvinistic teachings were so important, why did not Weber choose a practicing Calvinist rather than a deist of Puritan background for his ideal type? Actually, Franklin, who came from a humble Boston family with a history of dissent, and had been exposed to some Puritan influences from his parents and to Cotton Mather before his manhood, was a very good choice. Weber's purpose was better served by a man who had been secularized; modern research has tended to confirm that the Ethic is stronger and leads to more upward mobility among Protestants who absorb the ethos and accept the methods without internalizing the theological super-structure. Franklin, and those like him—a very large group in the 18th century—were better carriers of the Spirit of Capitalism be-cause they avoided doctrinal orthodoxy altogether or sloughed it off.

To what extent can Franklin's economic behavior be attributed to his Puritan childhood and Cotton Mather, to the British Nonconform-ist conscience and the mercantilism he imbibed as a book-hungry youth, or to the physical circumstances of the New World, par-ticularly Philadelphia in the 1720s? The affinity of Franklin's ideas with Mather's have been understated, but all these influences were operative, and their proportions uncertain. Perry Miller has noted the high overlap between Puritans and Englishmen in general; the average Puritan, he estimated, was only 10 percent distinctively Puritan, and the remaining 90 percent was middle class Englishman. Yet Franklin did befriend George Whitefield and pay tribute to Cotton Mather. Whether he acquired his "Ethic" from his parents, from *Essays to do Good,* or from mercantilist authors, it was present and helped to make Franklin the most active, practical, inventive and civic-minded man in colonial America, becoming a fair model of the Protestant Ethic for many generations in America and throughout the world.

The economic philosophy that contributed so much to Franklin's fame, and later attracted ambitious young men in underdeveloped nations, took shape between 1720 and 1740, when Ben was rising rapidly as an entrepreneur in the printing business. The bourgeois stress on industry and thrift, already prevalent in Britain, was par-ticularly attractive to the colonies at this time. In the Glacial Age, cultural developments were somewhat less conspicuous than the in-terest in business, land and the importation of Negro slaves. Cur-rency shortage and inflation were symptomatic of the times. The advent of the Board of Trade in 1696 had made the colonists be-come much more aware of the British mercantile system and the role they were designed to play in it. At first they were drawn to England by the Glorious Revolution and the new politico-economic era presumably inaugurated by the constitutional monarchy under William and Mary, but after 1720, stirred by inchoate nationalism, they were repelled by the homogenization and rigidity the colonial system produced. In both situations, the colonial consciousness of the shortage of a skilled labor force was strong; as much or more than Britain, the colonies felt the need to seek skilled immigrants and to train a lower middle class that could exploit the abundant resources of North America.

The Glacial Age was an important formative stage for the American economy. After 1740, although economic development actually increased, a great deal of public attention was diverted by religion, war, and above all, politics and nation-building. Not until the 1830s did a similar period of entrepreneurialism return to America.

Paper Money and Physiocracy

Paper money or "currency finance" was a smoldering issue throughout the 18th century; the colonists were generally favorable to it and the Britishers who were immediately affected—merchants and Anglican clergy—were distinctly opposed. On this question the mercantilistic outlook they held in common did not bring transatlantic agreement.

The colonists suffered from a shortage of hard money. They tried to attract it by paying a premium, but the fundamental problem was an adverse balance of trade. More was imported from the mother country than was exported, and their specie therefore slipped away. When this chronic condition was exacerbated by the colonial wars, the colonists added paper money to their circulating medium. Massachusetts began this practice in 1690 and the other colonies followed eventually.

In most of the colonies the experiment with paper was successful and engendered no class antagonism between creditors and debtors. In Massachusetts, Rhode Island, North Carolina, and South Carolina before 1731, agrarian legislatures did too little to sustain the issues and depreciation occurred. Results were most satisfactory in Pennsylvania, New York, and Maryland where the merchants gave strong support. Even some royal governors were persuaded of the benefits of soft money and recommended this medium to Whitehall.

The colonists had a vague notion of quantity theory and tried not to issue beyond current trade and price levels, knowing this would cause depreciation despite any guarantees. Paper money offered some obvious conveniences to the provincial governments. Revenue came in from the interest without resort to unpopular direct taxes, and since redemption was not in specie, retirement of the public debt was easy. Thus the debts of the French and Indian War were paid off quickly after 1760. The currency restrictions the Crown imposed, first on New England in 1751, and on the other colonies in 1764, were among the minor grievances of patriots in the American Revolution. During the Revolution, the new states were forced to go beyond prudent limits in issuing paper and there was depreciation, but this was a temporary necessity and may be regarded as a tax on those through whose hands the paper passed.

Franklin's pamphlet, *A Modest Inquiry,* written in 1728 when he was only twenty-two, was very popular at the time and remains the classic in the large bundle resulting from this long currency controversy. Drawing heavily on Sir William Petty, as he was to do on so many economic matters, Franklin made a good case for additional paper money in Pennsylvania. More paper would keep interest rates down, stimulate land and agricultural prices, and encourage settlement. Had not the first issuance of paper already raised land values somewhat? The proprietor would benefit from the appreciation of his vast landholdings, and the Crown would benefit from the addition of wealth and subjects in Pennsylvania.

Franklin believed that those who were resisting paper money were a small and selfish minority. He mentioned money lenders who lacked the courage for enterprise and preferred to lend their funds instead; they would have to accept lower rates. And lawyers might be deprived of some business because of fewer debts and lawsuits. In his analysis the chief villains were the land speculators. He described them as having capital and biding their time, lending at high and increasing rates while land values remained static; then when the common people were caught in this squeeze and had to sell in distress, these men would buy cheap. After they bought, their views would change and they would favor a rise in money and land. The Philadelphia printer's appeal here was frankly agrarian; he was subscribing to the perennial theory of conspiracy and manipulation by speculators at the expense of the virtuous husbandman. This was an early instance of an allegation that was made more frequently and vociferously in the 19th century by the later agrarians—Jeffersonians, Jacksonians and Populists.

Scholars have noted that Franklin stood to gain directly from his seemingly benevolent soft money views. As a printer, he received the very lucrative currency printing contracts; and, as editor of the popular anti-Proprietary newspaper, he took the debtors' side, a position most of his readers presumably found congenial. But in his defense, it should be said that he championed paper currency long after he had such a direct interest. He and Thomas Pownall supported an intercolonial paper currency backed by the Bank of England. They did not finally abandon the idea until it became apparent that the Crown, angered at colonial agitation, would demand too much in return for this economic concession.

The advent of Roosevelt's New Deal and Keynes' economics has definitely softened the attitudes of historians and economists towards the colonial currency experiments. They are no longer dismissed as un-Christian and unsound. "Currency finance" can now be considered as a means of welfare, but one consonant with the incipiently *laissez-faire* atmosphere of 18th century America. The colonists "primed the pump" as Franklin Roosevelt did in the 1930s to combat the Great Depression. The currency put into circulation amounted, in effect, to loans to farmers and other debtors. There were, of course, no banks at that time. It seems probable that the continuing inflation was not injurious to the country since there were few persons relying on fixed incomes and little liquid capital.

The most strenuous and notable opponents of the paper were, moreover, suspect on social and political grounds. William Douglass, the Scottish-born physician, was rigid and conservative in many ways. He also resisted inoculation and the Great Awakening. Jared Eliot, another hard money man, was an Arminian with aristocratic pretensions. Thomas Hutchinson, a later opposer, took a supine attitude toward British authority and wound up a tory. Both from a democratic and an intellectual point of view, the ranks of the soft money advocates were more impressive: Ben Franklin, Sam Adams, John Wise, Richard Bland and even the misunderstood Cotton Mather.

When the cause of an intercolonial paper currency became hopeless in 1767, Franklin suddenly turned to the Physiocracy of the French, but this conversion is hard to explain fully. Was it the result of the increasing friction with Britain, coupled with the Sage's ten-year residence in London, so close to European intellectual currents? Was Ben, the country cousin in the Enlightenment family, finally being caught up in the climactic surge of the Age of Reason?

The Physiocrats, the first formal school of economics, had been formed in 1757 by Quesnay and included Mirabeau, Turgot, Dupont and Barbeau. Franklin was in correspondence with the last two. Some of the Physiocratic tenets Franklin could accept readily; they coincided with what he already believed. The advantages of free trade had been obvious to him for some time. In a 1747 letter to Jared Eliot he had summarized the classic disadvantages of tariffs: reduced trade, retaliation, smuggling, and indirect taxation with higher prices to the consumer. Most American colonists, especially New Englanders, were chafing under the Trade laws and could find similar reasons for justifying free trade. The Sage could also agree with the Physiocrats' *laissez faire,* although they referred to self-regulation as the operation of the Divine Order and expected state intervention to inaugurate it.

Franklin was attracted by the humanitarian universalism of these Frenchmen. They proposed an economic system that had the grandeur of a world view, in contrast to the selfish, nationalistic doctrines of mercantilism. The philosopher was impressed; he admitted that America was as yet "far from conceiving what is best for mankind or even Europe in general." The primacy of agriculture in the system seemed plausible to a representative of America, still overwhelmingly agricultural itself, and involved with Britain, then the only industrial nation in the world.

Franklin was on record as a vigorous exponent of the labor theory of value. He had taken the theory from Petty and elucidated it. Money was merely a medium, and gold and silver were erratic; labor was the real basis of value. He maintained that it was not the quantity of gold or silver but the quantity and quality of labor the inhabitants were able to purchase that determined a nation's standing. In reviewing economic history, Karl Marx later chose to praise Franklin rather than Petty for exposition of this theory. "The first sensible analysis of exchange value as labor-time, made so clear as to seem to be commonplace is to be found in the work of a man of the New World. . . . Benjamin Franklin . . . formulated the fundamental law of modern political economy." Marx believed that Franklin had successfully challenged an outworn tenet of mercantilism. To conform to his new Physiocratic "line," Franklin merely made an amendment: the labor theory became the agricultural labor theory of value. Whereas previously value was imparted by any kind of labor, under Physiocratic influence Ben claimed that a product's value was determined by the food men consumed while processing it.

The Physiocrats believed that the only real wealth came out of the ground or the ocean. Manufacturing was secondary since it did not create wealth but merely transformed material into more convenient shapes. The value added by manufacture was offset by the provisions the workmen consumed. It followed then that proprietors and peasants in agriculture were essential and morally superior to people engaged in commerce and manufactures. Succumbing to this thorough agrarianism, Franklin could write that there were only three forms of acquisition: war, commerce, and agriculture. Only the last was "honest." Thus he cast a shadow over much of his earlier economic writing, the maxims of Poor Richard, and his own career as a businessman. He stopped just short of complete capitulation; refusing with Turgot to go along with the Physiocrats' repudiation of interest-taking as usury.

Franklin as an agrarian was not convincing. Such a position did not square either with his character or his experience. His long-standing concern for the "Publick Interest" and the "Common People" attracted him temporarily to the anti-industrial philosophy of the frustrated French gentry. The immediate precipitants were discouragement over the diverging economies of Britain and the colonies, added to the strong admiration of him evinced by the French *Économistes*.

It would be a mistake to interpret Franklin's Physiocracy as a belated romantic yen for the rural way of life. He never loved the land in the European sense; in this he was typical of the great majority of the colonists. Franklin and the majority of Americans valued the land for the feeling of independence and security it gave them. The miracle of spring was subordinated to the dream of resale. Franklin the deist and secularized Puritan shared with the Calvinistic colonists an aversion toward pantheism and any mystical confusion of man with the lesser creatures or the landscape. Ben had, on occasion, celebrated husbandmen in verse and prose; it was good for the almanac business. So had Jared Eliot, a Connecticut gentleman who was trying to arouse a neo-Roman sensitivity to the pastoral and thereby protect society from agrarian unrest. But the affinity of most Americans in this century and later was to a region and not a particular piece of ground. Perhaps American love of the land would have been more intensive if the land of America had not been so extensive.

Demography and Manifest Destiny

The population of the American colonies was doubling every twenty to twenty-five years by natural increase; in a century there would be more Englishmen in America than in England. When Franklin, America's most renowned scientist, made this announcement, Europe was surprised and England was alarmed.

Franklin was reacting to the Iron Act, a Parliamentary effort to restrain the colonists from processing their own ore. In his brief essay, *Observations Concerning the Increase of Mankind* (1751, publ. 1755), he tried to assuage British fears but aroused them instead. He claimed that the day when colonial manufactures would compete with English was still remote; it would take a long time to exploit the resources of a new continent. Indeed, colonial demand for goods was growing so fast that even the entire export of Britain would soon be inadequate. Therefore he opposed any restriction on colonial manufactures. "To weaken the children is to weaken the whole family," he added, because a nation is like a polypus: parts grow back when they are cut off.

In England, interest in economic subjects was high at mid-century and many earlier treatises were being reprinted. Criticism of orthodox mercantilistic theory continued to mount and British thinkers were vulnerable to imperial and national self-doubt when Franklin's analysis reached them. They may have been reflecting the shrill alienation of the *philosophes* across the Channel. More likely they were recalling the projections of their own demographers, John Graunt and Sir William Petty, who had set 270 and 360, respectively, as the number of years necessary to double the English population (as late as 1776 Adam Smith in his *Wealth of Nations* wrote that five hundred years to double was normal for European powers like Britain!). In 1741 the careful German, Suessmilch, reported that there were 17 births for every 10 deaths in Prussia but only 11 to 10 in England. The case of Spain was still being discussed; her decline in population and status was attributed to her vast holdings in the New World. Robert Wallace in 1753 took the side of Montesquieu against Hume and Voltaire in a controversy characteristic of the 18th century: the "populousness" of the ancient world. Wallace decided, on the basis of literary sources, that the ancients were more numerous because slavery was healthier than modern urban life. Britain should abandon the city and trade and revert to agriculture. The British, for so long concerned with overpopulation because of the enclosures, had come, after the Glorious Revolution, to fear its opposite.

Two years later Richard Jackson, a "friend of America" and soon to be Connecticut's agent in London, echoed this pessimism in a letter to Franklin. He noted that even the gentry were increasing in Switzerland and Scotland but not in southern England. In America an old man might gather about him a hundred descendants but in England it often happened that a man with eight children did not have a single grandchild. Children were liabilities in the mother country; they brought difficulties to a family. Servants were corrupted by the proximity of their betters; the result was a low birth rate. "There are few parts of this kingdom that have not been more populous than at present, but I dare not suppose that England is less peopled than before although judicious men have said so." Jackson was dubious about urban growth. Increased consumption in the city was offsetting any increase in productivity.

Dr. Richard Price, another Franklin correspondent, was also gloomy. He seems to have accepted the Philadelphian's figures but rejected his theories. Price believed that England and London had been losing people ever since the Glorious Revolution of 1688. He cited the large army and navy, three wars, emigration to the Indies, luxuries and high prices, taxes and public debt, paper currency and tribute to foreigners as factors in the decline. *Publicola*, a commentator of the 1760s, suggested that the best course for the British at this time was to neither encourage nor restrain colonial population but to find ways to make the colonies advantageous to Britain. He was offended at the prospect of the American child dwarfing the British parent but seemed to find a silver lining: "As mere friends they will become more useful to us than they are now as dependents."

Guadaloupe or Canada? This was the choice British statesmen faced as they finally contemplated victory in the long imperial struggle with France. By the rules of 18th century diplomacy, Britain could not keep both but had to choose its spoils: tiny, sugar-rich Guadaloupe or big, empty Canada. In the vigorous pamphlet war on this question, Franklin as spokesman for the colonies, urged the retention of Canada. In making his case, he encountered British self-doubt at high tide and had to meet some arguments that had been inspired by his own population forecast of the previous decade.

Orthodox mercantilists favored overseas plantations and saw Guadaloupe as an ideal acquisition. The West Indies island provided sugar, an exotic crop not grown in the mother country but for which there was a good demand in Europe. Guadaloupe would presumably be content to continue raising this staple. At the same time, leaving Canada in French hands might serve as a check to American expansion. The French to the north would prolong colonial dependence and forestall any sentiment for independence. Oliver Goldsmith said that big limbs made the body slow and clumsy; and would not the Turkish Empire be stronger if it were smaller?

Franklin was blunt in his reply to those who would use Canada as a check on the Americans. Check, he claimed, was a modest word for massacre; the French had encouraged the Indians to this end over the years. Any divide and conquer tactic would drive the colonists into the arms of the French.

Franklin wanted Canada added to the Empire and he used the growing population of America as a threat. Earlier he had hoped King George's War would add territory because the colonists were hemmed in by the mountains and the sea. His cry for "living space" was evident in his list of the various ways a leader could earn the title, "Father of the Nation." First on the list was "the Prince acquires new Territory, if he finds it vacant, or removes the Natives to give his own People room." He emphasized that Canada in French hands was stunting "our" growth. Quoting an "able" writer (himself, using a pseudonym), he invoked a theory of natural stages of civilization related to land and population—hunting, farming, and manufacturing. Apparently no statutes could keep the colonists from the manufacturing stage if they were confined and population density increased because of a shortage of farming land.

In his desire for Canada, Franklin stretched international and natural law to their limits. Canada had not been a declared object of the Great War for Empire, but he contended that Britain had a right to it as an incident of war. He took the high ground of self-preservation and natural right when he argued that Canada must become British for *security*. Critics, mindful of the many European frontiers, thought this claim excessive; on such a ground, each nation could annex its neighbor. But Franklin pointed to the long

1500 mile border of Louisiana and Canada. Because of the wilderness, sparse settlement, and autonomy of aggressive Indian tribes, American borders were more difficult to protect than were the European. Experience had shown that massacres, raids and even invasions could go undetected for some time. The good doctor believed that these conditions justified a much broader claim for security in the New World.

Yet Franklin was conciliatory in some ways. In 1757 he had become a colonial agent in London and needed to be more diplomatic. In his pamphlet he referred to the "American" colonists and to "our" and "us" when he meant British or imperial. British readers were assured that annexation would postpone "indefinitely" any colonial rivalry with home manufactures, and that the Great Lakes and navigable rivers would make Canada as accessible as Germany to British goods. By focusing on markets for finished products rather than on sources for raw materials, he could argue that English freeholders in Canada would offer a much greater potential market than the French-speaking Negro slaves of Guadaloupe. This point could also be made in asserting the superior value to the Empire of Pennsylvania over the West Indies.

At this time he even had convenient second thoughts about population in England. In 1751 he had been definite in stating that the home country had reached her maximum. He was wiser in 1760 in observing that, in contrast to a real mother, in the imperial situation, "the growth of the children tends to increase the growth of the mother." By supplying the expanding colonies, Britain could grow tenfold. How much stronger Britain would be when manufacturing occupied every corner of the island! (In the 1769 edition of his *Observations,* after his conversion to Physiocracy, he would still promise Britain a tenfold increase—if they would improve agriculture.)

Franklin liked to believe that his pamphlet arguments contributed in some way to the British decision to retain Canada and forgo Guadaloupe. The controversy added to his fame. It was the first instance of a colonial seeming to take a broad imperial view.

Some of the seeds of Manifest Destiny—America's ideology of expansionism—lay imbedded in Franklin's population and annexation writings of the 1750s and 1760s. Ben's "geopolitics" can be defended, however. Other colonial statesmen, notably James Logan, had also expressed fear of French encirclement. From 1740 on, the French and their Indian allies had encroached conspicuously on the security belt of the English colonies. They were a genuine menace and the American colonists had no reason to assume that a British victory was inevitable. By mid-century even British mercantilists acknowledged the danger and conceded the primacy of security over narrower domestic concerns. Franklin's emphasis on security was merely an extension of the mood of anxious British observers. Later, during the Revolution, some American leaders invoked security and Nature's design in seeking Canada, Nova Scotia and Florida. At the peace table in 1782, Franklin, acting for the new nation, tried to secure Canada although the American military had failed to conquer it during the war. In these matters Franklin was not bellicose but stressed natural pressures rather than the actual use of force. It is true nonetheless, that the principle that he asserted so explicitly in 1760—security or safety—would prove to be a more serviceable and flexible rationale for Yankee expansionists than the theory of the natural right of liberty in the years that lay ahead.

Ironically, Britain's despondency over its population trend seemed to lift somewhat even as their redcoats were losing the war in the colonies. In 1781 John Howlett offered convincing evidence that ten times as much beef as formerly was being consumed in the north of England. The English were assured that the nation's inhabitants had actually increased 33 percent since the Glorious Revolution, and a surprisingly high 16 percent between 1760 and 1780.

Demography as a science originated with John Graunt, a London functionary, who published in 1662 exact figures on births and deaths in the city. He was assisted by Sir William Petty who later provided similar vital statistics for Dublin. Petty dubbed this work "political Arithmetick," and announced he would express himself only by "number, weight, and measure." Although these men tried to speak in the quantitative language of science, they were motivated by tradition—it was customary to take a headcount after a plague—and by national pride. Had London become bigger than Paris? They had to combat 17th century prejudices. The freedom-loving, remembering William the Conqueror's Domesday book, viewed the census as an infringement on liberty; the pious, citing the Old Testament—"And Satan rose up against Israel, and moved David to number Israel."—believed enumeration could lead to death.

Graunt and Petty made many discoveries: that depopulation by the plague was offset in only two years by emigration from the countryside; that the city was growing three times as fast as the country but the birth rate was higher in the latter; that many London districts were "smoky and stinking" and had high death rates; and that more males were born than females.

Franklin relied heavily on Graunt and Petty and their successors. Their philosophy and statistics were congenial to the printer of *Poor Richard's Almanack*. Franklin accepted the idea that the rural births exceeded urban but agreed with Petty that cities and manufactures made for progress. If factories were too unhealthy, home manufactures were the answer. This, of course, was an easy solution from the American perspective because the colonies had scarcely reached this stage of industrial development. Writing at mid-century, Franklin could assume that a large number of landholders would of necessity lead to some manufacturers; he did not as yet feel compelled to choose between city and farm.

Franklin has left no account of the method he used to calculate his population estimates; presumably it was the simple differential between births and deaths. *Poor Richard's Almanack* had published some figures on colonial population; perhaps he consulted these. Somehow, he concluded that colonial parents produced eight children versus the normal four in Europe. Assuming that half these grew to adulthood and married by age twenty, America's people would double every 20–25 years; increase depended on the number and age of those marrying. In Europe the scarcity of land, low wages and the debilitating effects of city life postponed and deterred marriage. In America where land was plentiful and wages consequently high, early unions were natural and easy. He endorsed early marriages on several grounds: people were not yet set in their ways; youth could avoid dissipation; parents would still be living when the children grew up; young marriages were more fruitful. Besides, the philosopher added, the married state is the happiest because the temperaments of men and women are complementary.

Franklin was the first to report on a human population that was actually multiplying in a natural state, that is, on a virtually empty continent with all the Old World checks removed. He implied what Malthus would later emphasize—that all species, including man, multiplied by geometric progression if unchecked by the environment. This had been recognized in the 17th century and in the 18th became a valuable generalization in biology. Franklin's analysis of it was a rare instance of an American formulation having an impact on European thought. Almost all the intellectual traffic ran the other way.

The philosopher's population ideas had some influence in Europe for several generations. Adam Smith knew Dr. Price well and through him may have been acquainted with Franklin's work. Smith accepted Ben's estimate and in his *Wealth of Nations* drew heavily on America for examples. He may have consulted Franklin on these passages since both were in London during 1773–75, but evidence is lacking. Malthus did not become aware of Franklin's work until after the first edition of his famous *Essay on Population* came out in 1798; he acknowledged the American in the second edition five years later.

In the 18th century the tests for prophet and "scientist" were the same: results. How accurate were Franklin's population estimates? The world had to wait several generations for the complete answer. He had estimated eight children per colonial family in 1751. The first United States census in 1790 indicated 7.76 per family; since this was the average, some suspected that it might run as high as 15 in the backcountry. As a comparison, the underdeveloped countries today report an average of 6.5 to 7.3 per mother. By this standard, colonial Americans were certainly fecund.

The American people increased by 34.6 percent each decade down to the Civil War. Doubling every 23.4 years, they were in the middle range of Franklin's 20–25 approximation. After 1860 urbanization began to slow the rate. At what point in time did America contain more Englishmen than England? The 1850 census showed 1½ million more people in the United States than in Britain. The philosopher was right again. One could take the total population figure for 1790 and, doubling every twenty-five years, emerge with 62,947,714 for a century later, just 0.13 percent off from the actual 1890 census. The Philadelphia Sage made some shrewd or lucky guesses; but how characteristic that an American scientist-entrepreneur would set such definite quotas—and have them exceeded!

Franklin regarded immigration and emigration as natural rights and most colonists agreed with him. It was appropriate that a citizen of Pennsylvania was the champion of free movement. From the beginning, Penn's colony had profited from its founder's "open door" policy. The disaffected from Britain and the Continent had combined to produce great prosperity there. The colonists would not and could not admit that colonies ever weakened the mother country. Franklin insisted that it was national pride, idleness and "other causes" that reduced the inhabitants of Spain and not her settlements in America. Did Graunt and Petty make him recognize that in the long run, neither emigration nor immigration affected the population significantly? At any rate, this was a good 18th century *laissez-faire* position and it still has merit, although Americans have become dubious. A modern demographer concludes: "In general, the effect of migration on the population of the two areas concerned is so complex as to be indeterminate."

But Franklin was not consistent, and pointed out at least one special case. If immigrants were more industrious and skilled than the natives, the birth rate might be favorably affected. Again he may have had Pennsylvania in mind, although it might be argued that the Scotch-Irish, disembarking in Philadelphia, were industrious in moonshining and skilled only as squatters and fighters. When Britain increased its transportation of felons to Pennsylvania and the southern colonies, Franklin suggested that the colonists return the compliment by depositing a thousand rattlesnakes on England's shores. British mercantilists continued to think of the colonies as a place to dump undesirables and hope that they would somehow turn out to be assets to the Empire in their new environment; Franklin could not accept this and diverged from them on this point.

Franklin's views constitute an early manifestation of the American ambivalence toward immigrants. Although he inclined toward *laissez faire* and wanted America to be the asylum of liberty, he did worry about quality; there was a certain type of immigrant he preferred. The philosopher's demographic "science" was tempered by social considerations. The conflict between scientific and humanitarian *laissez faire* and the ethnocentric desire for homogeneity and identity has persisted ever since. The balance has fluctuated with the national mood, but what had been only a preference for Franklin, has come to be the rule of American immigration policy. Since the late 19th century, we have emphasized restriction, favoring those with some skills and bourgeois tendencies.

Franklin seems to have been a moderate in his approach to luxuries, the *bête noir* of mercantile theorists. He did not approve of them but did not belabor the matter. He did hope that Britishers would at least refrain from the purchase of foreign luxuries although he admitted that the demand for them could provide employment. On this point, Ben leaned a bit away from Shaftesbury and toward Mandeville whose dictum was "Private vices lead to public benefits."

Yet in matters relating to population, Franklin's enlightenment contrasted favorably with the European intellectuals of his day. Compared to him, they were fanatically nationalistic, statist and anticlerical. To Frederick the Great and his advisors, who were prescribing for the Germans—a "rising people" like the Americans—population was such a *summum bonum* that steps to forbid divorce, reduce the stigma on fallen women, operate state foundling homes and even condone polygamy seemed necessary. Everyone, particularly the French, attacked the celibacy of the Church—the "eunuchism of the West"—and called for awards by the state to prolific mothers. Some theorists wanted sumptuary laws to control the addiction of the poor to luxuries and opposed invention because it would reduce employment. The doctrines of mercantilism were harsh in many ways. Fortunately, American conditions and Franklin's humanity permitted him to take a broader and more optimistic view.

Chapter 5

Natural Rights and Real Whigs

The Enlightenment and the Glorious Revolution raised the status of secular reason, the printed word, and intelligent individuals. In America, essayists, printers and lawyers belatedly joined the clergy in the circle of opinion leaders. Most of the colonists had learned to read their Bibles and could easily augment religious with secular reading. The study of history and law gained markedly on religion in the 18th century, and lawyers—especially those born and educated in the colonies—were natural leaders in applying this learning to New World conditions.

Free speech and free press, so necessary to the development of public opinion, had not yet gained the status of natural rights and so fell short of modern American standards. Even the English constitutional monarchy was slow to concede these liberties, and slower to grant them to its colonials; and because of its religious character, America was not far ahead of the mother country in granting the kind of liberties involved in private judgment and the airing of obnoxious opinions.

In Great Britain the press had not been mentioned in the settlement or bill of rights resulting from the Glorious Revolution; its freedom was only implied. During the first Stuarts the Crown had claimed control of the printing press as a prerogative. After the

Restoration, licensing had been based on a Parliamentary act. In 1694, under William and Mary, the licensing law was repealed but this did not alter other British statutes. Publishing anything about the government was still illegal. Except for the first years of the Puritan Parliament, no printed reports of that body had been permitted. Even after 1688, Parliament clung to its gentlemanly secrecy. Members made a small concession to the public interest, however, when they allowed official printers to publish proceedings and votes in the Commons.

Under the guise of Parliamentary privilege, both houses tried to punish conduct they disapproved of, either by members or non-members. While they might allow the publication of an occasional factual account of the proceedings, they were sensitive and anxious to restrain critics. At this time "free speech" usually referred only to the right of a member of Parliament to speak against the government from the floor, and not to such a civil right of the citizen "out of doors."

But public knowledge was growing. Hand-written accounts of Parliamentary gossip were circulated in the coffeehouses that sprang up in late 17th century London. Coffee, compared to beer, seemed to promote sharper political dissent. Informers sold information to the proprietors and the resulting sheets were not covered by law. Printed pamphlets could be traced by the type font to the offending press, but the newsletters were much harder to track down.

As the century ended, Britain moved to redefine treason, making it more consonant with the new constitutional monarchy by narrowing the definition and granting more rights to the accused. In the 17th century, even "compassing" (imagining) the King's death had been a capital offense, but England was finally reaching that milestone in civilization, the day when death had become too drastic a penalty for mere utterances unsupported by overt acts.

When prosecution for treason ceased to be the major means of controlling criticism, the government relied instead on seditious libel. There were various kinds of libel: blasphemous, obscene, private and seditious. The last was defined as criticism of the government, tending to lower its esteem and disturb the peace. This was a misdemeanor punishable by whipping, the pillory, or prison. The authorities found that printers and editors could be so intimidated by court proceedings that a few convictions for this offense had the desired effect of circumscribing anti-government tracts.

The jury and judge had special roles in libel cases. The jury was asked only to determine whether the accused had in fact published the offending matter; such a decision was termed a "special verdict." To the magistrate was left the major decision: whether or not such material was libelous. Thus the protection of twelve men good and true was slight in these cases, and the discretion of a single judge was great.

Freedom of the Press in America

In America there were three instances of seditious libel in the late 17th century but for various reasons, none of them became intercolonial *causes célèbres*. In 1687, pastor John Wise verbally challenged the taxes imposed without the consent of the Massachusetts assembly by the notorious Governor Edmund Andros. The Ipswich minister was convicted, fined, and suspended from his pulpit for a time. There was some sympathy for him in other Massachusetts towns. In Pennsylvania five years later, printer Andrew Bradford criticized the deputies and predicted the name of the lieutenant governor would "stink." Bradford and a friend requested a jury trial and refused even to concede that they had published the offending material. Instead, Bradford took the offensive, demanding that the jury render a general rather than a specific verdict in his case; that is, to determine not only the publication question but whether the material was actually libelous. Juries, he insisted, should be judges of law as well as fact. Accepting this departure from precedent, the jury tried to decide this and became deadlocked—nine to three for conviction. The men were released and there was no second trial. In 1695 Thomas Maule, a Salem Quaker, was arraigned in Massachusetts as the author of a book that had been licensed in New York attacking the Puritan establishment. Maule complained of the high bail and stayed in jail, playing the martyr role and comparing his fate to the recently executed witches of Salem, an episode the magistrates were already coming to regret. Maule, like Bradford, asked for a general verdict and the jury acquitted him. They reasoned, however, that Maule's case was "ecclesiastical," and that they were protecting religious conscience in freeing him. The cases of itinerant Presbyterian Francis Makemie and Anglican convert John Checkley were seen as a threat to the establishments in New York and Massachusetts, and also turned on the religious aspect; so the secular cause of freedom of press did not receive direct benefit in these instances.

The case of the *New England Courant* was an exception. When that journal became too sensational and critical of the *status quo* in 1723, the editor, James Franklin—Ben's older half-brother—was charged with seditious libel. The grand jury released him, however, because the veniremen resented the colonial licensing system requiring prior approval, especially since its English counterpart had been repealed in 1694. The Franklin paper was sensational and aggressively anti-establishment, lampooning Harvard College and resisting Cotton Mather's inoculation campaign, and in one major respect it was progressive. The *Courant* published *Cato's Letters* on freedom of speech and press. These letters, reprinted from the *London Journal,* were the collaboration of the radical Whig popularizers, John Trenchard and Thomas Gordon. The essays of these men in *Cato's Letters* and the *Independent Whig* were destined to have a strong influence on colonial newspapers.

The Zenger Case

Rex vs. *Zenger,* colonial America's most celebrated case of seditious libel, began officially in November, 1734 when the New York Governor's Council ordered the sheriff to burn four issues of the *Weekly Journal* because they were "false, scandalous, malicious, and seditious." The newspaper was just one year old, having broken the monopoly of Andrew Bradford's *Gazette,* which carried the government printing.

In that time the *Journal,* printed by John Peter Zenger, had become a popular and effective critic of the new royal governor, William Cosby. The editor and guiding genius was a lawyer, James Alexander, and he was abetted by Lewis Morris and his friends—the Morrisite faction—who were disgruntled by rapid patronage shifts in Cosby's administration, including the removal of Morris as Chief Justice. In the *Journal,* Alexander lamented that when "a governor turns rogue, . . . it is prudent to keep in with him and join in the roguery"; he came closer to treason when he claimed that "Authority by which our laws receive their life do not depend upon the will and pleasure of any man, or upon the mere opinion of judges." Yet these opinions found an audience among many elements in New York who were dissatisfied with the governor. One historian described Cosby as a "greedy proconsul raping the public land."

The Council's "burn" order in itself created sympathy for the defendant, Zenger. Cosby and his Council had been unable to get an indictment from the grand jury or even co-operation from the Assembly and so had resorted to an "information," the simple complaint of an officer, which could be used in cases of battery, cheating, perjury, conspiracy, or libel when an indictment was not "available." While technically permissible, the "information" had been little used in America and seemed to the colonists a vestige of Star Chamber practice, not compatible with the rights of Englishmen, especially in the American locale. To them this procedure was highhanded and unfair.

When Zenger's lawyers, James Alexander and William Smith, even before the trial, challenged Cosby's "tyranny" by questioning the legality of his judicial appointments, they were disbarred. The lawyer replacing them as counsel, although competent, was not bold.

Alexander saw the handwriting on the wall and wisely sent to Philadelphia for Andrew Hamilton, the most famous barrister in the colonies, as an associate counsel for Zenger. He was a good choice because he had friends in New York who had been offended by Cosby. Arguing from a brief begun by Alexander, the aging Hamilton—the original "Philadelphia lawyer"—used exceptional experience and forensic ability to persuade the jury. In August, 1735, after deliberating less than an hour, the jury brought in a general verdict of not guilty, "upon which there were three huzzas in the Hall."

Hamilton's principal defense was truth. The British rule, "the greater the truth, the greater the libel"—that truth was even more damaging than a lie because it was more disruptive—should no longer apply, he argued, because it dated from the "terrible" Star Chamber courts of the early Stuarts. In a century, law and religion had changed very much. In fact he deemed all precedents before the Glorious Revolution of 1688 destructive and arbitrary. The precedents he did cite, however, were not very estimable. His best appeal was to truth as a natural right, to the "constitution," and "to the reason of the thing." The rhetoric of Hamilton was particularly elaborate in this case probably because—like James Otis and Patrick Henry at a later date—he had logic and the gallery with him but not history or law.

Hamilton readily conceded that Zenger had printed the material in question and was willing, moreover, to stipulate that the words used were scandalous and seditious and therefore a libel, if only the Attorney General could prove in court they were false. Needless to say, the government did not relish the prospect of the protracted inquiry into the Cosby regime that such a proof would entail.

The Philadelphia lawyer was on stronger ground when he called for a general verdict. When facts and law were intertwined—were virtually inseparable—as in this case, a general verdict was necessary; there were English precedents for this. His claim that Parliament had taken away from great men the power to decide what was scandalous and that the use of the information was therefore improper struck a responsive chord. The Morrisites and the *Weekly Journal* had already claimed that indictment should be by peers, not by the government. Yet bold as he was in asserting truth and decrying the information, Hamilton did not take this opportunity to go further; to repudiate the concept of seditious libel altogether; to proclaim true free speech and press and the unlimited right to criticize, without having to meet the legal test of truth.

In certain other aspects, Hamilton did take quite an advanced position. He affirmed the right of free men to remonstrate against abuses of power. The purpose of seditious libel proceedings was national, he said, to protect the king, not the colonial governors. The liberty of the country had to come before the preferment by the governor. When a ruler brings his personal failings and vices into his administration, and the people find themselves affected by them either in their liberties or properties, that will alter the case mightily; and all the things that are said in favor of rulers and of dignitaries and upon the side of power, will not be able to stop people's mouths when they feel themselves oppressed. Since the Governor's placemen in the Assembly made petitions to it ineffective, the press remained the only avenue of protest left. In New York, there was more freedom to discuss God than Governor Cosby!

As he proceeded, the incipient nationalism in Hamilton's arguments became more evident. He contended that, because of the expanse of ocean, it was too slow and expensive to seek redress from the King's Bench in London; that under such circumstances, the British "constitution" must provide the protection. In this he seemed to suggest that the farther English colonials were from the mother country, the more carefully their "constitutional" rights should be observed, that perhaps they deserved different or even more protection than their countrymen at home. Implicit was the idea that the colonies were coordinate, not subordinate, contradicting the more traditional assumption that on the edges of an empire, citizens might have to forgo some privileges for the sake of defense and administrative efficiency. Perhaps it is this implication about the rights of colonials that best justifies the overgenerous title Governeur Morris applied to Andrew Hamilton long afterward: "Morning Star of the Revolution."

Hamilton's defense met with considerable opposition. At the trial, the Attorney General asked, "Can a thing be lawful just because it is true?" And should not good motives also be required? Such a doctrine would endanger privacy by revealing human frailties and domestic discords; it might also threaten public order, he believed. He decried the colonial tendency of "levelling" that he thought was prevailing in this case. The severest critics emerged some time after the verdict; two gentlemen using pseudonyms (they wrote from the West Indies), claimed Hamilton's performance was a wild harangue that ran counter to long established precedents. They described his defense as "indecent," the work of a counselor with little legal knowledge and no morals.

The three principals drawn together by this trial—Zenger, Hamilton, and Alexander—were complementary; each contributed to the cause of liberty and nationalism in his own way. Their greatest impact was in the Middle Colonies, a region of considerable religious and ethnic diversity, where, compared to New England or the southern tidewater, political thought was lagging.

John Peter Zenger, the printer from the Palatinate, played the martyr's role. When the court set his bail too high, he stayed in jail for almost a year. He managed to publish the *Journal* anyway, and the bare subsistence of his family during that time created sympathy. Although Zenger had not written the words that most provoked the government, he followed the then current Anglo-American ethic of the printer's trade by assuming, as printer and publisher, responsibility for the authors in his paper. The name of Zenger as defendant drew frustrated and apolitical non-English elements to the cause and focused their latent resentments, aroused earlier by Leisler's Rebellion,[1] against English aristocratic dominance. Identification with Zenger made it easier for these people to imbibe the advanced principles of liberty advocated in the

Journal. Seven of the twelve jurors that acquitted Zenger were of Dutch ancestry.

Andrew Hamilton, serving without fee, lent the prestige of his name and profession to the cause. He demonstrated that a court case could be made against the kind of regime Cosby was operating. Because he was a Philadelphia resident, his role in the trial caused controversy in Pennsylvania. Ben Franklin, in the obituary of his friend, noted that although Hamilton had a "free Manner of treating Religious Subjects," that offended many, "he was compassionate in Nature," "the Poor Man's Friend," and steady in "the Cause of Liberty."

But it was James Alexander, operating behind the scenes much of the time, who was ultimately the most influential. From the outset, he had used his considerable talents to needle Cosby in the pages of the *Journal.* Compared to Zenger, he had a superior command of the language, and used invective, irony, satire and Swiftian humor to provoke the Governor. In a mock advertisement, he described a lost animal who bore a remarkable resemblance to Cosby's chief henchman: "a large spaniel, of about 5 foot 5 inches high who has lately strayed from his kennel with his mouth full of fulsome panegyricks." By juxtaposing libertarian essays with devastating news reports, Alexander was able to bring excruciating pressure on the provincial government. When Bradford's *Gazette* defended Cosby, the ensuing newspaper war stimulated interest in the case and in Alexander's ideas.

Alexander had the last word when he replied to the more temperate of the West Indies critics, a lawyer who had faulted Hamilton's courtroom reasoning and behavior as well as the jury's decision in the Zenger case. Boldly assuming that speech and press were natural rights, Alexander invoked history to show that men who would be despots naturally began by prosecuting mere words. His heroes of liberty were Algernon Sydney—"A British Brutus"—and Addison and Steele who were amiable yet "manly." The villians, obviously, were the Stuart kings. The unreasonable doctrine that the truth could be even more libelous than falsehood began in England, he claimed, only with the advent of James I. He blamed James and his successors, and their presumptions of divine right, for the Star Chamber and the harsh punishments for libel—the pillory, loss of ears, and branding on the face. He believed that a prosecutor had to prove both falsehood and malice to fulfill the charge of libel, and that Star Chamber proceedings not requiring this, had departed from civil law and natural equity. He regarded the free speech and press principle as a major pillar of free government; it gave vigor to republics and limited monarchies and, without it, constitutions dissolved.

Alexander did not come to grips with the legal points raised by his critic but rested his case on the lessons of history. He defended Hamilton's court behavior by explaining that in a popular cause, strict rules of pleading were seldom followed and it was customary for the counselor to mix appeals to the emotions with enunciation of legal principles. In this essay, appearing in Franklin's *Pennsylvania Gazette,* Alexander supported Hamilton and followed the line of Trenchard and Gordon, those radical Whigs whose views were already as familiar to Franklin's readers in Philadelphia as they were to Zenger's in New York.

Alexander and his supporters then tried, unsuccessfully, to give New York "something of a constitution" by perfecting the separation of powers, circumscribing the governor, and reforming the judiciary. Perhaps his interest in mathematics predisposed him to go beyond a "mixed" government and demand one with checks and balances. He objected to Governor Cosby sitting on the New York Council when it met as a legislative body; he wanted real separation of powers. Whereas the British authorities and royal governors were inclined to the position that English precedents applied unless exceptions had been granted, Alexander was inspired by the writings of radical Whigs to argue that the colonies should make their law primarily from local experience, supplemented only by English rules that the colonials thought were beneficial and compatible with liberty in the New World.

The Press and the Truth After Zenger

The other major case of seditious libel in the colonies also arose in New York; it was a by-product of the Revolutionary agitation. Alexander MacDougall, self-made merchant and Son of Liberty, was charged with libel for writing a broadside which attacked a New York Assembly act for provisioning redcoats in the City. This was part of a lengthy resistance to quartering and was also a challenge to the DeLancey faction, then in control of the provincial government. When arrested in 1770, MacDougall preferred martyrdom in jail to freedom on bail. While a prisoner, he enjoyed enormous popularity not only in New York, but also in Boston. The authorities delayed the trial, and when the chief witness died, charges were dropped. Later MacDougall, with the other New York radical leaders, Isaac Sears and John Lamb, opposed the landing of the tea, and strongly supported non-intercourse with Britain and the idea of a Continental Congress.

In his behavior and remarks MacDougall sought to emulate the great English Whig, John Wilkes. In 1763 Wilkes had aroused the masses as well as some intellectuals with his criticism of the autocratic behavior of George III and his minister, Lord Bute. Essay No. 45 in his journal, the *North Briton,* had been aimed at the King himself and Wilkes was cited for seditious libel. In jail Wilkes became the symbol of resistance to tyranny and defense of British constitutionalism. Cries of "Wilkes!" were heard everywhere. Mac-Dougall, although less talented, was just as zealous for liberty, and the cause was even more popular in the colonies. When Mac-Dougall was behind bars, the Sons of Liberty set up Liberty poles, and there were riots and demonstrations like those during the Stamp Act crisis. He was hailed as the American Wilkes and in memory of the "immortal No. 45 of North Briton," 45 gentlemen dined with him, 45 ladies had tea with him, and 45 pounds of beef and 45 bottles of Madeira were bestowed on him.

The Scottish ancestry of the men involved in these Middle Colonies libel cases is noteworthy. James Alexander graduated from Edinburgh; his mathematical talents led him to be Surveyor General of New Jersey and a charter member of the American Philosophical Society. Andrew Hamilton was a graduate of a Scottish university but obtained his legal education on the eastern shore of Virginia. At age thirty-seven, he spent a year at Gray's Inn to enhance his professional prestige. Alexander MacDougall emigrated from Scotland with his parents in 1738. William Smith, co-counselor in the Zenger case, and John Morin Scott, MacDougall's attorney were also Scotsmen. These men were successful in America and their subsequent careers suggest that they were radical largely on the question of liberty. They were levellers only to the extent that they would favor those with common sense and freehold property—the upwardly mobile like themselves. They may have borne resentment toward upper class Englishmen and, as a result, toward English legal precedents.

The effect of the Zenger verdict on extending freedom of the press in the colonies has often been overstressed. At best the decision gave the press the right to use "truth" as a defense in criticism directed elsewhere than the assemblies. In any case, truth was an inadequate defense, usually expensive, and sometimes difficult or impossible to prove in court. The Zenger case did seem to discourage subsequent trials for libel in court, but did nothing to alter the growing tendency of colonial legislatures to flex their muscles and emulate Parliament by asserting privilege. Again and again these bodies indicated that they would not permit "affronts," "indignities" or anything construed as reflections upon members, their procedure, or even the provincial government itself. Thus the colonial public was free to criticize England, or the king and his agents, but had to be more careful in observations about the local government where tyranny of the majority was a danger. Down to the American Revolution, the major barrier to the principle of the free press was not English-born judges or the common law of seditious libel; it was the abuse of privilege by the assemblies who retained judicial power and could try offenders directly. Colonial legislators evidently believed that they were obligated to punish everyone who assaulted the colonial governments with mere words.

Otherworldly defenders of religious conscience contributed little to the emancipation of the press. They continued to agree with Roger Williams, the 17th century champion of conscience, that mere scandal to the civil state *should* be punished. The pietists were content with free speech among their brethren or susceptible other groups and did not seek to arouse the general public. Freedom of the press—the right to attack the government openly with words, risking the disturbances that might ensue—was a more dangerous but ultimately more precious principle.

The religious impulse tended to work the other way in 18th century America: it retarded press freedom. The colonists continued to be zealous Christians, whether "pressing into the Kingdom" or across the Appalachians. As Protestants and incipient republicans they were hardly willing, as the Revolution approached, to countenance Papists, atheists, or divine right monarchists. As true believers, they already *knew* what the proper forms of religion and government for a godly people should be.

While the Zenger case may have been exaggerated as a landmark auguring real freedom of the press, it was significant in revealing that the colonials, even in the Middle Colonies, were staying abreast of British libertarians. British juries about 1735 became bold enough to render general verdicts in cases of seditious libel. In an English libel case in 1731, the truth as a defense was flatly rejected. The oratory of Andrew Hamilton and the prose of James Alexander dramatically publicized the radical Whig position on natural rights and the constitution. Hamilton, Zenger and Alexander nurtured these ideas in the Glacial Age, and libertarianism made gradual headway.

Before 1763, some newspapers openly questioned the restrictions on the press, claiming the government did not have that power. The right to think included the right to think aloud and in print; actions, not opinions, should be punished. Improved laws would result from putting grievances into print and before the public. Freedom of press was not dangerous because it was self-correcting. Critics of such freedom could also put into print their reasons for opposition. A man's loyalty should be to constitutional principles, and not to a person, a king or governor. If these newspaper arguments were representative, the concept of seditious libel was being undermined in the colonies.

After the Peace of Paris, the journalistic sector grew rapidly. Circulation of the city newspapers was extended to the countryside and the colonies began to learn much more about each other, whereas before the war, each colony had looked to Britain for news and guidance. By 1776 all but Delaware and New Jersey had their own newspapers. Intercolonialism developed slowly however, and state particularism was still strong during and after the Revolution as the difficulties of the Confederation illustrated.

Even though many devices and rites were used to stir the people after 1763—poems, bells, flags, bonfires, effigies, and tar and feathers —the chief reliance was always on published work of a certain kind —plain, abstract, systematic expositions of political and constitutional matters—strong in logic and relatively free from belletristic adornment. The colonial press lacked the elegance of its English counterpart, but this very fact enhanced its impact upon the colonial reading public.

Prior to the Revolution, no colonists asserted the principle of a free press, unlimited by seditious libel. When people spoke of a free press, they meant the absence of the prior restraint of licensing, not freedom from subsequent action for libel. The Americans, who had purchased almost as many copies of Blackstone as the English, agreed with the great legal authority on this point when he wrote, "Every freeman has an undoubted right to lay what sentiments he pleases before the public: to forbid this is to destroy freedom of the press; but if he publishes what is improper, mischievous or illegal, he must take the consequences of his own temerity." Apparently everyone—Whigs, tories, deists and New Lights—felt some restriction on political discussion was necessary to preserve the safety and stability of provincial governments. The natural right of a free press continued to be circumscribed, even after the Zenger case, because the rule of truth as a defense was not fully established, the seditious libel laws were still operative, and the assemblies took their privileges too seriously. A full recognition of the natural right of free press did not come until the early days of the republic, when Jeffersonian editors challenged the Federalists' sedition law.

The failure of the colonials to either lay the groundwork or elaborate the modern version of this principle is not surprising. The concept is advanced; it presupposes a highly literate, objective public and a stable political state. While the colonists were exceptionally literate—especially the New Englanders—they were far from detached (many of them were New Lights), their desire for liberty was strong, and their own sovereignty was not as yet secured. Despite this, press coverage was candid and lively; the editors could still find ample copy and fair game in the tories and in the factions and personalities of the time. Even with limitations, the American press was the freest in the world.

Lawyers and the Saxon Myth

In the 18th century, land transactions, large fortunes, and the use of paper currencies stimulated litigation. Professional lawyers emerged and became influential in the colonies despite folk prejudices. In the previous century the law had been at a pioneer stage when every man was his own lawyer and even the judge was a layman; the magistrate's judgment was often summary, with the reasoning omitted, and so precedents did not accumulate. After 1700 some students made the expensive voyage to London for legal education at the famous Inns of Court, where they could observe the most distinguished practitioners of the law in action in the courts of Westminster. The majority of the neophytes, however—especially the

New Englanders—remained at home and learned the profession while acting as clerks in the courts or in the offices of attorneys. By the time of Revolution, local bar associations were requiring a collegiate education in the liberal arts as a prerequisite for legal training, and the colonies had begun to make the English distinction between attorney and barrister, the latter advocate privileged to argue in the superior courts. Yet the typical lawyer in colonial America had to be versatile. Although many of his cases involved stray cattle, others required that he be cognizant of Mosaic, common, and admiralty law, as well as of the English and colonial statutes.

Lawyers were conspicuous as bibliophiles and pamphleteers even in this colonial society where religion, the printing press, and a rural middle class had made tradesmen and farmers as literate as the gentlemen of most other countries. These advocates cherished their books and reacted strongly to them by making notes in the margin and at the foot. Interest in law and history tended to reinforce each other; the two categories together, constituted the largest proportion of volumes in colonial libraries. Significantly, these interests were very strong in Massachusetts and Virginia, the oldest and most populous of the settlements. Native-born and American-educated lawyers from these provinces proved to be the boldest defenders of American rights as the relations between Britain and the colonies worsened.

At Massachusetts Bay the Puritans had tried to operate their commonwealth without lawyers. Instead, the clergy gave advice in administering justice with the result that Mosaic rivaled English common law. Apparently the Saints tended to identify the common law with the hated Stuarts and their officials. In any case, the Puritans came largely from a class that was unfamiliar with the intricacies of the common law courts. The lesser borough courts became their models for the New World, and they may have been adequate for the 17th century. The 1679 Reform Synod condemned lawyers. It was at least 1720 before Puritan prejudices receded and respect for the bar began to rise sharply.

In Virginia, lawyers were similarly suspect in the early days. Through restrictive legislation, the Old Dominion had attempted to prevent and retard the development of professional lawyers as a class. Many planters claimed that such a group would exploit their ignorance of the law and challenge their social status. Yet because

the origin of Virginia was relatively secular, the colony was somewhat more amenable to the common law than Massachusetts.

By the Revolutionary decade, the original differences between
Massachusetts and Virginia had declined. Both had replaced their
early aversion to lawyers with high standards, and could boast some
erudite professionals; and the Pennsylvania bar, having overcome
the anti-legal prejudices of the Quaker faction, was also developing
some astute political thinkers.

In Massachusetts, John Adams was the most learned member of
a distinguished bar that included among the patriots, James Otis,
Oxenbridge Thacher, Josiah Quincy, Jr. and Joseph Hawley. Adams,
the son of a Braintree farmer, was the heir of first generation settlers
and a graduate of Harvard College. Early in his career he became
identified with his more radical cousin, Sam Adams, and the "country" party that resisted the royal prerogative in Massachusetts.
Adams joined some other members of the Suffolk County bar in the
"Sodality," a club for legal research; this and the concomitant Stamp
Tax crisis inspired *A Dissertation on Canon and Feudal Law* (1765).
In this essay, Adams began with the assumption that the Normans
brought feudal institutions to Britain with them in 1066. He saw
feudal law—in contrast to the common—as military, designed for a
society of encamped soldiers; the executive had the despotic powers
of a general on a battlefield. Adams claimed that under Norman influence, the spiritual and temporal "grandees" acted in collusion, and
that the people were held together in servile clans. Romish priests
persuaded the people that God had entrusted them with the keys
to heaven.

With this perspective, Adams defended the motives and principles
of his colonial forebears; they were refugees from the canon and
feudal law the Normans had imposed during the Conquest. The
first settlers brought to the New World an abhorrence of passive
obedience and hereditary or divine right. They were not fanatics.
They knew their classics and were better read than the Anglican
Churchmen of the time. And even if they were tinged with enthusiasm—and he did not concede this—"no great enterprise for
honor or happiness is achieved without that noble infirmity." By
demolishing "diocesan episcopacy," the colonists formed a church
more consistent with scriptures and a government more in accord
with human nature. With these essentially conservative ideas, Adams
started down the road to Revolution and Independence.

When he looked across the water to Britain, he was reminded of cyclical theories of history. It seemed that frugal, vigorous, brave people inevitably degenerated into the proud, the luxurious, and the decadent. Britain had reached her peak of power, he suggested, in 1763 when the treaty with France made her the greatest Empire on earth; but a nation at its peak was highly vulnerable and could begin the downswing quickly. The seeds of the impending decline had been apparent long before 1763. The king and the court had been corrupting the English people; the attack of a venal Parliament on American liberties immediately after that date confirmed Adams in his belief that Britain was on the wane. Aware of Franklin's projections of a large population for the colonies, Adams believed that America would be Britain's successor as the champion of liberty in the world. American principles and habits were similar to those of Rome on the upgrade. Later he was to view the triumph of Washington's armies in the Revolution as a confirmation of the superior virtue in American society.

Although Adams had faith in American virtue, he was also a Newtonian. He believed that politics was governed by natural laws. When the Revolution came, he feared that the unusual opportunity to create a republic might be bungled unless the form of the government erected was "scientific." Yet he was cautious; he did not want to experiment. If the new republic imitated colonial governments, the transition would be easier; and he liked the idea of a confederation of separate state governments. A continuing emphasis on the assemblies would be wise because the greatest happiness in Britain had occurred during Elizabeth's reign, during the years of the Commonwealth, and after 1688, the periods when the Commons were dominant.

Because America really had only one "order" of people and the land was so well distributed in contrast to Europe, Adams saw no need for extensive changes in the electorate. Given these conditions and the virtue of the colonists, a republican form of government was required; yet even the virtuous had some temptations, so the people could not be given unlimited political power. The American republic would need laws, checks and balances, and a written constitution inasmuch as the withdrawal of British sovereignty might lead to social instability. He wanted to make sure that experts such as himself, so well grounded on the weaknesses of earlier governments in the world, had plans ready to avoid similar mistakes. The

Massachusetts statesman was not really at ease with the disturbances the patriots caused after 1764. He defended his friends, the Sons of Liberty, in the Stamp Tax and Tea Party episodes, and resisted any description of these incidents as mob action. In addition he tried to make a tenuous distinction between good and bad mobs; there were "public" mobs defending their principles and there were "private" mobs following a leader for revenge or booty. Nonetheless, he thought that even the "public" mobs were of a dangerous tendency and justified only in the extremity, when fundamental liberties were in jeopardy. It was probably vestigial Puritanism that made John Adams define virtue in personal and negative terms. Virtue for him was self-restraint, the will disciplining the selfish passions. Despite this conservatism, Adams still found it possible to praise the Americans for their moderate behavior during the Revolution; he ignored the treatment accorded tories and those who resisted the boycott of British goods.

In Virginia the roster of patriot lawyers was longer and even more distinguished. Among them were Thomas Jefferson, Richard Bland, George Mason, George Wythe, Edmund Pendleton, and Patrick Henry. Jefferson, although seven years younger than Adams, proved to be his counterpart in the Old Dominion. He wrote his first tract on government, *A Summary View of the Rights of British America* (1774), in reaction to the Coercive Acts which had closed Boston harbor and reduced Massachusetts' right of self-government. The short essay was intended for the Virginia delegation to the First Continental Congress, but received wide circulation.

Jefferson began the *Summary* with the bold premise that the American colonists were not British subjects. He claimed that the prospective settlers had exercised their natural right of emigration, subtracting themselves from the kingdom of the Stuarts and withdrawing from the social compact that bound 17th century English society. They arrived in the New World as free agents. He likened America's first colonists from England to the ancient Saxons who had swarmed out of the woods of northern Europe in the early Middle Ages. The Saxons conquered England and settled down, living according to the common law. They accomplished this on their own with their own sweat and blood; their Saxon homelands had made no claim on them. In the same way, Jefferson argued, the American colonists had triumphed over the wilderness and the

Indians of the New World through their own efforts and sacrifices. In England each Saxon soldier had gained his piece of land through conquest; by analogy, the land in America belonged, not to the king, but to the individuals who had conquered and occupied it. The English Crown had not provided the initial financial backing and had shown interest in the settlements only when the commercial potential was evident. Therefore, Jefferson reasoned that the Crown was not entitled to any return; England had no more rights over the colonies than Denmark or Saxony had over England because of the emigration of Danes and Saxons to her shores.

But how did Jefferson account for the revered charters of the 17th century, the documents in which Stuart kings had granted lands and governing rights to companies, proprietors, and other groups? He explained that the prospective colonists became free agents when they decided to leave England; *then,* and in that capacity, they made new compacts with the king. The charters were not gifts but contracts whereby these free agents made themselves subject to the king personally. Even so, the colonists had been unwise and had weakened their case by accepting these charters. They erred because they were laborers, not lawyers. Thus America was settled, according to Jefferson, by subjects of the king and not of the kingdom.

We tend to associate Jefferson with progress, democracy and "the people." He stated that the earth should not be bound by the "oppressive" past, but his study of history and law made this distinguished Virginian quite conservative in some respects. Jefferson was really taking an aristocratic position in stressing the individual's right to land by conquest. In this he favored Saxon and American freeholders but passed over the small but growing non-landowning portion of the population. His case for American rights was legal and historical rather than philosophical. He broadened his views later, but in his *Summary* Jefferson was asserting the rights of his freeholding ancestors rather than the natural rights of all men.

An older Virginia lawyer, Richard Bland, had actually anticipated Jefferson's political views, and had phrased them even more gracefully. Bland was the first to publicize the right of emigration, together with the theory of settlement by compact. Like Jefferson, he invoked John Locke, common sense and self-evident truth. Bland's long experience in the House of Burgesses had convinced him that a government dominated by the legislative branch, when it was composed of gentlemen of virtue, was an ideal arrangement. Most planters and lawyers could agree with this stand. Jefferson and Bland were in the vanguard on the road that political thought was taking in the Old Dominion.

Traces of this Saxonism could be found in many places besides Massachusetts or Virginia, and not just among members of the legal profession. Benjamin Franklin was not a Philadelphia lawyer but, as we have seen, was a champion of emigration, and after reading many of the same books, seemed to agree with Adams, Jefferson and Bland on the matter. Like the Saxons of ancient Germany, the Saxons of modern England had emigrated to America at their own expense and "therefore supposed that when they had secured the new Country, they held it for themselves, and for no other people under heaven." "Have not all Mankind in all Ages had the right of deserting their Native Country when made uneasy in it?" "Did not the Saxons desert their Native Country when they came to Britain?" Franklin asked in 1773.

Many colonials with an inclination for law and history were attracted by the Saxon Myth. They believed that the Germanic peoples had an innate capacity or genius for liberty, and, also that this quality had been nurtured by superior political institutions. They saw the distinguishing features of Saxon government as the consent of the governed, elected kings and judges, an annual parliament, and a volunteer militia in contrast to a standing army. Above all, Saxons had held their land outright rather than subject to feudal tenure. This fact, conceded even by English legal authorities, obviously impressed Adams and Jefferson and many other colonial lawyers and landowners who were concerned with land titles and resented quitrents, primogeniture and other practices that seemed feudal and incompatible with the public good in America. In the colonial setting, scholarly men closely identified freeholding with liberty.

Modern historical research does not support the claim that all the Saxons lived in freedom, or that their ancient society resembled a modern democracy. Actually theirs was a society of warriors that imposed itself on a servile peasantry. But colonial men of affairs believed the Myth and it provided them with some good historical arguments for liberty. The Myth also better served English libertarians than were many of their philosophizing Continental counterparts. Instead of having to hypothesize natural rights originating in the remote caveman past, they could point to a more recent and authentic golden age that they believed was fully confirmed by English historian records: the period after 449 A.D. and before 1066, especially the days of King Alfred.

Proponents of the Saxon Myth drew heavily on Tacitus' *Germania* for their knowledge of Saxon customs. Thomas Gordon's 1728 translation was very popular in America. The *History of England* (1732) by a Frenchman, Paul Rapin, provided another translated source; and the legal researches and antiquarian speculations of Sir Henry Spelman, Bishop Samuel Squire, and Lord Kames had some influence. *A Historical Essay on the English Constitution* (1771), published at a crucial time, summarized the Saxon virtues the colonials had been reading about. Adams and Jefferson liked this anonymous work attributed to Obadiah Hulme. English-speaking colonists everywhere in America were susceptible to the Saxon Myth but it was developed and expressed best by the essayists and lawyers of Massachusetts and Virginia, and by those of Scottish or Puritan descent in the Middle Colonies.

Bookish colonists were drawn to the ideas of a small group of talented Britishers who, disillusioned with the limited amount of freedom even after the Glorious Revolution, began to use the Saxon Myth as the basis for an elaborate ideology and historiography. These writers, usually denominated True or Real Whigs, defined progress as the advance of civil liberty and offered a radical, libertarian interpretation of English history since the Conquest. They saw its course since that time as a seesaw struggle between Saxon freedom and Norman tyranny. They praised the persistence of common law after 1066 and the concessions John made to the barons in Magna Carta. They identified Parliament as the heir of the Saxon *witan* and generally approved of its evolutionary gains. While the break with the Pope and the Roman Church was a step forward from feudalism to freedom, there were also major setbacks. The Tudors, the Stuarts, and Oliver Cromwell had exerted arbitrary power, and the Restoration of Charles II had proved to be especially luxurious and retrograde. For the Real Whigs, the biggest strain on this Stuart's reign was the execution of Algernon Sydney for the mere act of writing (not even publishing) his *Discourses* attacking despotic government.

Real Whig historiography was the political aspect of a more

general movement in Britain and on the Continent to elevate the Germanic and reduce the Roman component in the culture of the 18th century. To the romantics of the Enlightenment the Goths were noble savages, intuitively wise, just, pure and democratic. They benefited from the vogue even more than the American Indians. Men of letters paid homage to "the race of Odin" and in their enthusiasm extended the definition of Goth to include not only the Angles, Saxons and Jutes who had descended on Britain, but also the Goths themselves, the Vandals, and the other Germanic tribes that had earlier conquered the Romans—in fact, almost everybody and everything that was non-Roman; this included the culture of the Middle Ages, before the Roman heritage was recovered in the Renaissance, and even the Celtic Britons. Thus King Arthur acquired some Gothic attributes, and a few extremists claimed that the Celtic druids had civilized the Greeks.

In the political application of the Saxon Myth, the Real Whigs had actually been preceded by the "Gothicists" of the 17th century. Colonials probing the roots of America in England would have come upon a strong "anti-Normanism" in the propaganda of Parliament against the first Stuart kings. When royalist theorists claimed the divine right of the Stuarts as a legacy from William the Conquerer, partisans of Parliament called for research to refute this with historical evidence denying the legitimacy of such a strong monarchy. Scholars responded by finding an etymological relationship between "Jute" and "Goth," thus forging a closer link between England's invaders and the Germanic tribes Tacitus had chronicled so favorably. They emphasized that the Goths really had no king at all, only a general to lead them in war, who could be demoted afterward. Above all, they stressed the organic development of Parliament from the ancient *witan;* presumably this institution had functioned without interruption during both the Danish and Norman invasions and was the legitimate locus of governmental power. Opponents argued that the *witan* had actually been a military council, thus making it a poor precedent for Parliament; Gothicists rebutted this with citations from Tacitus suggesting its democratic character. The claims of the latter naturally reached a crescendo when the Parliamentary armies closed in on Charles I during the Civil War. Afterward, during the Commonwealth, the champions of the Goths were challenged by the Levellers who rejected tradition and a Saxon golden age in favor of an even greater antiquity—Biblical Paradise or the lifetime of Christ. In reaction, the Gothicists of the late 17th century became more conservative, developing and advocating "Gothic balance," a system of checks and balances whereby aristocrats and commoners limited each other.

For those who dreamed of the full restoration of the Saxon constitution, the bright prospects of the Glorious Revolution and the settlement of William and Mary proved disappointing. Just as the behavior of the Long Parliament in the 1640s had indicated to many Real Whigs that a group could be as tyrannical as one man (although John Adams found the Interregnum acceptable), after 1688 it became apparent that a strengthened Parliament did not necessarily mean greater liberties for the average citizen. The Septennial Act of 1716 changing Parliamentary elections from every three to every seven years was a move away from the Saxon ideal of assemblies chosen annually. The Real Whigs became bitter in criticizing the Hanover kings and the long Walpole ministry (1721–1742). The standing armies of the Hanovers reminded them of William the Conqueror and Cromwell, they were troubled by the moral decay of the English people and, above all, dismayed by the political corruption that mounted rapidly early in the 18th century.

The Real Whigs, in making their case against Georgian England, took care to invoke Greece and Rome but they also publicized the fate of liberty in contemporary nations. The colonials gradually became acquainted with these philippics during the 18th century. Viscount Robert Molesworth, the first identifiable Real Whig, in his *Account of Denmark* (1694) described the ignorant populace, selfish nobility and standing army that brought on a revolution in that little nation, and how a French circle at the court was able to induce the Commons to surrender their precious gothic constitution to a despotic king. In Sir William Temple's *Observations on the United Provinces* (1690), Emperor Charles V of Spain was the villain; he violated Dutch provincial customs, imposed a standing army, and exacerbated religious differences by erecting new bishoprics. The Scottish historian, William Robertson, wrote the *History of Emperor Charles V* (1769), a very popular account that drew an ominous parallel between the Spanish ruler and George III. William Molyneaux's *The Case of Ireland* (1698) became relevant to America later. He argued that since Ireland had never been conquered but had submitted voluntarily, only her own parliament could impose taxes. Irishmen were free men entitled to the rights of Englishmen, including the right to be taxed only by consent. Colonial readers also learned of the loss of liberty in Sweden, Portugal, Rome, Russia, Morocco, Egypt, India and Ceylon. Turkey was the worst example and France the nearest. Real Whigs were discovering just how precious and vulnerable liberty was.

In the colonies the most influential Real Whig authors—measured by reprints in newspapers and books in libraries—were Trenchard, Gordon, Rapin, Locke, Sydney, Robertson, and Catherine Macauley. The works of Molesworth, John Milton, James Burgh, James Harrington, and Gilbert Burnet were also on many shelves.

The most popular writers, Trenchard and Gordon, began their brief collaboration in 1719. The *Independent Whig* and *Cato's Letters* in the *London Journal* made them famous, but the collaboration ended when Trenchard died in 1723. Their satirical and polemical attacks on High Churchmen, political Jacobites, and standing armies drew much attention in England and on the Continent. For colonial readers, however, their essays on libel, free speech, and civil liberties were the most relevant; their blows at tyranny were also useful in justifying the assemblies in their struggles with the royal governors. The effect of Trenchard and Gordon—and of the latter's translation of *Tacitus*—was to sustain the Saxon Myth and to revive some of the religio-political mood of the Interregnum. While the Real Whigs had virtually no effect on the corrupt politics of the Walpole era in the mother country, they were offering ideas that were compatible with the traditions and experiences of many who lived in America. From these writers the colonials learned to appreciate their own virtue and political practices and eventually to compare themselves favorably with Britain for having retained more of the ancient constitution and Saxon simplicity.

The lawyers who received their education solely in the colonies were somewhat more apt to be tinged with Saxon libertarianism than those who traveled to the Inns of Court in London (although the latter showed some signs of budding American nationalism and studied harder than their English fellows). One reason for this was the limited number of technical legal works available in America; casebooks and textbooks were scarce and expensive. The renowned legal commentators were Edward Coke and William Blackstone, but Volume I of the latter's famous *Commentaries* was not published in England until 1765, too late to contribute to the basic education of the leading lawyers of the Revolutionary generation. For them, Coke—his *Reports* and *Institutes,* especially *Coke on Littleton*—stood almost alone as an authority. Patrick Henry's legal preparation consisted largely of puzzling over *Coke on Littleton.* Coke was obscure, crabbed and undigested, but he acquainted novices not only with the complexities of land tenure but with the sacred and historic nature of the British constitution. As a student, Jefferson called Coke an old dull scoundrel but his later recollection was more favorable: "*Coke on Littleton* was the universal elementary book of law students and a sounder Whig never wrote nor a profounder learning in the orthodox doctrines of British liberties. Our lawyers were then all Whigs. But when his black letter text and uncouth but cunning learning got out of fashion, and the honeyed Mansfieldism of Blackstone became the student's horn-book, from that moment, that profession began to slide into Toryism and nearly all the young brood of lawyers are now of that line. They suppose themselves to be Whigs because they no longer know what whiggism or republicanism means." Those who persevered with Coke were obviously proud of their achievement. If they pondered his career, they were impressed by his defense of an independent judiciary and his assertation of the Higher Law binding the tyrannical Stuarts.

Coke's influence had been evident in the colonies from the beginning. He had participated in the drafting of the charter of 1606, providing for the settlement of Virginia and New England. The Puritans of Massachusetts Bay incorporated his ideas into their first codes and Jeremiah Dummer later invoked him in protesting the spread of the juryless admiralty courts. William Penn was indirectly guided by his opinions in drawing up his frames of government for Pennsylvania. Daniel Dulany the Elder, of Maryland, cited Coke in 1728 in making a Real Whig case for the rights of Englishmen in the plantations. Coke's decision in the famous Calvin's Case involving a Scotsman, encouraged colonial lawyers who wanted to believe that persons living in English territories outside the realm owed their allegiance to the king only, and not to Parliament. To James Wilson, Pennsylvania's ablest constitutional lawyer, and himself a Scot educated at Edinburgh, the precedent seemed important. Coke was preferred to Blackstone by such men because, in contrast to the latter, he was ambiguous and inconsistent on the vital question of Parliamentary supremacy, although he seemed to concede it occasionally. In speculation about the charters, the constitution, and the relationship with England, American lawyers found Coke quite useful, especially because he aligned English common law and the rights of Englishmen so carefully with the Higher Law, *i.e.*, God's law and natural rights.

The Conspiracy Against Colonial Liberty

The lawyers and other colonials had hoped the settlement of William and Mary meant constitutionalism, a mixture of the classical forms of government—monarchy, aristocracy, and democracy—with the checks and balances necessary for liberty. Early in the 18th century, they shared the pride of all Englishmen at the victory over Louis XIV and the peace of Utrecht; the British Empire seemed to be rising fast and its citizens were the freest in the world. Not long afterward, however, the Real Whig attack on the Hanovers and the corrupt Walpole ministry took their toll and the colonial confidence in the Empire began to turn to doubt. Gradually colonial lawyers came to understand that the British constitution they had admired was not very effective in the mother country, that in practice the powers of government were not separate enough to ensure liberty.

On paper the English and American versions of the British constitution seemed much alike, yet in operation the systems were quite divergent and this heightened the misunderstanding between the colonial leaders and the Crown. The final break between the colonies and British occurred over a fundamental constitutional difference; the colonists believed, indeed knew from experience, that a diffused and segmented sovereignty was viable, and were convinced that such a structure was consonant with the Saxon heritage and the best interpretation of the British constitution. King George and his ministers had no such confidence in the separation of powers. British politicians knew from their experience that although the educated class might revere the formal British constitution, Britain actually operated under a "private" or "informal" constitution in which "influence," rotten boroughs, virtual representation (only 10 percent of the populace was enfranchised), and heavy patronage oiled the wheels of government. These leaders assumed that the stricter separation of powers favored by Real Whigs and their American sympathizers was simply unworkable in 18th century British society. They were probably right. Despite rapid change, theirs was still too much of a traditional society with different orders of men: nobility, gentry, peasants, and a burgeoning urban rabble. The colonies clearly were different in that the population, except for the slaves, fell into gradations within the middle class; and in this kind of society a system of separation of powers could work.

Colonials interested in the law found fresh reasons for suspicion when George III came to the throne after the French and Indian War. Certain government actions lent credence to theories of a conspiracy against liberty. In 1761 the Crown, at the behest of customs officials, attempted to renew and extend into peacetime writs of assistance that permitted search and seizure in private homes without specific warrants. There were English precedents for the writs, and they had brought to book many wartime smugglers, but to colonials they seemed a dangerous departure from the constitution, from the common law dictum that a man's home was his castle. James Otis gained immediate fame when he invoked natural law against the writs. Then in 1763 the Crown proclaimed a line along the western mountains beyond which the colonists were not to settle. Ostensibly this was to keep the colonists accessible to commerce, reduce conflict with the Indians, and provide for orderly settlement but the Americans chose to ignore the proclamation, suspecting that it was designed to limit their population and favor English speculators. The next year Parliament imposed the Sugar Act, signalling a postwar enforcement of the trade laws combined with a new search for revenue. The stated purposes of these measures, to increase the colonies' contribution to the costs of Empire and to remind them of their subordinate status in a mercantilistic system, were not fully satisfying to those who had become sensitized libertarians. The fact that the mysterious and reactionary Scotsman, Lord Bute, who had not apprenticed in the cabinet, was the close adviser of George III, suggested that the regime was developing new unconstitutional and despotic tendencies; and there were rumors again of an American bishop.

Did the King and Parliament merely intend to enforce mercantile restrictions and extract imperial expenses, or were they plotting something more: to make uniform in the Empire the lower level of liberty then prevailing in the corrupt homeland by reducing it in America? Many colonials inclined to the latter view when Parliament enacted the Stamp Tax in 1765. Because in form it was not a duty but a tax to be levied internally, the colonists questioned its constitutionality. Given their developing legal tradition, it was natural and easy for colonial lawyers to use their lawbooks to support the pocketbooks affected in this instance. They could invoke Coke; he had championed the interpretation of Magna Carta requiring that the people be taxed only with their consent through their representatives; therefore only colonial assemblies, and not the Parliament in London, could levy such a tax.

Parliament in repealing the Stamp Tax within a year was staging a strategic retreat, but it soon substituted the Townshend duties. Although the imposition of duties in place of taxes was an apparent victory for the colonials because London seemed to be accepting the principle of no internal taxation without consent, the Townshend measure expanded the jurisdiction and power of the vice-admiralty courts. Since these tribunals had English-born judges and no juries, this was an additional instance of erosion of traditional rights. To make their economic restrictions work in America, the imperial authorities were willing to impinge on rights the colonies had come to regard as traditional and almost sacred.

In passing the Quartering Act of 1765, Parliament managed to strike two nerves of the colonial Real Whig psyche at the same time. The law required local governments to make available unoccupied dwellings for British troops and to provide them with certain provisions. Despite a formal request from the British commander in America, New York's Assembly balked. The colony's treasury was ample enough, but legislators regarded the Quartering Act as another form of taxation without representation. They acquiesced only when other colonies failed to join them in resisting. Real Whig fears of a standing army were also aroused by the prospect of redcoat encampments near centers of population, although the colonials appreciated the presence of British regulars on the frontiers to keep order and check the Indians. These fears seemed to be substantiated five years later when British troops in Boston—four thousand of them occupying a town of twelve thousand —fired into a crowd of demonstrators, after provocation, killing five unarmed men who became the patriot martyrs of "the Boston Massacre."

Even the Declaratory Act of 1766 that reaffirmed Parliament's right to tax the colonies took on hidden meaning to lawyers versed in Real Whiggery. Its wording closely resembled Ireland's Declaratory Act of 1719 in which the English Parliament had affirmed its supremacy there; that act had come in answer to Irish separatism and claims of dominion status. As noted earlier, one of the first Real Whigs, Molyneux, had argued that inasmuch as Ireland had never been conquered but had actually submitted to the English Crown, Irish law still prevailed and English laws should have no force unless re-enacted by the Irish Parliament. While the native Catholic Irish remained silent, Anglo-Irishmen and Scotch-Irishmen followed Molyneux and emerged as spokesmen for this 18th century Irish nationalism. Not regarded as fully English or Scottish in the lands of their birth, neither were they considered Irish in Ireland. Because of their marginal status, they developed a particularly acute sense of the rights of Englishmen overseas. Their motives were a blend of reactive nationalism and self-interest, since the Irish economy suffered terribly from the colonial status assigned to it in the trade and navigation laws. The ideas of these transplanted Whigs in Ireland and Ulster were therefore quite appropriate to the American situation that arose later. American lawyers were bound to be suspicious of the 1719 precedent and invoked the Irish Whigs in discussing and rationalizing their own relationship to Great Britain, its Parliament, and the king.

The British move in 1773 to offer East India Company tea cheaper than the smuggled Dutch variety the colonists were drinking, was given a sinister interpretation by the Real Whigs. They convinced themselves that the plan to sell the Company tea in America was a sign that the British were still determined to extract revenue by unconstitutional means and to undermine their liberty. They saw the issue of the Company tea as an insidious device for luring the Americans into paying the single Townshend duty still on the books. Prominent citizens were among the "Indians" who staged the Tea Party in Boston harbor. When the British overreacted to this destruction of private property by passing the so-called Intolerable Acts, closing the port of Boston and reducing self-government in Massachusetts until restitution was made, new elements in the colonies joined the opposition to the Crown.

These particular threats to the British constitution, and additional circumstantial evidence, account for the extravagant rhetoric and emotionalism in American political tracts during these years. The prospective economic burdens of taxes, duties and quartering acts—in view of the relative prosperity of the American colonies—cannot alone explain the opposition to these measures. Yet until 1774 the belief in deference, in rule by a gentlemanly elite, was strong enough in most colonies to restrain the population, and the democratic spirit was not evident except where the New Light flared. By the next year, however, Patrick Henry's words, "Give me Liberty, or give me Death!" were very much in season.

Those who believed that the British were engaged in a vast conspiracy to take away colonial liberties were not altogether wrong. George III, the Privy Council, and Parliamentary leaders may not have met in midnight secrecy to "design" the colonies' downfall step by step, but the tightening of mercantilistic and bureaucratic controls did tend to move colonial ways closer to those of the homeland, hence closer to corruption. And the particularism of the colonies, although reduced from the 17th century, was still resented in London. George's definition of a good king was one who presided efficiently over an empire in which the outlying parts were properly dependent on the home country. The Seven Years' War had hastened Britain's oncoming industrial revolution; to the king and his advisers there was a concomitant need to perfect relationships with her most valuable overseas possessions. After the figurehead administrations of the first two Hanover rulers, George III wanted to take up where William and Mary had left off in rationalizing the Empire. The colonials were victims of the times and divergent development.

The Declaration of Independence

The Continental Congress made the Declaration of Independence official on the Fourth of July, 1776, when the thirteen colonies were finally unanimous for separation. For the moment the doubters were silent, and the one-third of the population who were patriots held the center of the stage. These patriots, out of "a decent respect to the opinions of mankind," announced to the world the principles they were fighting for and the grievances they had endured. Jefferson was their scribe. He was a master of style, and he did not need to reread Locke or any other philosopher for the ideas; the language of natural rights had been in the air for more than a decade and was common property.

The novelty of the Declaration was the section we skip over today: the long list of charges against King George himself. The king was the symbol of British nationality and it was important to diminish any reverence for him that lingered among the folk. Earlier in the year the Quaker radical, Tom Paine, in his *Common Sense* had begun the process by attacking the monarch and the institution of monarchy itself, going beyond the evils of a ministerial coterie or a particular administration. Among the very pious, the specific enumeration of the king's "crimes" no doubt reinforced their image of him as the despotic Anti-Christ to be loathed as much as the Pope. It was also necessary to persuade the more timid Whigs, those who had hoped for a negotiated agreement in lieu of civil war, by underscoring the king's villainy in addition to the unconstitutional measures of his regime. In the theory of the Real Whigs, the Empire was composed of coordinate units connected through the person of the king; this single link was one of sentiment and consanguinity, and many were therefore reluctant to break it. The charges in the Declaration, phrased impressively, and emphasizing the king's responsibility in British violations of so many of the specific liberties Real Whigs held dear, sought to sever that remaining tie, and move the timid over the line and into the company of their more radical countrymen. Whether the charges against George III were exaggerated by conscious design or unconscious ideological fervor, they of course served to rally the patriots, bringing together pietists and rationalists for the military struggle already begun.

The Declaration proclaimed the conventional natural rights; it asserted the sovereignty of the people, the consent of the governed, the right of revolution and the individual right of life and liberty. The American version, replacing "property" with "the pursuit of happiness" as the third natural right, was a modification of Locke that reflected the expansive mood of the Americans, and perhaps also the more generous spirit of the Enlightenment in its last stages. It is interesting that the freethinking Jefferson at first wrote, "we hold these truths to be sacred," and was corrected by Franklin who substituted "self-evident," a term more appropriate in the Age of Reason, but one still quite acceptable to pietists who were in the tradition of Ramus and common sense.

Teachers perennially pose the question: just what did the draftsmen mean to say in their famous 18th century pronouncement: "all men are created equal."? The founding fathers were saying that, after studying the nature of man firsthand in America—this being as close as they could get scientifically to Man stripped of the accidents of time and place—they had concluded that all men everywhere possessed the same basic instincts and, consequently, the same natural rights. They had learned from their New World experience what the *philosophes* of the Old World could only assume; that environment and not heredity made the man. This was a philosophical affirmation of the brotherhood of Man. Yet in this theory, of course, the Americans occupied a special position. Because of so favorable an environment, their character already approached the optimum in God and Nature; what the Americans were, all men could hope to be someday. In the race to develop God-given talents and assert God-given rights, the Americans had a head start. As Louis Hartz has put it, they were "born free."

This emphasis on the environment gave our statesmen a liberal and progressive cast for the time, especially when contrasted with the few Calvinists in America who held an orthodox view of predestination—that God in the beginning elected only a few, and "passed over" the vast majority of the world's inhabitants. But as the chapter on the heathen has already suggested, environmentalism had its conservative implications also. If a man could retain his God-given liberty only as a noble savage in the forest or as a yeoman with his firing piece, freehold, and franchise in a republic—and nothing in-between would do—most people had in effect been passed over in this scheme, too. The great difference was assumed to be the possibility for change; environmentalists ought to have more realistic plans than Calvinists or sectarians for ameliorating the conditions of this world. They would do it by delegating power to the most reasonable men, a rational elite, who would establish the proper institutions. Americans were more hopeful about changing the world than their European brethren, but that optimism was highest when they contemplated what reasonable white men from Europe could still accomplish on the rich North American continent. When they thought of other peoples and continents, they lost much of their confidence in Man and became gradualists.

When French friends consulted Jefferson a few years later on their plans for a revolution in that country, he counseled against it, predicting a fiasco because the French peasant, untutored in liberty, was not rational enough to assert his natural right of revolution against the Bourbon monarchy. Did Jefferson mean that although everyone had natural rights, most people were not in a position to exercise them effectively? The French had their Revolution anyway.

Secular natural rights advocates, like their religious counterparts, deduced too much from a few "self-evident" truths. What they created was a historical fiction drawn from Gothicism and Puritanism about the sacredness of the individual personality. When challenged by a levelling spirit after 1770 and 1774, the conservative aspects of that individualism came to the fore. The need for law and order, checks and balances, and the protection of reasonable people in their persons, property, and opinions seemed self-evident to them.

If we ask what the common people thought of the Declaration, with its egalitarian phrases, the answer is easier and less qualified. The feelings of a large fraction of the people were so completely aroused, that their sentiments in this direction far exceeded those of their presumably liberal leaders. They had long subscribed to "self-evident" truths, and as the final chapter will suggest, were rather suddenly relishing the equality of men—or at least those men who could sing hymns and fire muskets. This was the Spirit of '76.

NOTE

1. Jacob Leisler seized power in 1689, prematurely proclaiming William and Mary, and ruled New York for more than a year in the name of the poorer classes. The demand of "Yorkers" for a legislative assembly like the other colonies, the dissatisfaction with Andros and the Dominion of New England (of which New York was a part), together with the beginning of the Anglo-French War and rumors of a Catholic plot by an ex-governor combined to ignite the uprising. When Leisler was hung for treason, he became a martyr in the eyes of the democratic faction in Manhattan.

Chapter 6

God's Sovereignty and a More Perfect Union

The Great Awakening sundered the delicate balance between rationalism and pietism among Calvinists themselves, and in the colonies generally; the decade from 1740 to 1750 was a watershed in American thought. Although the revival produced many offshoots, it was comparable to the 1660 Restoration in England in auguring a deep division that took a theological form; there were the proponents of the "evangelical Scheme," and the opposers, who were the adherents of the "legal Scheme." The former consisted of Calvinistic New Lights, New Sides, Separates, and Baptists; the latter included Old Lights, Old Sides, Old Baptists and Anglicans who were crypto- or outright Arminians.

Rationalism continued to percolate into the colonial society, but what happened to the New Light between the time of the Great Awakening and the Revolution? Did the colonials, those stirred but not converted during the religious excitement, lapse into that state of self-indulgent privatism and pursuit of individualistic prosperity, later dubbed "normalcy"? For a decade or so they did. The opposers of the revival (those "soft" on predestination), became bolder and some admitted openly their Arminianism; they were largely urban, and therefore quite receptive to the Enlightenment science and humanism that was crosing the Atlantic with new speed and frequency; their ranks were small but their rationalism was conspicuous. Yet the parallel with 1660 was not complete because the New Light did not turn inward to quietism; instead, after 1744, it continued to smolder and flare as it burned through the hinterlands from Maine to Georgia. Some churches aroused in the revival were dormant for as long as a decade afterward, but elsewhere the New Light was spreading. The evangelicals had not attained power and been discredited as Cromwell's Puritan coalition had; on the frontier, among the common folk, and among the clerical elite, they retained their strength and dreamed of a more perfect union, despite the influx of worldly ideas into the towns of the seaboard.

In the northern colonies the intense excitement of the Awakening had almost disappeared by 1745. When Whitefield returned to New England a year later, he was much less effective. Harvard and Yale had turned against him because he intimated that their faculties were without grace. The influx of new members to the churches had slowed noticeably, as if all those susceptible to the New Light—or reacting to it—had already been gathered in. (In the western communities affected by the Frontier Revival, admissions after 1740 were not as large.) By that time the Separate movement had begun in New England and would continue into the next decade. In the Middle Colonies there was a similar ebb. Gilbert Tennent had settled down in a Philadelphia pulpit; like Davenport, he apologized for his excessive zeal and his rash judgment of colleagues during the revival.

The New Light in Virginia

The Great Awakening was far from over below the Mason-Dixon line, however. In the South, in fact, it had scarcely begun. The New Light followed settlers into the backcountry, and even touched some places in the gentlemanly tidewater region. Populous Virginia was the first to feel its warmth. Although it has been noted that Whitefield failed initially to arouse the tidewater planters, he may have had some indirect effect. There was a mysterious upsurge of piety in Hanover County in 1739; some respectable citizens began reading devotional works and meeting in private houses to discuss them. Evidently they found the Anglican parish services too formal and latitudinarian. They were fined repeatedly for neglecting them. In their ignorance, they at first described themselves as Lutherans because they admired Luther, but others more familiar with theology identified their beliefs as Presbyterian. Governor Gooch, a Scotsman, was willing to recognize them as such and extended all the protections that recognized dissenters were entitled to under the toleration laws. When New Light missionary William Robinson visited them in 1743, these "Presbyterians" gave him a very friendly reception. During the next three years, other New Lights visited the county attracting large audiences, but they strained their tolerated status by failing to register with the authorities and casting aspersions on the established clergy and the few Old Side ministers settled in the west.

Then Reverend Samuel Davies, with the approval of the New Light synod, came to settle in Hanover County. At once he began to offset the adverse reactions caused by the New Light itinerants. He complied completely with the toleration laws, and "spent no time in exposing the Peculiarities of the established church." Although delicate in health, Davies was physically effective in the pulpit; his voice was commanding, his delivery was affectionate yet emphatic; yet he was not boisterous but grave and dignified. His congregation grew so large that it spilled over into four adjacent counties. He reached them by riding on horseback around a circuit of four and later seven meetinghouses; even so, some pious folk had to travel forty miles to hear this man. His largest meetinghouse, seating five hundred, could not accommodate the worshippers, and he had three hundred communicants, including a few blacks.

The eloquence of Davies, who was of Welsh ancestry, was instinctive. His grandfather had come to Pennsylvania from Wales in 1684. The family had been Baptists until Samuel's parents found that group theologically lax and shifted to the more aggressive New Light Presbyterians. Young Samuel followed, joining the Presbyterians at the age of twelve, after a brief religious experience. He was educated by the Reverend Samuel Blair at Fagg's Manor. Blair, a Log College graduate, of course took Tennent's school as his model and mixed the classics thoroughly with the scriptures. Thus Davies was able to augment Old Testament strictures with Cicero and the ancients.

His New Light characteristics were evident in many ways. He

liked to spend several days in composing sermons and always had one before him in the pulpit, yet he often committed them to memory, or extemporized as the Spirit moved him. He enumerated as many motives as he could, religious and secular, for being good and used rhetorical questions and many facts to build his case. He perceived that sermons were even more effective than Bibles or catechisms. He echoed Locke as interpreted by Edwards when he spoke of trying to "make the hearer sensibly feel, as well as clearly understand." If the hearer's reaction was too physical, Davies was charitable in his judgment. And he followed Whitefield when he decried denominational competition and urged catholicity; he claimed to exult more in being a Christian than a Presbyterian, and to "not care what church men went to Heaven from." Methodists, as well as Baptists and Presbyterians could sing his hymns; a favorite was

> Lord, I am thine, entirely thine,
> Purchas'd and sav'd by Blood Divine,
> With full consent thine I would be,
> And own thine sov'reign right in me.

Except at the height of the colonial war, love was a stronger theme with Davies than justice; and like the Great Awakener, he did not explore in the pulpit the recondite or unpopular doctrines of Calvinism. Instead, he inveighed against "lukewarmedness" in religion and the "deadly poison" of posing as a Christian without the inner conviction. "To maintain a secret walk with God, to be as holy as he is holy, this is the labour, this is the work."

In his first years in Virginia, Davies seems to have maintained the proper New Light "weanedness" towards the things of this world. He dwelt on death, perhaps because in his youth sickness had put him on the edge of it. The corruption and worldliness of Britain and the Old Dominion filled him with foreboding. He was sure that God, in causing the Lisbon earthquake, intended more than a warning to Portuguese Catholics. There was in fact a simultaneous tremor of modest severity in America and this was reassuring to him since, unlike the European Newtonians, he preferred to believe that even in modern times God could stop the machinery of natural law and intervene directly in the world. The catastrophic defeat of General Braddock's army on the nearby frontier the same year was another sign of God's displeasure with the colonists for their neglect of Him.

Yet in his attitude toward the war, Davies departed from most of the Edwardsian New Lights in the north. Even if the Empire and Virginia were deserving of punishment he could not remain aloof. Instead he emphasized the inherent evil nature of the French Papists and their savage allies whom God was using as His instruments as He had long ago used the Assyrians against "His children." God intended a warning; it was unthinkable that He wanted a French victory and a Catholic occupation of Virginia with the accompanying loss of civil and religious liberty. Davies used his oratorical talents to rally the citizenry, especially the dissenters, to the cause of king and country, land and liberty. He became the best recruiting officer in the colony, thereby raising the status of all dissenters in the eyes of the governor and the Church people. In his sermons to potential fighting men, he was blunt. Men who would not serve God and country were unmanly and by inference were unregenerate. Show that you are "men, Britons, and Christians," he said, reversing the usual order of the pietists. In 1758 when recruitment lagged, he preached on "The Curse of Cowardice," and enlistments were oversubscribed. Confronted directly with the war in his own colony, Davies seems to have amended the New Light creed by offering anxious Calvinists an alternative to the lonely spiritual pilgrimage on this earth, namely a crusade against the French Papists in the uniform of the Virginia militia.

But Davies did not submerge his piety completely or permanently in the imperial cause. Before the war he had decried the corruption in British public life. During the conflict he appeared Whiggish in his praise of the British constitution with its marvelous balance of monarchy, aristocracy, and democracy, and when the redcoats had their backs to the wall in 1756 and 1757, he pictured Britain as a Christian state, a veritable Israel, beleaguered by minions of the Devil. When a British triumph seemed certain, however, he was ready to reassert the thesis of the New Lights: *i.e.*, Britain was doomed as a nation unless reforms were made immediately. He reasoned that God gave the victory to the English, not because they were deserving, but to vindicate His own honor.

Staunch Anglicans envied Davies' success in Virginia. They accused him of sophistry and subterfuge because he was ecumenical in his preaching, yet his Presbyterian followers were coalescing into a political faction and had begun to examine candidates for office about their positions on questions of the day. While the dissenters were emerging in politics, and Davies was attracting hundreds to every sermon, some parish churches had to close for lack of attendance. Davies' selfless labor in recruiting during the war contrasted sharply with the materialism of Anglican rectors who complained at being paid their salaries in paper currency instead of the much more valuable tobacco their contracts called for. Although their claim might have been just, it reinforced the image of greedy time-servers and was dramatized in the Parson's Cause, when one minister, not content with a British decision against the currency, sought back pay in tobacco. Patrick Henry, a young lawyer who learned his eloquence from Davies, defended Virginia and the plaintiff was awarded damages of one penny, which was about what a rector was worth in the minds of most Virginians at that moment.

Davies' effectiveness in the tidewater was due to his moderate evangelism that met a latent need for many nominal Anglicans. And his Presbyterian polity was not a great novelty to them either. The Anglican Church in Virginia was a "low church" establishment that had a 17th century character, as much presbyterian as episcopalian; to this the New Lights merely added evangelism.

From their beachhead in Hanover County the Presbyterian evangelicals spread through the tidewater and the frontier, and on the eve of the Revolution, were heavily reinforced by the invading Separate Baptists. When a moderate New Light was combined with the moralistic constitutionalism of the leading planters, the result was a new regime in 1776 with some democratic modifications of the polity and society in the Old Dominion.

Separates and Baptists

The Baptists became important in America in 1755 when Shubael Stearns and Daniel Marshall, Separate Baptist preachers from New England, traveled to the North Carolina backcountry and gathered a flock at Sandy Creek. From this mother church at the forks of the Cape Fear River, the denomination spread in both directions and by the time of the Revolution, its churches dotted the map from northern Virginia to the new lands of Georgia. The great and rapid success of the Separate Baptists in the South must be attributed to an element already at work for the New Lights and New Sides in awakening the Reformed churches; namely an evangelical Calvinism that was effective under frontier conditions.

Prior to 1755, the Baptists had played a very minor role in colonial life. In the 17th century, the deep-seated Puritan fear of antinomianism and anarchy had resulted in the persecution of Baptists as well as Quakers in most of New England, although freedom prevailed in Roger Williams' colony of Rhode Island and there was some toleration in Plymouth. In the 18th century the fear changed to contempt, but the Toleration Act was only grudgingly and imperfectly extended to Baptists and Quakers. The early New England Baptists were humble, otherworldly folk; there were no Boston Baptist "grandees" comparable to the aristocratic Quaker merchants of Philadelphia. But the Baptists did parallel their dissenter brethren in some degree by turning their piety inward during the Restoration period, and following various New Testament "principles"—the love feast, foot washing, and the laying on of hands. Although they were General (Arminian) Baptists with no interest in theology or a learned clergy, they adhered to a congregational polity. This combination had sufficed in the days of excitement and persecution but lacked vitality when persecution ceased. The congregations became female-dominated and static, lagging far behind population growth; and denominational historians describe this period euphemistically as one of "consolidation."

Because of the decades of inwardness and Arminianism, very few of the Baptists in New England were stirred by the Great Awakening; like the Quakers, they remained aloof, untouched by the New Light. Partly this was a resentment that amounted to a class antagonism toward the established Congregationalists. When so many of the Congregational majority were converted in the revival, the New Light somehow did not seem as attractive or emancipating to the lowly Baptist minority. Although the three flocks of Baptists that were Calvinistic experienced moderate gains, the Awakening brought forth no leaders from the ranks. As the history of the Quakers already indicated, a revival of messianic religion could not easily be built up on quietistic foundations. If the Baptists were to be reborn, it would be very largely under new leadership and in new places. After 1740, New England Baptist leaders came either from the "western brethren" in the Middle Colonies or from Congregationalism, via the Separate movement.

The pre-eminent leader in the "new reformation" of the Baptists in New England was Isaac Backus, a Congregationalist stirred by the Awakening. His ancestry is a clue to a major source of the radical New Light there. His mother traced her descent from the Winslows, a founding family in the Plymouth Colony; his great-great-grand-father had come from England to Connecticut in 1638. He was proud of this lineage but the reputation of the family in the 18th century was merely local; the Backuses held land and offices in Norwich, a town in eastern Connecticut, near the Rhode Island border. Al-though they had the means, they did not send Isaac to college.

The evolution of Backus from covenant Calvinist to Separate to Separate Baptist was typical of many New Lights. After he was awakened, he realized that his regular pastor, although showing some sympathy with the revival, was not lively enough in his preaching or strict enough in his Calvinism. New Lights usually be-gan by complaining about the dullness of a graceless minister, but they soon focused on the lax admission policies that prevailed in the Puritan churches. In Norwich, Backus and his brethren reflected a common New Light attitude when they called for the abandon-ment of the Half Way Covenant and the written statement of con-fession—in general, the kind of "large" policy that Stoddard and the Brattle Street Church had inaugurated—and a return to the standard of the founding fathers: an oral public confession, to be ratified by a majority of the church members.

The New Light desire for a church limited to visible saints stemmed from the perception that religious feeling was generated by a peculiar togetherness. Backus "sensed" that he could not com-mune with worldly men who had made merely a perfunctory writ-ten statement. The New Lights yearned for that harmony, that "beauty of union," as Edwards phrased it, that they believed came only when saints took communion together, apart from worldlings and graceless conformists.

For four years Backus and his New Light brethren tried to re-form the Norwich church from within; they failed because Con-necticut's consociationism reinforced the *status quo* and the Old Lights, who were in the majority, feared for their own souls in the event that the insurgents triumphed and imposed high standards.

Finally, Backus and his friends "came out" from the Norwich church in order to found their own. Their Separate church was one among some 125 in New England gathered by New Lights who had despaired of reforming from within. Separation was a civil offense, but the radical pietists risked other hazards also—financial and political as well as religious. Assessors labelled them "schismatics" and refused to accord them the toleration extended to Anglicans, Baptists, and Quakers; they pressed the Separates for religious taxes and if they refused, their goods were seized and sold at auction or they were jailed, or both. Nevertheless, Backus forsook a business career to become a Separate preacher and served several jail terms in the cause of religious freedom. "Schismatics" was the charge again when these people sought to protect themselves by invoking "liberty of conscience" provisions in charters and toleration acts. Without tax support, Separate preachers had no choice but to live up to their principles and rely on free contributions from worshippers. Most of them barely subsisted since New Englanders were traditionally stingy; Backus was the exception because he had independent means.

Once they had withdrawn, the Separates had to resist the inevitable Protestant tendency to subdivide further. Backus stoutly resisted the few perfectionists who claimed that they were without sin and above the moral law. One man let his married daughter, whose husband was on a voyage, cohabit with a soulmate "for they lay with the Bible between them." When her husband returned and found his wife pregnant, he sued for divorce, being ignorant of the New Light on spiritual wifery.

In addition to outside harassment and outcroppings of perfectionism, the new sect suffered from an agonizing internal division; even after separation from the Old Lights, they found they could not always take communion in ineffable harmony. This dichotomy, and not persecution, made the movement chronically unstable and led eventually to its demise. The fatal split was over the baptismal rite. Which was Biblical: baptism in infancy or in adulthood? The Puritans did not hold that infant baptism remitted for sin as the Catholics implied, but they did claim it was scriptural, that it was a "seal" and indicated that the child would be raised under the watch and care of the church, and that there was some slight presumption that he would eventually prove to be one of the Elect and be regenerated. To the New Lights, this Puritan version of baptism was at best meaningless and at worst pernicious in implying that grace ran "through the loins of the saintly parents," thus encouraging "carnal security" (complacency about salvation) in those merely sprinkled as babies. The New Light antipedobaptists were in agreement with their archfoes, the Catholics, at least to the extent of believing the rite of baptism should signify an important change. In conducting their churches, Backus and other Separate preachers tried to follow a policy of open communion, hoping to harbor both views —antipedo- and pedobaptist—within the same congregations, but the two would simply not mix.

When Backus felt compelled to make an extended study of the question of baptism, he was surprised at just how weak the Puritan case was; he could find no scriptural passage specifically sanctioning it. The chief evidence the Puritans offered was that the apostles had baptized families; presumably children were included. On the other hand, the Baptist claim that infant baptism was a device added later by priests to increase their control over the laity was congruent with the Separates' anti-institutional bias. Backus concluded that the Baptist position was the historically sound and the logical one.

In converting to the Baptist faith, Backus and other Separates— more than half the group—had to overcome the strong socio-religious prejudices that dated from the Reformation. In the Puritan view, Baptists were not only the ignorant heirs of the Munster fanatics, but their claim that baptism was valid only for adults was dangerous because it implied that the pious majority was unsaved, that the Christian commonwealths they erected were in fact not Christian. The evangelical power of the Great Awakening, however, enabled many of those born into the Puritan establishment to take the plunge and become Baptists, accepting the ridicule and contumely of neighbors. The Separates who could not go this far eventually drifted back into the fold of the orthodox churches. The sect of Separates was an unstable compound, that did not survive the 18th century.

Those who joined the Baptists were treated with scorn and envy by the orthodox. Once Separates became Baptists, they were no longer liable for the support of the settled minister; this led tax-paying Puritan neighbors to regard them as hypocrites who were "dipping to wash away their taxes." As people shifted to the tolerated sect, the tax burden increased for worshippers remaining in the establishment. Thus the exodus created a crisis grave enough to cause extensive hard feelings, although not enough to topple Puritan rule. The Separate Baptists were probably not tax dodgers as the critics claimed; believers' baptism was a natural and logical development for those following the New Light. Backus and the other converts, having added the "further light" of baptism to their New Light, took their brand of Calvinism to the "Old Baptists" of New England (largely Arminian) in the decade after the Awakening and thereby enlarged the "beauty of union."

In the Middle Colonies, English and Welsh Baptists were among the first dissenters attracted by Pennsylvania's religious freedom, but the diversity of belief in the New World soon led them toward creedal orthodoxy; like their contemporaries, the Scotch-Irish Presbyterians, their leaders wanted to maintain group identity by subscription. More in response to these immigrants than to the Awakening, the Philadelphia Association eventually decided in 1742 to adopt the Calvinistic confession of the English Particular Baptists. Where it could, the Association imposed this creed on the scattered flocks. Thus the Calvinistic Baptists, called Particular because of their belief in Election and limited atonement, gained control of most of the churches. This was a pyrrhic victory, however, since up to 90 percent of a congregation sometimes deserted in the process; worshippers accustomed to Arminianism could not be made to accept the legalistic Calvinism of the European-oriented clergy. In New England a few of the General (Arminian) Baptist churches were able to resist the aggressive campaign and linger on, but all were extinct by 1794.

After the Awakening, with the emergence of the Separates and the decline of the Arminians, the Particulars took the name of Regulars. Thus after 1742 the major competition within the Baptist denomination was between two kinds of Calvinists, the Regulars and the Separates—the orthodox Old World and the evangelical New World. Colonial history was to indicate that neither Arminianism nor Calvinism of the Regular or Old Side type could be well sustained by a congregational polity; to thrive these creeds needed the episcopal or the presbyterian form. At peaks of religious concern various combinations of theology and polity might be viable, but at other times only evangelical Calvinism could draw in and hold a male laity, yet retain enough organization to make the church vital in the community and reinforce home-rule democracy.

Were the Separates actually Calvinistic in theology? Some hesitant authors have reserved that term for the Regulars only. It is clear, however, from the mode of preaching and the wording of individual church creeds, that the Separates followed the spirit of the Association's 1742 confession, that they were indeed Calvinistic. The term "moderate," while it does not suit their exhortations or gestures, has been used to suggest the character of their creed, to indicate that, although generally adhering to the Calvinistic scheme, they conveniently ignored many of its deep implications. (For clarity, I have substituted "evangelical" for "moderate" in this book.)

In Connecticut Stearns had received a divine "opening" to go westward; Marshall followed and married Stearns's sister. They eventually found religious conditions in the Carolina backcountry conducive to their Separate Baptist message. The Carolina proprietors had encouraged religious toleration and diversity from the beginning; this had resulted in clusters of Quakers, Moravians, German sectarians, and a few Lutherans. The Anglican establishment was only nominal; S.P.G. missionaries had found the frontier population intractable early in the century, and the Church was very weak in the tidewater; in 1765 there were only five rectors in the colony, and there were no learned clergy of any denomination settled in the backcountry before 1770. But many newcomers, following the interior valleys from Pennsylvania, entered Carolina after 1730; the large group of English descent formed a natural clientele for the New Lightism of Stearns and Marshall.

The success of the Separate Baptists with such folk was immediate and spectacular. The Sandy Creek Church soon became the mother of a large association. The genteel tidewater people became alarmed. They described the Separates as deformed, ugly, primitive, illiterate—as "vulgar enthusiasts." Particularly annoying to the better sort was the "holy whine," a preaching style that had a hypnotic and nasal quality. The justification for it originally was said to be the need to reach large audiences in the open air and wind. Evidently the Separates had copied this mannerism from James Davenport, and like him they engaged in spontaneous and euphoric singing. Carolina preachers who had only the whine and other "gifts," but no formal education, naturally produced trembling, "jerks," "barking," and fallings more extreme than the northern colonies had witnessed in their revivalism; these manifestations recurred in Kentucky and elsewhere on the Southwestern frontier during religious excitement in the 19th century.

When Whitefield passed through Carolina in 1764, he learned of the spreading New Lights. Did he recognize and acknowledge them as heirs of the 1740 Awakening, as his disciples? Far from it. He refused to identify with the New Lights or let them use the name "Methodist," a term he reserved for his followers and those of the Wesleys—groups within the Anglican faith. He also reaffirmed the propriety of infant baptism. In his old age the Great Awakener had become a more orthodox Anglican, accepting the Church judgment that the New Lights were mere "enthusiasts." Earlier Whitefield had seemed more philosophical: when told that many of his converts had gone from separatism to the Baptists, his retort was "My chicks have turned to ducks."

The Separate Baptists did not make a major advance in respectability until the middle of the 1760s. Despite the great difference in religious temper between Separates and Quakers at this time, outsiders in Carolina recognized the historical connection: like the Quakers, the Separates resented a paid ministry, dressed plainly, and encouraged female participation. The Separates' chief rivals, where they had any, were the non-evangelical Regular Baptists who were more sedate and cerebral in their Calvinism. These two branches of the denomination shared a common theology and polity, but their colonial beginnings were different; the Regulars derived from English and Welsh immigration to Pennsylvania; the Separates sprang from Connecticut Puritanism at a revivalistic apogee. Efforts to merge the two were often made, but were thwarted by the Separate laity who found the Regulars' sermons too dry, their dress too worldly, and their behavior too lax. Young Separate males who were contemplating the ministry were impressed, however, by the superior erudition of the Regular clergy, and disappointed that a merger could not be effected. In the meantime—the situation was similar to the Presbyterian Old Side-New Side schism—the Separates completely outdistanced the Regulars in the canvass for converts. On the eve of the Revolution, the Separates even penetrated that citadel of respectability, the Virginia tidewater; by 1774 they had five thousand members there, outnumbering the Regulars six to one. The union of the two branches finally occurred in 1787 (in North Carolina, 1777). The Separates agreed to accept the Regulars' Confession of Faith "but to prevent it from usurping a tyrannical power over the consciences of any, we do not mean that every person is bound to the strict observance of everything therein contained." Thus did the Separates guard their freedom against any tendency of the Regular minority toward subscription and hyper-Calvinism.

The Separates' spectacular sweep of the southern colonies was accompanied in its final stages by persecution and prosecution. In colonial history we customarily condemn the Massachusetts Bay Puritans for whipping, mutilation, and execution of invading Quaker and Baptist itinerants, but we sometimes overlook the severe treatment the Separates received a century later in the Virginia tidewater. There a strongly prejudiced populace, abetted by some persons in the Anglican establishment, permitted beatings, whippings, and mayhem against the evangelicals. Separate preachers had to endure continual physical abuse and threats of death from the rabble. Samuel Hariss, gentleman-turned-Baptist, was pulled down by a ruffian and dragged alternately by the hair and the leg until rescued. Elder John Waller was attacked at once by a parson, a sheriff and a clerk; the parson thrust a whip down Waller's throat, and the trio pulled him down and lashed him. Attempts to finish off a preacher while he was in jail were common; when James Ireland was in the Culpeper jail, antagonists first tried to blow up his cell, and later put poisonous fumes under his window, but he survived.

Persecution was as much a quirk of the age as of the Puritan mind. The identification of the Separates with the Anabaptists of Munster raised the usual specter of immorality, sedition, and anarchy. The Baptists were described as cruel because they denied baptism to infants; if children died before adulthood and immersion, they were lost. Of course the critics echoed the refrain the Anglicans used against revivalists everywhere, namely that the New Light preachers were power-hungry hypocrites, "enthusiasts" who were taking the plain folk away from their labors, only to delude them and unhinge their nervous systems.

But the real danger of the Baptists was believed to be more behavioral than creedal, more social and political than religious. It was not only shrewd but appropriate therefore, when the Baptists were brought into the courts, that the prosecutors based their charges on behavior and not directly on beliefs. Usually the Baptists were accused of disturbing the peace; this meant assaulting strangers with Biblical citations and inquiries about their souls; or with vagrancy, because Baptists insisted that God had called them directly, and therefore disdained to conform to the toleration acts, itinerating as freely as mobs would permit. Even when they complied with the laws, juries and judges were rigged against them; yet they accepted their "sufferings" and prayed for more. The Separate Baptists were crusaders for religious liberty. The martyrdom of the Separates in the Old Dominion confirmed Jefferson and Madison—two gentlemen who were far from the New Light in religion—in the conviction that the time had come to move beyond toleration to complete religious freedom.

When the Revolution came, the Great Awakening was still visible in the South. The New Lights—Presbyterian and Baptist—had gathered in a good percentage of the unchurched English and Welsh, as well as some Scotch-Irish on the southern frontier, and had effectively penetrated the tidewater with their message of the Terrors of the Law, the New Birth, and the Kingdom to come. Puritan Calvinism had spread from New England to Georgia and, modified only slightly by Middle Colony influences, was a vital force in all the colonies.

Edwards on the Will and Original Sin

The Great Awakening affected behavior patterns more than theological beliefs, and the ideas of English writers with Arminian tendencies continued to make inroads in the colonies after the revival, especially in eastern New England where Colmanism had taken root. The Awakening may have actually hastened the spread of such ideas. Those who instinctively rejected the fervor of the revival looked anew for an alternative to the Calvinism that they identified with excessive emotionalism and a pessimistic view of human nature; they found it in the Enlightenment with its bias against religious authority, and its emphasis on the rationality of man. The Enlightenment reinforced their native common sense in rejecting predestination and original sin, with its barbarous corollary of infant damnation.

Thus Calvinistic theology benefitted less from the revival than might have been expected. Calvinists found their system—although temporarily shored up in the countryside—still being undermined by urban intellectuals. In Europe their brethren were discovering that the traditional Calvinist defenses had become somehow ineffectual and obsolete, no longer intellectually respectable. Old

World Calvinists were heartened therefore when they learned that Jonathan Edwards, the renowned New England theologian, was coming to the rescue with a full-scale refutation of the Arminian scheme; they hoped that his polemical skill and relentless logic could demolish Arminian thinkers once and for all. John Erskine, the leader of the Scottish Calvinists, was conspicuous in his encouragement, and Scotsmen accounted for 44 of the 425 subscriptions to Edwards' *Freedom of the Will*, (1754). Partisans were not disappointed. Edwards produced a formidable tract on the will that provoked theological controversy for a hundred years. The Reverend James Dana attempted an answer in 1770, but no complete response was printed in the 18th century. *The Freedom of the Will* (1754) together with Edwards' other post-revival writings—the *Religious Affections* (1746), *Original Sin* (1755), and *Virtue* (1757)—eventually provided the doctrinal texts for a small body of new believers that emerged from the Awakening—the Edwardsians or New Divinity men.

Edwards wrote the last three works at Stockbridge, the small community of Housatonic Indians in the Berkshires, where he was serving as missionary. In 1750 he was dismissed from his Northampton pulpit, largely because of his New Light demand for a closed communion, *i.e.*, the abandonment of the Half Way Covenant and the restoration of public confession. In his Farewell Address to the Northampton congregation, he reminded them that Arminianism was still growing, that the danger was greater than when he had given his first warning in 1734.

In *The Freedom of the Will*, Edwards was returning to a theme of his youth, elaborating questions he had put to himself in *Notes on the Mind*, written when he was a student at Yale. But his immediate concern was to defend the Reformation and the Calvinistic system from rationalistic scoffers who had made some specific attacks. He was answering the "fashionable notions" of Daniel Whitby, Thomas Chubb, Samuel Clarke and especially John Taylor. These English Arminians were seeking, in the name of common sense and practicality, to sweep away the deterministic assumptions of the Calvinists. Edwards' task was formidable because the ethos was strongly toward individual accountability and *ad hoc* reasoning. His defenses—determinism, logic, and revelation—ran counter to the social forces of the time.

Yet Edwards made a good case; he held that to understand ourselves we had first to understand God, and not the other way around. He could not accept the Arminian implication that man had free will—that is, that his will was somehow independent of the network of causes outside, or was in equilibrium before it made a decision. In a world of cause and effect, an individual's will could not be self-determining; there had to be a determiner, and obviously and logically that force was God (with some interference from Satan). If the will were free to choose, God's foreknowledge would be hampered and His omniscience compromised; assuming a moral universe, there had to be determinism.

In his revival sermons, Edwards, while driving home God's sovereignty, had sometimes made Him seem capricious, but later he insisted that the Almighty acted only by design, never hastily or accidentally. To underline this, he entitled one chapter, "No Event without a Cause." Cause was defined broadly to include all antecedents, whether natural or moral, positive or negative. Whatever man did, he did for a reason. In this way he sought to put the Arminians in the ridiculous position of suggesting that an individual could operate outside the world of cause and effect, and could act from no discernable motive. Edwards saw only two choices: either limiting divine omniscience or denying human freedom, and he naturally "inclined" toward the latter. To assume that man, like God, had a creative will not only seemed contrary to logic and history, but to Edwards' personal experience. His best ideas and "inclinations" had come to him as "openings" from the other world, as promptings from his unconscious.

Edwards tried to make the most of the limited freedom available under his system. Following Calvin, he defined freedom as the power to pursue an inclination, that is, to act without compulsion. In following his inclination, however, man was accountable even though he had no choice in the matter. He made the philosophical distinction between natural and moral necessity; in the first case, man was not accountable, but in the second he was, although both were absolute. With this small concession to freedom, he thought he had avoided being classified with certain freethinkers, Hobbes, Leibnitz, Spinoza—"philosophical necessitarians" they were called —who subscribed to the conception of a completely determined, mechanistic universe, where men were robots and were never responsible for their actions.

In *Freedom of the Will*, Edwards did not discuss sin extensively enough to satisfy himself or his critics; three years later in the *Origin of Sin* he perfected his position. Taylor had seemed vague in explaining this great problem, suggesting that sin occurred because of evil example (without explicating the example and its origin), and because of our "weak natures." Edward countered, of course, by asserting that Adam's fall was historical and plausible, the best explanation of the universality of sin in the world.

With his renowned consistency, Edwards began by denying that Adam ever had free will even before the Fall; to maintain otherwise, as many Calvinists did, would again infringe upon God's foreknowledge. He made another startling departure from 18th century Calvinism when he described Adam's relation to mankind. The orthodox account was that Adam was the federal head of the human race, that he represented generations unborn, and that all men were "in" Adam and therefore were guilty with him when he broke his covenant with God; Adam's sin was "imputed" to men. That mankind should be held accountable and suffer by transference of blame for the actions of its federal head so long ago seemed feudal and farfetched to the rationalists of the 18th century. They were reluctant to accept the claim that individuals, even infants, had to suffer for acts over which they had no control. When Edwards substituted a metaphysical conception for the federal theory, he may have presumed that he was remedying this weakness. He argued that mankind was a complex person and when Adam sinned, mankind actually participated in the sinning, because all men, having a collective consciousness, were identical with Adam; thus Adam's sin was also each man's. This novel position may have mollified a few who found it an improvement over imputation, but the theory smacked too much of the Realism of the Middle Ages to have any vogue.

Probably the most telling of the points Arminians made against the Calvinistic system was that it made God the author of sin; this state of affairs was presumably unthinkable and could do nothing but turn many people toward skepticism and atheism. Edwards' exposition did little to meet this objection. He conceded that God had "permitted" Adam to sin, and had then withdrawn His "superior principles"—"The Holy Spirit, that divine inhabitant, now forsook the house," and Adam was left with only his natural propensities, *i.e.*, an inclination to sin.

There was one claim Edwards could in no way refute. It was the personal testimony of Arminians who, unlike himself, were convinced by their own consciousness that they were free. Freedom was self-evident; they felt it. Edwards' mystical bias conditioned his theology and his life, denying him such a facile view. He sensed man's deep alienation from his Maker, and his yearning for reunion with the collective unconscious. Edwards was closer in mood to a newly Protestant Celtic lower middle class—in Wales, Scotland, Ulster, and America—struggling with only partial success to free itself of Catholic suppositions, than he was to other Anglo-American intellectuals. Ineffable sensations reassured him, as they did other New Lights and pietists, that the other world was close by. His Arminian opponents, on the other hand, whether in the cities of the homeland or the towns of the colonies, had no such sensations; for them the other world was fading and only individualistic rationalism mattered. By their standards, Edwards was a medieval anachronism.

Until the middle of the 20th century, scholars judging the encounter between Edwards and the Arminians over free will have usually concurred in this contemporary decision. They gave Edwards good marks for his intellectual footwork but downgraded him for the wrongheadedness of his premises. Gradually, however, respect for various aspects of Edwards' thought has revived, including even his view of the will. The recent ethos of the relative, the unconscious, the Neo-Orthodox and the existential—of Einstein, Freud, Neibuhr and Kirkegaard—has contributed, and so has Perry Miller with his sympathetic exegesis of Edwards' works. The truth was on both sides. Edwards did rely too much on revelation. His claim that mankind was a complex person was too metaphysical for the time and place. Yet in his acceptance of Locke, Newton, and cause-effect—or sequence as he shrewdly called it—he was as modern as his opponents or perhaps more so, and certainly more original. For their part, the Arminians stretched logic and made assumptions in favor of the free, autonomous individual. Man was not quite as free as the Arminians implied, nor quite as circumscribed as Edwards contended. The 18th century contest over the nature of the will and sin must now be rated as closer to a draw than was previously supposed.

Yet Edwards, no matter how much time elapses, can never be proclaimed the winner in this controversy; he made a fatal blunder. He assumed that all he had felt and seen in his lifetime could be best understood in a formal Calvinistic scheme, in fact one closer to Calvin's original than the covenant theology of the Puritans. Once that assumption was made, it was eminently logical to defend absolute necessity and original sin as fundamental principles upon which the other points in the system rested. Actually the position of the New England Calvinists—and even of Edwards in his works—on the controverted points was not far from that of the Arminian opponents. The latter conceded that man did not have complete or ultimate freedom, that he was circumscribed by a network of cause and effect, but had only the power to choose, free from coercion. They did, however, try to make something more of this freedom than Edwards did, and denied that moral necessity was an absolute like natural necessity. But the differences were small, and the form of the debate profitless. After the Awakening, when the Spirit had withdrawn and rationalism was resuming its advance, Edwards tried to stop the Arminians with logical argument and direct confrontation; this was a New Light compulsion but was the wrong strategy, of course. Had Edwards' defense been more oblique, had he rested the case for piety on the empirical findings that he had made during the Awakening and the Calvinistic implications that could be drawn from them, he would have withstood the test of history much better. Perry Miller believed that Edwards' writings constituted an "immense cryptogram," but in this case he seems to have been too explicit. In retrospect, gadfly Whitefield was more prudent than philosopher Edwards. The Great Awakener insisted on the necessity of the New Birth and the "efficacy" of New Light Calvinism in bringing it about, but he never attempted formal explanations of these phenomena.

Unfortunately too, Edwards' logical efforts to defend his piety produced some followers who reacted to the post-Awakening *milieu* by overemphasizing theology in relation to piety. In fact, this small clique known as the New Divinity men—less than 5 percent of the New England clergy, all from Connecticut and Yale—became almost as hyper-Calvinist as Scotch-Irish Old Siders in their creedalism and warfare on heresy. To be consistent, they conceded openly that God was the author of sin, despite the warning of Arminians that such teaching would repel good and reasonable people. And to make the distinction even sharper between themselves and compromising Arminians and Old Lights (who retained their vague, pre-1740 covenant Calvinism), they firmly denied the efficacy of means, asserting the power of grace alone. Their only redeeming tenet was a disinterested benevolence that they shared with New Lights in general. Samuel Hopkins, as noted earlier, was a dedicated champion of the slaves but this benevolence could not flower adequately when coupled with other New Divinity doctrines.

The ministers in this group, except for Joseph Bellamy, were dull and legalistic in the pulpit and had some difficulties with their flocks. In their hands the New Light was subordinated to Calvinistic theology and so lost much of its power. The New Divinity men, of course, proudly claimed to be the direct heirs of the great Edwards, but to regard their arid detour as the major highway of his influence, as some scholars have done, is to miss much of the contribution of Edwards to the New Light in American history.

Arminians and the Enlightenment

The small but influential coterie of urban Arminians (known also as Liberals) were not disposed to answer Edwards and the New Lights directly on the matters of will and sin. Although they were disciples of reason, logic-chopping was not their style. They counted on rationality once more making headway, at least among the better educated, when the "enthusiasm" subsided. Extreme distaste for revival emotionalism confirmed their preference for reasonable religion, an outlook that had already seeped into Harvard and taken root in eastern Massachusetts. In contrast to the Calvinists, the colonial Arminians drew their religious ideas much more directly from contemporary England, and from freethinkers (whose influence after 1740 was finally being challenged at the lower levels, by the Methodists and the Anglican Evangelicals).

The Arminians began with the observation that contemporary men—at least Europeans of the better sort—were eminently rational. From this they deduced that all men, not just the Elect, had retained a moral sense and most of their reasoning power after the Fall. Since men were rational, so must their creator, God, be also. God was knowable, not inscrutable, and His fundamental wishes could be ascertained by observing natural law, supplemented and improved by reading the Bible. The scriptures, however, should not be accepted as truth intuitively, but only after passing the tests of common sense. Biblical rituals were acceptable if they seemed comparable to those of the secular world. With respect to communion, the Arminians agreed with Stoddard that all but the profane could partake, since only God knew who were the saved.

The Liberals tried hard to accommodate to the Age of Reason by seeking as a sanction for morality an alternative to the doctrine of God's sovereignty. They believed man was a free agent with a conscience, yet denied that this interfered with God's foreknowledge or led to a world of blind chance. They carefully deduced God's excellence from the universe He had designed, then called upon their hearers to be grateful, to imitate Him, and to live by His laws. As teachers of knowledge and morality who opposed sudden crises, they inevitably preached means and slighted justification by faith. In any case, for them faith meant assent, comparable to "owning" rather than conversion. Therefore they implied that the proper use of means stimulated the growth of faith and was bound to be rewarded by an amiable and reasonable Almighty.

The colonial Arminians stopped short of freethinking, however, by standing firm on immortality and endorsing the possibility of miracles in modern times. Life after death was plausible, although biblical evidence of it was scant. God could, on rare occasions, stop the machinery of the universe and intervene directly; miracles would have a favorable effect on the populace and the heathen by increasing their desire for rational Christianity.

After the Awakening, the orthodox watched the Arminians carefully, suspecting that they would develop unsound views of the Trinity. This was part of the rationalist syndrome and had proven true among English Arminians earlier in the century. In anticipation, the New Lights and the orthodox tightened the pertinent creedal provisions in the churches. They were right; in 1755, the Liberal Jonathan Mayhew of Boston ridiculed the three-in-one principle of the Trinity as nonsensical. Subsequently, anti-trinitarianism percolated into the colonies slowly. Historically, the two most common departures from the Trinity of the Athanasian creed were Arianism and Socinianism. The Arians held that Jesus was one with God but had been created separately before the world began, and was therefore subordinate although divine. The Socinians were more radical, suggesting that Jesus was a man, albeit perfect and with special authority. Charles Chauncy began to refer to Jesus as the "Son of God" rather than the conventional "God the Son," but none of the Liberals would take an open anti-Trinity stand. There was no

Socinianism before the Revolution but Arianism seeped in gradually, and the alarmed New Lights preached up the Trinity.

The deists, those who denied revelation altogether and assumed the fierce anticlerical attitude of the Enlightenment, apparently had no open advocates in colonial America. Deistic influence was accordingly indirect, largely through the writings of Englishmen. In the colonies, English deists—including Bolingbroke, Tindal, and Collins —were so universally regarded with alarm and disgust, that the Arminians had to labor diligently to distinguish their halfway position—rational, but retaining a role for the supernatural—from the fearsome infidels.

After the Glorious Revolution, the deists in England had mounted quite a successful attack on organized religion and priestly obscurantism. They had dismissed the Bible as a "cunning fable," an uneven literary production by many hands, and exalted reason alone. Was it reasonable, they asked, that God would offer His revelation to the Jewish people only? They denied miracles, of course, and they were Socinians, suggesting that Jesus was a mere man, more rational than mystical, and not a superhuman agent. All men—and not simply the Elect as Edwardsians believed—had a moral sense, an ability to discern right from wrong and therefore could be saved. Anticlericalism was evident in their charge that the natural religion of the Grand Architect had been subverted by centuries of priestly domination.

Deism reached its peak in England during the 1720s. After the deists had destroyed many of the scholastic assumptions, they quarreled about what to replace them with and the movement lost its momentum. Although the colonies were somewhat more receptive to reason in the immediate wake of the Great Awakening, deism could not gain a foothold. The colonists' fear that British and French military officers would spread freethought among America's pious yeomen was not substantiated until the Revolution. The Arminians clung stubbornly to their position of "supernatural rationalism" with revelation and miracles and hoped everyone would notice that they drew the line at overt deism. In 1763, Mayhew could write, "There is no such monster as an *Atheist* known amongst us; hardly any such person as a *Deist*."

The economic views of the Liberals were quite conservative. Like the mercantilists in England, the colonial Arminians sought to press a Puritan ethic of industry and frugality on the populace. As advocates of reason and morality, they fretted over the lower orders of society who were constantly tempted by luxury and idleness. While these "sins" must have been less prevalent in the colonies where wages were threefold higher than in England, gentlemen still pondered strategies for motivating the workingman to produce, and as an inducement shared with him their dreams of exploiting the resources of the new continent. Chauncy has not acquired the notoriety of Alexander Hamilton, but he too hoped to save women and children from idleness and dissipation by giving them Christian employment in factories. Eager for material progress, the rationalists tended to think of the workers—uneducated and vulnerable to their emotions—as a reactionary force that had to be converted into an effective factor of production.

After the Awakening, the Liberals were haunted by the spontaneity and passion of the New Lights, and by the disorder and anarchy the "enthusiasts" seemed to presage. Their anxiety was further heightened by the appearance of mobs in British cities after mid-century; this suggested that any sequel to the religious upheavals of the 1740s would result in a decided levelling spirit in the colonies—a mood not conducive to maintenance of private conscience, judgment, or property. The Arminians, in contrast to the Calvinists, did not find religious or secular crises exhilarating or inspirational. While they acknowledged business cycles, they strove to flatten them out; their consistent opposition to paper currency reflected their desire for social and economic stability. Their view of progress was realistic—a rapid development of resources and a slow education of people.

Evangelical Calvinists, Liberty, and the Millennium

The strength of the New Lights in the decades after the Awakening lay chiefly in their re-discovery and cultivation of an aesthetic feeling for the "beauty of union," the communal piety of the saved. This feeling, and not sensational preaching or theological defenses of predestination and original sin, was to be the real legacy of the Awakening and, more subtly, of Jonathan Edwards. The beauty of union was the joy the awakened felt when they worshipped together, apart from Arminians and other worldlings. The surrender of individual pride, the oneness of the group with God, renewed their spirits on these occasions and brought them a satisfaction that was beyond description. The search for happiness was a particular pre-occupation of 18th century philosophers. The New Lights found it in holiness—in revivals, in communion with fellow saints, and in the prospect of the Kingdom to come. The longing for purity—the re-cognition that the power of God's light was directly proportional to the number of saints gathered in one place, and that it was cor-respondingly diminished by the number in fellowship who were unregenerate—was the motive for Edwards' unsuccessful demand that his Northampton flock abandon Stoddardeanism and restore the oral confession of faith. With the same motive, Isaac Backus turned to the closed communion Baptists when, in the mixed communion of the Separates, the beauty of union was constantly broken by dis-agreements over the baptismal rite. Edwards and Backus agreed that such divisions resulted in "moral ugliness"; but "union," Ed-wards noted, was "one of the most beautiful and happy things on earth, which indeed makes earth most like heaven."

The quest for perfection and union of course gave rise to millen-nialism, a natural outgrowth of the revival. God's power in the Awakening suggested that the pace of history was accelerating, that the Second Coming was close at hand. Puritan historians, after the failure of Cromwell's regime in the 17th century, had introduced cycles to modify their view of history as progress toward the King-dom of Light. God would advance His Kingdom, not along a smooth upward path, but by "times" and "seasons," periodic leaps toward perfection, with troughs of complacency in-between. With the long decline of piety in the early 18th century, however, the pious some-times exaggerated their pre-millennial fears; the world would get much worse before it got better, and many would perish on Judg-ment Day before His reign began.

The Great Awakening raised the hopes of the evangelicals again and they shifted to the more optimistic post-millennial view; God's reign of a thousand years on earth would precede, not follow, Judgment Day. With this postponement, the New Lights could anti-cipate His Coming with unmixed joy. Those who understood Ed-wards knew that the Good Society would begin simply with God's restoration to the Elect of the powers man lost at Adam's fall. Ed-wards envisioned no destruction or reconstruction, but rather a massive renewal—a bigger and better revival. God would turn this world into Paradise, that is to say, into a Christian commonwealth.

Of course the New Lights believed the millennium would begin in America. Their arguments were traditional and logical: that Paradise was to be found in the west; that according to scriptural prophecy, on the New Day, the sun of righteousness would rise in the west; that logically God would begin His great work in a new country and where His people were concentrated, because it was not "God's manner" to introduce a new excellence into the churches of an old, corrupt region. Cotton Mather had referred to the colonies as the New Jerusalem, and Edwards had predicted that "the latter-day glory," would probably begin in America. After his *Narrative* of the Frontier Revival, some English dissenters had speculated that the center of Christendom had already moved from Europe to America, presumably to the town of Northampton.

In assuming that America was the center of God's interest in the world, the New Lights were behaving like the Chosen People. They were returning to the Puritan conception of "a city on the hill," not to the idea of a "howling wilderness." They reflected the growing conviction of all colonials that the New World could produce a better society than the Old World had ever known. The evangelicals hoped to build on the Awakening, using various strategies to induce heavenly showers, and to extend them to more people, so that the earthly Kingdom—the better society—might be hastened. Indian Work, for example, was revived by the combination of interest in the west and the millennium. The New Light tendency to ignore religious and political boundaries and press for a continental union was a force that would emerge on the eve of the Revolution as a deep and pious nationalism.

One strategy that Edwards proposed was the Concert of Prayer, quarterly meetings for fasting and prayer. He hoped that the crowds would grow and the practice spread, gradually creating conditions for another great revival. The plan implied that the collective will could influence God. Chauncy was critical, arguing that these efforts, when accompanied by fasting that overstimulated the imagination, would not necessarily be pleasing to God. Edwards replied, however, that the prayers were not so much to please God as to please supplicants with each other, to make visible and intensify feelings of dedication and solidarity.

These special sessions were tried with some success, generating a series of modest and sporadic sprinklings that fell short of heavenly downpours. Some people thought that prayer contributed to the capture of Louisburg from the French in 1745. Later, prayer sessions also stirred the dry bones of the student body at the College of New Jersey (Princeton), touched off a more general outpouring of the Spirit in 1764–65, and brought scattered "quickenings" right down to the Revolution. When the New Lights confounded the millennium with independence from Britain, the royal authorities rightly regarded their meetings as subversive. The New Lights used these "concerts" to depict graphically just what the earthly Kingdom of Christ would look like once the cloud of sin were removed. They were certainly different from Quaker meetings where everyone ceased creaturely activity to hear the Inner Voice. The Concert of Prayer resembled in some ways New England's traditional days of humiliation, but the emphasis was on looking forward to the millennium, not back to the covenant.

The evangelicals assiduously tried to project into society the love generated by the Saints in fellowship and by the contemplation of the millennium. They made works the criterion, rather than inner state alone, yet the Spirit in the doing was more important than the acts themselves. After the Awakening, Edwards' goal, "love to Being in general," gradually came to mean a disinterested but organized benevolence toward those of low station in this world. The continental union would not be complete until the lowliest had felt the New Light and been drawn into the circle.

Davies' military sermons had aroused the New Lights of Virginia, and ultimately everywhere, from a drift into antinomian complacency. But after the French and Indian War, the Calvinists for the most part were aloof from politics, and the more pious were trying to understand the subtleties of the New Divinity. While they were not as well informed as the city Liberals or Real Whig lawyers, for their own pious reasons they were wary of George III and any bishopric he had in mind for America. Whereas a bishop posed a political and social threat to the other groups, the New Lights' fear of an American bishop was primarily religious; his theology disturbed them more than his polity. The bishop would reinforce an already powerful Arminianism, strengthen rationalism and discourage evangelical measures to hasten the millennium.

The New Lights relished the Boston Tea Party and the subsequent crisis of the Intolerable Acts. The open conflict with Parliament ended a drift that had begun with victories over the French in 1759, and augured the final stage of the Work of Redemption; they yearned for a union that was free from the contamination of British tyranny and corruption.

More than the Liberals, however, they were mindful of the sins of America. These were great, especially among the town dwellers who had been seduced by European finery and ideas. More distressing to them than sins of the flesh (New Lights were sometimes guilty of these too), was the pride of rich and covetous colonials toward their neighbors, and their sycophantic and unmanly pursuit of English gentility.

The New Light orators, with their spontaneity and rhetorical talents, moved early to activate the people's will to resist. Only a handful of lawyers—Henry, Otis, Thacher, and especially Hawley— had the gifts of New Light rhetoric and could compete with them in this. Yet because the New Lights left fewer literary remains, historians have generally failed to acknowledge that it was the evangelical orators, rather than the Liberals, Old Lights, or lawyers who fanned the flames of the Spirit of '76, making a civil war and a military victory possible. Whereas Liberal sermons were controlled performances by men seeking to channel public passions, the New Lights used their Plain Style unsparingly against king and Parliament to galvanize the people into military action.

When evangelical orators defined liberty, it did not mean the right to participate in material prosperity or the right of each individual to commune with God privately in some esoteric fashion. For them liberty was the serenity of soul, the almost pantheistic joy that came from living in an orderly community with fellow saints. Opponents accused the Calvinists of promoting anarchy, but they were very much for order. They were free to do God's will, not to act independently or selfishly.

When the ruler, George III, broke the law of love, specifically when he failed to consider the welfare of the colonies as distinct from the realm, the obligation to obey was broken. The behavior of the British, especially their ministers, indicated that they were without grace and therefore both contemptuous and envious of those who retained their manly Christian character. Considering the advanced state of sin in Britain, the New Lights did not really expect reformation or any concessions.

Evangelical preachers pushed their followers off the neutral fence, urging them to come out and be separate—preparing them for military resistance. By separating from the British Empire, the colonists might be able to preserve their virtue, remain true to the founding fathers and halt the inroads of British rationalism. Many descendants of 17th century settlers were actually filled with filiopietistic desire to reclaim their country from a decadent empire, and renew the errand into the wilderness.

These real Calvinists welcomed economic privation; it was a good test of character. The non-importation and non-consumption agreements were wise not because they punished British exporters, but because they taught the colonials to do without luxuries, to regain their Puritan ethic and weanedness from the world.

The New Light in Revolutionary New England

Connecticut was the pre-eminent example of the affinity between Calvinistic evangelism and radical politics; the New Light took on geographical and political as well as religious meaning there. In the western towns nearer to New York, people tended to be conservative, only moderate in their New Light or more often Old Light or Anglican, but east of the Connecticut River—chiefly in Windham and New London counties—where Separates and Separate Baptists as well as Congregational New Lights had been cultivating communal piety, the evangelicals had early success as a political faction because of "their superior Attention to Civil Affairs and close union among themselves in Politicks." In 1764, New London was the first community to protest the Sugar Act as an unconstitutional attempt to collect revenue without consent. The next year after passage of the Stamp Tax, "People of all Professions" in the eastern towns watched mobs hang effigies of Jared Ingersoll, Connecticut's Stamp Distributor. A few months later, five hundred men from Windham—very largely New Light Sons of Liberty—intercepted Ingersoll on his way to a special session of the legislature. They did not like or trust this New Haven lawyer who had opposed the Awakening and afterward acquired English airs while acting as the colony's agent in London; the fact that he had advised the Crown on the Stamp Act made him a traitor to liberty in their eyes. While Ingersoll tried to explain himself, the crowd grew to a thousand; many men were in uniform, they all held staves and were not in the mood for parley. When they demanded his resignation as stampmaster, Ingersoll decided not to be a martyr to the stamps, a tax he had thought unwise from the outset. He tried to appease the mob by resigning and uttering a few reluctant huzzas for liberty. The reputation of Ingersoll, and of Governor Fitch who was from the western town of Norwalk and had urged obedience to His Majesty and the Stamp Act, proved to be insurmountable political liabilities to the Old Light party. In the spring elections of 1766, the New Lights, who already controlled the assembly, gained the Governor's chair and a majority in the Council. In their campaign, the New Lights evidently convinced a large majority of the voters of their thesis: "an Arminian, and a Favourer of the Stamp Act signify the same man."

From 1766 to the Revolution the New Lights maintained their political control of Connecticut, and after the Boston Tea Party and the 1774 elections, the opposition conservative "old Party," finally disintegrated. The radical New Lights were notable for arousing "public spirit" against the Townshend duties, the Coercive Acts and the drinking of tea. They vociferously championed charter rights over the prerogative of the Crown, and at least one citizen invoked the Real Whig claim that the first settlers had come on their own and owed nothing to the English government or king. As relations with the mother country worsened, the radicals became bolder and their tempers shorter. They used rails, tar and feathers to intimidate "inimical persons," whether these folk were hesitant Old Lights or open tories, nor did they defer to the cloth. Anglican rectors sympathetic to the Crown had to ride rails out of town. While patriotic committees of correspondence and safety were chiefly phenomena of the eastern towns, New Light pastors worked hard to gain political converts among their Old Light parishioners in western Connecticut. Sometimes reluctant citizens were forced to make public testimonials to the justice of the patriot cause, and even moderate New Lights were inclined to excuse rash behavior and mobbism when "liberty" was at stake. While the New Lights called for an early meeting of an inter-colonial congress to solidify opposition to the Crown, they would not forgo vigilante enforcement of non-importation against retailers in the interim. They invoked the "Curse of Meroz" against those who would not take a public stand: those who are not for us must be against us. The Connecticut New Lights did not flinch from armed resistance to the Crown; in fact at the last they seemed to relish the prospect of separation from the decadent Empire.

The come-outer spirit of Connecticut's New Lights was also revealed in their attitude toward new settlements on the frontier. They supported the political fortunes of the Susquehannah Company promoters who were trying to develop Westmoreland, a township in Pennsylvania, by making the tenuous claim that it lay within the boundaries of Connecticut under the sea-to-sea provision of its charter. While both parties, Old Lights as well as New Lights, were subject to the temptations of land speculation, the difference was that the Susquehannah group had popular support from New Light farmers, potential emigrants with land hunger and a westering impulse, who were tired of low fertility and crowding in Connecticut. Beneath the obvious desire for more land and the status that accompanied ownership, the farmers had a religious yearning for the pilgrimage to Paradise, and an inclination to withdraw from the Old Light-Anglican culture that impinged on the communities near the seaboard.

A few Old Lights dared to defend their middle ground despite the atmosphere of mob rule. Chiding the radicals for taking the name Whig, these conservatives saw themselves as in the true tradition of Real Whiggery. They favored not "licentious" but "lawful" liberty, the kind that was best secured by mixed government and not by mobs, committees, or all-powerful assemblies. They claimed the right of private judgment and condemned the intolerance of the patriots, their lack of restraint and impatience with due process. Better informed about the Empire, they feared the retaliatory power of the Crown, and contemplated the conquest and occupation of the colony by redcoats and the loss of precious charter liberties. With such fears, the Susquehannah scheme seemed to them foolhardy and needlessly provocative to the royal authorities. Some conservatives, when prospects for victory at the polls faded, looked across the ocean to the Crown for encouragement and rewards for defending true Whiggish principles in the face of such a militant and hostile populace. Thus the excesses of the radicals, and their Curse of Meroz attitude, polarized Connecticut and finally drove some Old Lights into the arms of the king. Significantly, the tories, who thought they recognized the historical antecedents of their persecutors, dubbed the radical New Lights, "Cromwellites."

On the surface, there was little political concern in western Massachusetts before 1774. The people were preoccupied with settling the west beyond the Connecticut River; Berkshire county was carved out of Hampshire in 1762. The Baptists gathered some New Light flocks out there, but they were at first apolitical and ill-informed about events to the eastward. Along the Connecticut River, the River Gods, especially the "monarch," Israel Williams, maintained surprisingly cordial relations with Lieutenant Governor Hutchinson and the Crown officials in Boston; as late as 1770, Sam Adams fretted over the tory potential in the western towns. The westerners have been described as "laggard revolutionists."

Beneath the placid façade, however, some New Light currents of liberty were flowing. Major Joseph Hawley, the only River God touched by the New Light, was the beacon of radicalism in western Massachusetts. He had impressive social and religious credentials for the role. He was the third Joseph Hawley in Northampton, the grandson of "Pope" Stoddard, the cousin of Jonathan Edwards, and the son of the melancholic Hawley who had slit his throat during the 1735 revival. Young Joseph had studied with Edwards after graduating from Yale, but a book by Experience Mayhew, the Nantucket patriarch, seduced him into Arminianism and he gave up the ministry for the law. Estranged from Edwardsian Calvinism, he was one of the town leaders responsible for Edwards' dismissal in 1750. About the time of Edwards' death, however, he recanted his Arminianism and abjectly apologized to the people for his part in Edwards' downfall. Soon after, Hawley became the west's leading lawyer, renowned for his integrity and low fees as well as his telling arguments. The New Light he had recovered deepened also; sometimes, when he heard an inadequate sermon, he would mount the pulpit himself.

The only tremor the Stamp Tax controversy produced in western Massachusetts was in the tiny village of Lanesborough. There a group of ten men plotted to restrain the sheriff from arresting any more debtors until stamps were available, because without stamps for their bonds, jailers would not grant the privileges of the jail-yard (which usually was construed to include the town). If debtors had to stay in their cells, the loss of liberty would be complete. The men used stones and staves to interfere with the sheriff; they were arrested, and nine of them pleaded guilty and were sentenced. The tenth man, the ringleader, declared his innocence and hired Hawley as counsel. Hawley offered the defenses of a good lawyer: that the writ of arrest was unstamped and therefore invalid; that the men had not conspired but were peacefully assembled; that conditions were extraordinary in the province, with the courts closed and stamps unavailable. Nevertheless, the Superior Court with Chief Justice Hutchinson presiding, finally found the ringleader guilty and he went to jail. For his "free remarks" at the trial, suggesting that Hutchinson did not respect the "constitution," Hawley was disbarred temporarily. He explained his thinking in this case—"the Berkshire affair"—more fully later in the *Boston Post*. Hawley claimed, citing Lord Coke, that with the courts closed and writs invalid during the stamp crisis, the positive laws of the society had been suspended and that the laws of nature had come into operation. People who "have the principles of the English constitution interwoven with the constitution of their mind" would understand him, he said. (In 1761 Hawley had copied into his journal the natural rights arguments James Otis made in the writs of assistance case.)

When the British authorities virtually demanded that the legislature compensate those who had suffered from the stamp riots in Massachusetts—Hutchinson was the most conspicuous because he lost valuable manuscripts and furnishings—Hawley countered with a demand that the rioters also receive amnesty. He managed to sell this radical proposition, so obnoxious to conservatives, to a majority of his fellow legislators. He was sympathizing with rioters protesting an unconstitutional tax, rather than being solely concerned with his jailed client in Berkshire county. The Crown disallowed the measure as an infringement on the Crown's pardoning power, but the episode demonstrated Hawley's growing influence in radical politics. In resisting British pressure in 1766, Hawley blurted out: "The Parliament of Great Britain has no right to legislate for us." James Otis is said to have retorted, "He has gone farther than I have myself." Writing his conservative friends, Israel Williams tried to account for Hawley's radicalism by blaming Otis' influence, and then he added, "if he is not distracted then the devil is in him." This was a reference to Hawley's spurts of excessive zeal, and to the recurrent melancholia he had inherited from his mother as well as his father. In Hawley, the rationalism of Real Whiggery was overbalanced by the piety of the New Light and the conflict between this world and the next created a tension that was often unbearable, even for one raised in the Puritan tradition.

Western Massachusetts may have seemed dormant between repeal of the Stamp Act and the Boston Tea party—1766 to 1773—but Hampshire county gave Hawley its support and that was radicalism enough. Eastern radicals were impressed with his efficiency in financial and military affairs. In 1774 he was chosen for the first Continental Congress in Philadelphia but declined because of poor health. John Adams took his place. In his advice to the younger lawyer, Hawley revealed the New Light creed at its tolerant and optimistic best. He wanted the Massachusetts delegates to avoid giving an impression of Boston snobbery; "It is highly probable . . . that you will meet gentlemen from several of the other colonies fully equal to yourselves or any of you, in their knowledge of Great Britain, the colonies, law, history, government, commerce . . . very likely you may meet divers gentlemen in Congress, who are of Dutch or Scotch or Irish extract; their blood is as warm as ours; everything should be very cautiously avoided which could give the least umbrage, disgust, or affront to any of such pedigree." The success of the Congress would depend on "the harmony, good understanding, and I had almost said brotherly love, of its members." Yet towards the mother country he was not so forbearing: "We must fight if we cannot otherwise rid ourselves of British taxation . . . it is evil against right."

Hawley's desire for union was strong even for a New Light. He had favored the Albany Plan in 1754; twenty years later he spoke of a "Continental Covenant," hoping Canada could become the "fourteenth colony" to join the struggle against Britain. When he read Tom Paine's *Common Sense* in February, 1776, it sunk into his "well-prepared heart." Several months before this he had decided that independence was the one thing needful, but he was willing to adopt delaying tactics until military preparations could be made.

As the Revolution unfolded, Hawley was one of the few leaders whose opinions stayed ahead of the people, even when they were fully aroused in 1775 and 1776. He remained steadfast in his radicalism, hoping for a democratic constitution and free trade. He disapproved of slavery and regarded suffrage for adult males as a natural right, and when the Massachusetts constitution of 1780 fell short of such hopes, he opposed it. Despite increasing spells of mental cloudiness, Hawley remained liberal; he was a more consistent libertarian than the New Light rank and file, perhaps because he was a member of the clerical elite who had been deflected from his true calling, the ministry.

In describing the Revolutionary years in Rhode Island, political historians need to examine the "Ward-Hopkins Controversy" that preoccupied the colony between 1757 and 1770. The specific origins of the "Controversy" are obscure, but two factions fought hard for colonial offices when these posts finally surpassed in importance the town offices in politically backward Rhode Island. These groups have been portrayed as parties comparable to those in England, seeking public office to promote private fortunes and favor local interests and thriving on personality clashes and family connections.

Samuel Ward was a farmer and merchant from Westerly. His father had been governor and he retained strong ties with Newport, the capital city. Among his allies were the Greene and Cooke families. He built his following very largely in the Narragansett country, in the smaller towns near Newport. Ward sat in the Governor's chair for four years versus nine years for Hopkins in this period. It would seem that the Ward group was slightly less persistent, organized, and articulate than its opponents.

Stephen Hopkins was a prominent merchant and skillful politician who gathered a large following in the north with booming Providence, his home city, as his base. He had in his camp the Browns of Providence, a famous mercantile family, and in his rival's territory to the south, the Wantons of Newport. Hopkins gained an early reputation for Whiggery by warning the legislature against the effects of the Sugar Act and the impending Stamp Tax. In his *The Rights of the Colonies Examined* (1764), he wrote: "they who are taxed at pleasure by others, cannot possibly have any property . . . can have no freedom, but are indeed reduced to the most abject slavery." This pamphlet gained him an inter-colonial reputation. Yet Hopkins and his party were conservative on economic matters; in 1763, when they had the votes, they pushed through a currency reform bill that would stabilize Rhode Island's chronically inflated paper money. While both sides, when they were in power, manipulated the colony's tax structure to favor their regions, and spent heavily in the elections, the Hopkins faction appears to have spent more in buying votes and paying opposition voters to "lay still."

The Ward and Hopkins parties were quite similar in socio-economic composition; both had some patrician leaders and included farmers as well as merchants; this has proved frustrating to historians of the progressive school who prefer to depict clear-cut conflicts between agrarian and mercantile interests. When the religious factor is introduced, however, this similarity is lessened somewhat. Ward was an ardent Sabbatarian Baptist from Westerly, a community on the Connecticut border that had been deeply stirred by the Great Awakening, and had given birth to Separates and Separate Baptists afterward. His followers had a Congregationalist-New Light-Separate Baptist cast to them.

By contrast, the Hopkins party had an Arminian complexion; the leaders tended to be Anglican, Old Light, Old Baptist, and Quaker; the group was an amalgam of the *nouveaux riches* of Providence and its satellites and prominent Old Baptist and Quaker Rhode Island families. Hopkins' own ancestry reached back to the first settlements in Rhode Island as did those of his Quaker wife.

From this perspective, the Ward-Hopkins Controversy was more than simply the tale of two cities—established Newport versus rising Providence—because it also reflected a much older antagonism in religious life styles, namely the difference between Roger Williams' tolerant and "catholic" Rhode Island, and the influence of its evangelically pious neighbors, Connecticut and Plymouth. The 17th century difference had persisted, flaring up during the Revolutionary crisis.

New Light libertarian sentiment surfaced only briefly in Rhode Island politics, but on these occasions—1765 and 1774–1776—it was crucial. When word came in 1765 that Parliament had passed the Stamp Act, Hopkins was already on record as a foe, but Ward was Governor and his views were less well known. Ward took an unexpectedly hard line, refusing to take an oath to execute the Stamp Act. He caught the attention of the Boston patriots when he issued a proclamation urging "the ministers and people within his jurisdiction publickly to implore Almighty God 'That our RIGHTS, Liberties, and Privileges may be precious in His Sight,' and that 'He will be pleased to frustrate every Attempt to deprive us of them . . . '" The Governor, with the help of the Sons of Liberty, pressured the Stamp Distributor, Augustus Johnson—an Anglican affiliated with the Hopkins faction—into resigning, and then wrote the Lords of the Treasury that no one could be found to distribute the stamps. This ended Johnson's political career in Rhode Island, and he accepted a vice-admiralty judgeship in South Carolina. Two Congregationalists of the Ward faction maneuvered a mob into burning effigies of Johnson and two Newport tories, but Ward did little to stop them, leaving for Westerly before the planned riot occurred. Later the Governor was praised for his attitude of "steady Opposition" to the Crown in this affair. Ward left office in

1767, and after losing the race for Governor in 1770, retired from politics to Westerly.

But the Boston Tea Party and subsequent Intolerable Acts brought Ward and his followers back into action four years later. He held an indignation party in his home protesting the closing of the Boston port. His influence revived enough so that he was chosen—with his rival, Hopkins—as delegate to the Continental Congress. During the Congress in Philadelphia, the political divergence between these veteran antagonists became quite explicit. Ward was the radical who denied Parliament's right to regulate trade under any circumstances, and would not accept Galloway's plan for a colonial union presided over by a Crown appointee; as early as November, 1775, he was for independence. Hopkins was the moderate who disagreed with these positions and shrank from total separation from Britain.

The Hopkins group, vociferous defenders of colonial rights in the previous decade, showed a discernable trend toward conservatism after 1770. Moses Brown, a mainstay of the party, converted to Quakerism in 1773, and the Inner Light diminished his interest in politics and in resistence to Britain. Although the Hopkins men were at pains to distinguish themselves from the small group of tories known as the Newport Junto, they did not succeed; the public began to detect toryism in their ranks. Hopkins himself was accused of drinking tea, and it was said that tea stains followed party lines. Tolerant and affable Governor Wanton, a Hopkins man and an Anglican, suffered from this accusation, but managed reelection for a sixth year in the spring of 1775. A few days later came the word of Lexington and Concord and the Assembly ordered a call up of fifteen hundred men. The Ward partisans believed that their suspicions and charges were confirmed when Governor Wanton pleaded for "respectful behavior towards His Majesty and both Houses of Parliament," warned against levying troops for war on the king, and refused to sign commissions for the officers. For his hesitancy in liberty's cause, Wanton was stripped of his powers and ultimately replaced by a Ward man. Some months later, Wanton's son was arrested as a tory when he refused to take an oath of fidelity. Hopkins went on to serve Rhode Island and his country honorably in the Congress, but the Reverend Ezra Stiles, Newport's renowned Old Light, had to modify his earlier judgment and pronounce Ward the abler of the two leaders. In Rhode Island as elsewhere in the north, it was the evangelical rather than the constitutional elements, sometimes less active initially, who proved bold and intransigent when aroused; ready—almost eager—to defy British authority, and unafraid of the consequences independence might bring.

The troubles of wartime, the grinding inflation, the hardships in uniform they accepted at first, but inevitably the perfectionists were disheartened by worldliness among the patriots. They discovered too much corruption and too many unsaved even on the American side. Some recoiled from these impurities and retreated to the frontier wilderness or withdrew to the other world. Others, caught up in the crusade, sloughed their religion as they became absorbed in the crusade for the republic.

The "Fair Experiment" in Church and State

The populous old colonies of Massachusetts and Virginia that were the ideological leaders in the Revolution were again the major arenas in the ensuing controversy over church and state. The war had increased religious toleration for Anglicans and Papists *if* they took the patriot side, but in Massachusetts and the other Puritan colonies, dis-establishment proved difficult because the established Congregationalists supported the American cause so fervently. Isaac Backus rallied the dissenters under the Baptist banner, but the tradition of a settled ministry was strong enough in New England to survive even the libertarian propaganda of the Revolution. Dis-establishment came slowly to the region, and Andrew Jackson was President before the last state, Massachusetts, finally eliminated the privileged status of the Congregationalists in 1833.

In Virginia, however, the Revolution created conditions highly favorable to dis-establishment and religious liberty. While the Anglican establishment was venerable and "low church," it was visible and vulnerable as the king's Church and its clergy had a reputation for indolence as well as a measure of toryism; and in the booming western part parishes had never been organized. With the inroads of New Side Presbyterians and Separate Baptists, the dissenters by 1776 amounted to two-thirds of the population in the Old Dominion. And for leadership, the Virginia tidewater elite could provide some Anglicans with strong Real Whig and free-thinking views—notably Madison, Jefferson, and Mason.

In addition, Old Dominion leaders were impressed by eminently practical considerations. Pennsylvania and New York had obviously profited from liberal religious policies, and the gradual extension of the Toleration Act of 1689 had been beneficial. There were ten major denominations—and outside of New England, none with a majority—yet actual church membership was low (one estimate for a later period, the post-Revolutionary trough of piety, was only 4 percent). These facts certainly suggested to the statesmen that the Old World concept of establishment would have to be modified further or abandoned altogether in such a diverse colonial society.

When the religious section in Virginia's bill of rights came before the Assembly, Madison made the historic move to substitute "freedom" for "toleration" and it was accepted, despite the majority of Anglicans in the legislature. From that day in 1776, everyone knew that the Anglican establishment was doomed, but the dismantling proved to be slow. Although the rationalists revealed their suspicion of organized religion by preferring the word "sect" to church, persuasion or denomination, the religious provision they gained was firm yet gentlemanly: "That religion, or the duty which we owe our CREATOR, and the manner of discharging it, can be directed only by reason and conviction, not by force or violence, and therefore all men are equally entitled to the free exercise of religion, according to the dictates of conscience; and that it is the mutual duty of all to practice Christian forebearance, love, and charity, towards each other."

The religious ideas of Jefferson, Madison, Mason and other latitudinarians drew heavily on the conclusions John Locke had reached after the Glorious Revolution. Locke's four letters on religious toleration were only slightly less influential in the colonies than his *Second Treatise on Government* or the *Essay on Human Understanding*. The English philosopher inspired not only the political but the religious philosophy of the founding fathers. Locke, however, had been unwilling to grant religious liberty to Papists or infidels on the ground that they were intolerant and jeopardized the public welfare. In the 18th century, Joseph Priestley, the English Unitarian pastor and scientist, updated Locke by recommending that Catholics and infidels be included, and citing the material success of Holland and Pennsylvania, suggested the axiom: the more toleration, the more prosperity. The Virginia liberals took this more generous view.

Despite their anticlerical views, Jefferson and Madison, like Locke himself, seem to have been dutiful Anglicans. Jefferson refrained from deriding Anglican worship and Madison regularly attended it. There is the tradition, however, that Madison avoided William and Mary College because of its official Anglicanism and chose instead the College of New Jersey (Princeton), which was technically non-sectarian though Presbyterian in fact. John Witherspoon, Princeton's president, was enlightened on the church-state question; this no doubt confirmed Madison's prejudice against "a corrupt and mischievous" establishment.

As the Revolutionary War dragged on, Jefferson and Madison encountered some political resistance when they sought to implement Virginia's bill of rights. At the outset the legislature had abolished Parliament's limits on religion, exempted dissenters from church taxes, and suspended fixed salaries, but balked at speedy dis-establishment and total freedom. In 1779 Jefferson called for a "fair experiment" in pluralism but could not get action on his bill for complete separation.

When the Revolution ended, religion and public morals were in a low state in Virginia, as in the other colonies. The legislature reflected this mood by drifting from the spirit of freedom in the 1776 bill of rights to consider tax support of the various Christian denominations in order to strengthen public morals and stabilize postwar society. Under the proposed general assessment, a tax would be levied for public worship but the taxpayer could designate the Christian sect the money would go to; if he were not a church member or a Christian, the money could go instead to an educational fund. As the postwar depression deepened, and the problems of the new republic became more apparent, conservative elements in Virginia society, especially Churchmen, were drawn to this measure.

The friends of religious freedom were alarmed by this trend and managed to get consideration of the bill postponed until the public could be alerted to its dangers. They prevailed upon Madison, who already had a reputation on this issue, to draft arguments against it, and the bill was printed and circulated to stimulate reaction. The result was a *Remonstrance* (1784), which was widely distributed and received the endorsement of all the dissenters, notably the Baptists and Presbyterians, but also Quakers and Roman Catholics. Even some Methodists and Anglicans of the establishment were signers. In fact, the only prominent groups who disagreed with Madison were Churchmen who stood to lose status if the very precarious position of the established church were eroded further.

Under fifteen headings, Madison made his case against general assessment and for total separation of church and state. Man, he noted, was the subject of God before he was a member of society, and man's natural and unalienable right to religious freedom was not in any way abridged by the social contract and the formation of a society. Religion should therefore be totally exempt from regulation by society or its creature, the legislature. The purity of primitive Christianity before Constantine made it a state religion indicated that only with establishment did pride, corruption, superstition and bigotry set in. Christianity was not dependent on human invention but found its power in the other world.

The practical considerations he injected were also effective. He noted that even if the civil state adopted only the Christian religion in general, this would tempt one sect to gain precedence, and involve magistrates in defining Christianity and delimiting who exactly were Christians. He added significantly, "we cannot deny an equal freedom to those whose minds have not yet yielded to the evidence which has convinced us," and urged forbearance towards sects with fantastic beliefs and overheated imaginations because they would be circumscribed by reasonable majorities. Madison approved of Voltaire's aphorism: "If one religion only were allowed in England, the Government would possibly become arbitrary; if there were two, the people would cut each other's throats; but as there are such a multitude, they all live happily in peace." Jefferson had said that uniformity of belief was no more desirable than of face or stature; he shared the conception of the safety in numbers. Later, Madison drew upon his *Remonstrance* as well as on Voltaire when he defended the separation of powers in the 1787 constitution, observing that the security for civil rights had to rest on the same basis as the religious: "it consists in the one case in the multiplicity of interests and in the other in the multiplicity of sects."

Madison warned that enactment of general assessment would be an admission that the legislature could act in this area, and would be a retreat from the position of freedom taken in 1776 in the state bill of rights, one that could undermine the other rights enumerated. He claimed that it would bring an Inquisition of minor degree, would ruin the Old Dominion's new image as an asylum for the oppressed, and might trigger emigration to more tolerant neighboring colonies. He reminded the Assembly of the dissenter majority in the population, noting the overrepresentation of tidewater planters and Churchmen in their body; he suggested that, in all fairness, a decision so important to the dissenters should not be taken until a reapportionment was effected. In later remarks on the Assembly floor, however, Madison reassured the more conservative by explaining that the decline in piety was temporary, purely the result of wartime conditions and not attributable to the partial disestablishment that had occurred.

Madison's arguments and leadership, backed by organized dissenter opinion, won the day and general assessment was defeated; he then used the ideological momentum his *Remonstrance* had created and tried again for the goal he and Jefferson had sought for a decade, complete religious freedom. Jefferson was on diplomatic duty in France, but Madison re-submitted his friend's bill of 1779 and it passed by a close vote, actually becoming law in 1786. This Virginia statute, an early instance of "the great collaboration" of Madison and Jefferson, became the model for most other states and its spirit was echoed in the First Amendment of the federal Constitution. Even the small groups on the margin, the Catholics, Jews, and Quakers were happy with it. Jefferson was so proud of this measure that he had it translated into French and Italian for his European admirers and later had it listed on his tombstone, with the Declaration of Independence and the charter of the University of Virginia, as one of the three great accomplishments of his life. The act reaffirmed freedom of religion as a natural right and provided in part:

> "that no man shall be compelled to frequent or support any religious worship, place, or ministry, whatsoever, nor shall be enforced, restrained, molested, or burthened in his body or goods, or shall otherwise suffer, on account of his religious opinions or belief; but that all men shall be free to profess, and by argument maintain, their opinions in matters of religion, and that the same shall in no wise diminish, enlarge, or affect their civil capacities."

Thus Christianity was formally separated from the state for the first time in 1400 years; finally it had been acknowledged that man could be trusted to form his own religious opinions.

Contemplating this new freedom, the rationalists were as confident that reason would prevail among the people as the pietists were of God's grace. Jefferson had put this so strongly in the preamble to his bill that Madison excised some phrases to make it more palatable to less liberal lawmakers. Jefferson deplored emotional and sectarian dogma, but assumed that in ethical teachings, all the religious "persuasions" were similar and relied on this to stabilize the commonwealth. He eagerly anticipated what has actually come about only in the 20th century: that systems of public education would supplant the churches as the established teachers of morality and civic duty to the populace. Jefferson's expectation that sectarian rivalry would consequently diminish has been realized, but the improvement in man's rationality that he assumed would occur, has not been as spectacular.

While the rationalist leaders got onto the lawbooks most of the phraseology they wanted in describing the church-state relationship, there were other, more pious, traditions contributing to the victory. Any discussion of church and state in colonial America must inevitably mention Roger Williams, the Calvinistic Seeker who was banished from Massachusetts Bay in the 17th century for his heretical opinions. The enigmatic founder of Rhode Island had some slight impact on the Revolutionary era, but it was largely indirect. Williams' church-state views, mingled with those of other high Puritans, filtered down through the toleration essays of Locke. He died in 1683, and because the Puritans were so successful in pinning the heresy label on him, only a few curious colonials read Williams' works in the following century. Isaac Backus was among the handful—Williams had been a Baptist briefly—but not until 1773 when Backus' own ideas were far advanced. Backus alluded to him in his *History* but preferred to invoke Locke in his politico-religious pamphlets apparently because of Williams' low standing. Other writers on toleration also mentioned Penn's Holy Experiment, the legacy of the Dutch in New York, or the Baltimores in Maryland, but Williams' "lively experiment" in Rhode Island was not as often noticed.

Williams had a Celtic strain although he was born of English parents in London; he was educated at Cambridge and served briefly as a clerk for Sir Edward Coke. The quality of his piety, presumably shaped by Anglo-Dutch thinkers, together with his extreme separatism, suggested a Continental admixture. In his famous controversy with John Cotton, who represented the oligarchy, Williams took an extreme position on church and state. He claimed that the two spheres were not organically related but properly distinct and should not be confounded. God had ordained no particular form of government. Christian states or peoples had no more rights in this world than pagans. The parable of the tares and the wheat applied, not to hypocrites within the church, but to Christians and pagans in the world, and so it followed that ungodly men retained their civil rights. A civil magistrate could not punish violations of the First Table (the first four of the Ten Commandments) because these involved man's duty to God and coercion did not make believers: "forced worship stinks in God's nostrils." This position, of course, made Williams something of an "internationalist" for his time, more tolerant of Indian life than his Puritan brethren, and willing to endure Quaker "incivilities" although opposed to their beliefs.

Williams' sole reliance on God's grace, and the power of the Word unaided by the state, was almost as extreme for the 18th century as it had been for the 17th; only the rationalists who had substituted morality for gracious piety believed progress was possible under such conditions. As so many historians have pointed out, Williams was not an "enlightened-democrat" but a pre-millennial Puritan whose religiosity led him to seek protection for the churches from the worldly policies of the state; this was in sharp contrast to Jefferson who wanted to free the new republic from "priestcraft" and revealed religion. Williams had no effect on Jefferson, and their motives were very different, yet their goal was the same: total separation.

When New Light ardor for the Revolution rose dramatically in 1774, it was accompanied by a demand for separation of church and state. The New Lights, with the Baptists in the forefront and the Presbyterians wavering, took a more pragmatic and less consistent position than that of Roger Williams or the rationalists. Their views grew out of post-Awakening friction with the establishments in Massachusetts, Virginia, Connecticut, and Carolina.

Isaac Backus was the longtime spokesman for this large element (although fellow Baptist John Leland, a friend of Jefferson's, was prominent later in completing Virginia's dis-establishment). Whereas Williams wanted no denominations or pastors, and Jefferson denied America was a Christian state, Backus expected the new nation to be Christian, Protestant, and Calvinist. He never went on record with a clear-cut statement favoring liberty for all dissenters, regardless of their errors; to him Universalists and Shakers were almost as heretical as Papists. Liberty of conscience as Backus and most of the New Lights defined it, actually consisted of voluntary obedience to God's will as revealed in the scriptures, obviously a narrower conception than that held by Jefferson, Madison, and the rationalists. It was merely the freedom to go at one's own pace on the pilgrimage of this world, not the right to reject the approaching Kingdom altogether.

In making his case for liberty, Backus portrayed his denomination, the Baptists, as the most faithful heirs of the New England Way; they had departed from the founding fathers in only one respect, the rejection of infant baptism. He praised the congregational polity of the Cambridge Platform of 1648 and rejected the consociationism that developed afterward. He quoted at length from the works of John Robinson, the Pilgrim pastor in Amsterdam. To a man of Backus' ancestry, this comparison of late 18th century Baptists to the first generation of New England settlers came quite naturally (Leland, the other Baptist leader in the Virginia campaign was also of pre-1660 Massachusetts stock); and in fact the attitudes of the organized dissenters of this era did turn out to resemble the "well-bounded toleration" of the first Pilgrims in Plymouth, before the invasion of semi-presbyterian ways from the more populous settlement of Massachusetts Bay.

While the rationalists and the pietists both emphasized morality over theology, and hoped that free churches would be conducive to good public morals, they seemed to differ on the role the state would play in the system. The pietists, or at least the evangelical majority among them, did not really favor a *total* separation of church and state; they still believed that the state should impose a Christian morality on its citizens. The rationalists, however, while they might wish to set limits if the public welfare were threatened by eccentric behavior, were much more willing to rely on man's rationality and on the general good effects of the moral teachings of the "sects," and were reluctant to resort to state intervention. What the New Lights actually wanted was not total separation but friendly co-operation, a "sweet harmony" between church and state. And in spite of constitutions, laws, and the "high wall" Jefferson and Madison intended, within a few years they got substantially what they wanted. In many different ways, from Bible-reading in the local schoolhouse to nationally proclaimed days of concern and thanksgiving, Protestant Christianity flavored the state and federal governments and the Fundamentalist heirs of this tradition seemed not to perceive any inconsistency in their support of laws against blasphemy, liquor, or the teaching of evolution in public schools. Even today, although Supreme Court decisions have buttressed the separationism of the 18th century rationalists, it is doubtful whether the American people as a whole yet agree with these decisions; a majority may still favor friendly co-operation over total separation.

The influence of the evangelicals in the Virginia legislative victory should be emphasized. That Jefferson and Madison were aroused by the sufferings of the Separate Baptists can be assumed. Madison was explicit, however, in attributing the 1786 law to direct pressure from organized dissenters on the lawmakers and not to the arguments or acumen of himself or his fellow rationalists. Because the New Lights made this historic measure possible, it was perhaps fitting that their interpretation, *i.e.*, friendly co-operation, prevailed for so long; but as a consequence, our national policy has lacked a rationale, and Jefferson's "fair experiment" has had only middling success.

The dislocations of the Revolutionary War and the influx of freethinking that came with French money and officers as a result of the alliance put rationalism into an ascendancy over evangelical piety for the next twenty years, but, as we have seen, the pietists cooperated with rationalists long enough at several points to secure new religious freedoms, and the evangelical denominations grew rapidly in frontier areas.

The "Spirit of '76," the kind of religious likemindedness apparent on the eve of the Revolution, recurred on a smaller scale in 1798, and Jefferson and his party were the beneficiaries. Despite Jefferson's identification with intellectuals, deism, and a revolution in France that had exceeded the norms of the American experience, he was still the symbol of equalitarian nationalism to the evangelicals. Jefferson would erase the plutocratic distinctions raised by Hamilton and the Federalist presidents. His vision of an agrarian republic destined to extend the area of liberty into the American hinterland attracted nationalistic utopians left unsatisfied with the results of the Revolution. At the prospect of Jefferson's election in 1800, a Second Great Awakening arose in the west.

When Jefferson and his cohorts were swept into office in the "revolution of 1800," Calvinistic piety entered a new era. From that time to the Civil War, it played a major role in reform movements, especially abolition, although challenged by other, newer forms of piety.

It seems clear that without the large evangelical component in the colonial population, there would have been no military victory over the redcoats, and beyond that no Independence, no Constitution, no legalized religious freedom, and no dramatic opportunity to be a beacon to the world. The rationalism of East Anglian Puritans, Old Lights and secularized Real Whigs, while conducive to individual liberty, due process, private property and the "hard" sciences, could not by itself have commanded the numbers to bring off the American Revolution; the oral tradition of north and west England, the "West Country," Ulster and Wales, seasoned by Calvinism, and reinforced by the American environment, was the essential ingredient in the Spirit of '76. If colonial society had resembled that of the Continent—as it showed some signs of doing early in the 18th century—and consisted predominantly of rationalistic planters, lawyers, and merchants, and quietistic or apolitical peasants and artisans—it would have evolved much more slowly, even though most of the traditional rights of Englishmen would have been retained. The Enlightenment assumptions about the reasonableness of the mass of men, and their ability to govern themselves, would have remained almost as much of a conjecture on this side of the water as in the Old World. As it was, however, while Enlightenment ideas filtered into America from the 1680s, the surge of them after 1750 only confirmed the colonials in their predispositions, giving them a rationale for developments long in the making.

The colonials approved in general the Calvinistic scheme not because it was reasonable but because it worked and its determinism was provocative; preaching God's sovereignty brought immediate and self-evident changes. It produced seasons of revival in which white men as well as women, children, Indians and Negroes felt God's power. It gave men who were moral athletes a special confidence that they were of the Elect and therefore ready to fight and die to hasten the millennium. Its converts pushed church polities in a democratic direction toward congregationalism, and away from presbyterianism. In the 18th century evangelical Calvinism was a technique for reclaiming those who had "warped off" from religion, for politicizing farmers on the frontiers and arousing guilt among descendants of the first settlers who had strayed from their errand into the wilderness. Pastors convinced of God's sovereignty were better able to convey a sense of urgency than their more complacent Arminian rivals; they were also more graphic in depicting the democratic union of true believers. Yet, the formal, non-evangelical Calvinism professed by the European-educated Old Side clergy—and imitated to a degree by the New Divinity men—was a closed intellectual system foreign to the empirical temper of the colonial majority. There is truth in a remark about Americans that was intended to be derogatory: they urge you to have faith, but the specific faith is not important. This is a back-handed way of indicating that while Americans want you to give conscious consent, to be committed to pious action, they recognize that fixed creeds inhibit godliness and stifle individuality, that an open society needs open minds, and that nothing is final because the Almighty will continue to provide "further light."

Bibliography

I have listed more journal articles than is customary in the hope that interested students can now find them in libraries and reproduce them easily. Sometimes an author offers a more concise and ordered presentation of his theme in an article than he does in the more extended space of a book.

An asterisk after the title indicates a useful bibliography, not just of primary sources, but of the critical literature on the subject.

General Works

For a lucid and comprehensive introduction to American thought and culture, see the early chapters of Merle Curti, *The Growth of American Thought* (1964 ed.).* Daniel Boorstin, *The Americans; The Colonial Experience* (1958),* is interesting but more fragmentary and opinionated. Vernon L. Parrington, *The Main Currents in American Thought: the Colonial Mind* (1927), is still worthwhile although rather unfashionable now because of his flagrant progressivism. The same is true for Max Savelle, *The Seeds of Liberty: The Genesis of the American Mind* (1948), who reflects the historians' celebration of America that took place between 1933 and 1950. Michael Kraus, *The Atlantic Civilization: Eighteenth-Century Origins* (1949), is very readable. The outstanding treatments of the Enlightenment are Carl Becker, *The Heavenly City of the Eighteenth-Century Philosophers* (1932), and Peter Gay, *The Enlightenment: the Rise of Modern Paganism* (1966).

References directly pertinent to the theme of this book—the role of religion in developing separatism and nationalism in the century prior to Independence—are perhaps less well known. William W. Sweet, *Religion in Colonial America* (1942), follows the progressive school of historians in de-emphasizing theology and the role of New England, and stressing instead the frontier and its effect on democratizing church practices and polities. Thomas C. Hall, *The Religious Background of American Culture* (1930), discerns three religious traditions in America: the Anglo-Catholic, the Calvinist, and the Dissenter; the last, he contends, has been the most pervasive, and he traces it to the pre-Reformation days of John Wyclif and the Lollards. John M. Mecklin, *The Story of American Dissent* (1934), is more inclined to credit the frontier, or even the Continent, than the Lollards. H. Richard Niebuhr finds the dominant idea of American Christianity from the outset to be *The Kingdom of God in America* (1937). Several of the essays in James Ward Smith and A. Leland Jamison, eds., *Religion in American Life Volume I. The Shaping of American Religion* (1961), are relevant and Volumes III and IV: *A Critical Bibliography of Religion in America** (Nelson R. Burr, ed.), are indispensible; because these are accessible and so extensive, I have been inclined to emphasize, wherever possible, works completed since 1961. Burr will publish a new bibliography, *American Religious Life,* shortly. Edwin S. Gaustad, *A History of Religion in America* (1966),** is a good, recent work on the general subject.

Chapter 1
Colonial Religion in the Glacial Age

The Nadir of Puritanism. For the Glacial Age of New England Puritanism, Perry Miller, *The New England Mind: From Colony to Province* (1953),* is without equal; also relevant is "Declension in a Bible Commonwealth," in *Nature's Nation* (1967), 14–49; *Errand into the Wilderness* (1956), is his concise and mature statement of what the Puritans believed. When the Age was under attack, Clifford K. Shipton defended it in four articles: "The Shaping of Revolutionary New England, 1680–1740," *Political Science Quarterly,* L (1935), 584–597; "The New England Clergy of the 'Glacial Age,'" Colonial Society of Massachusetts, *Publications,* XXXII (1936), 24–54; "Immigration to New England, 1680–1740," *Journal of Political Economy,* XLIV (1936), 225–239; and "Literary Leaven in Provincial New England," *New England Quarterly* IX (1936), 203–217; he refuted the claim that these years were politically and culturally stagnant. Gerald J. Goodwin, "The Myth of 'Arminian' Calvinism," *New England Quarterly,* XLI (1968), 213–237, pushes uphill, arguing that the covenant Calvinism of the Puritans was not at all compromised by crypto-Arminian influences. Ernest Benz, "Ecumenical Relations between Boston Puritanism and German Pietism: Cotton Mather and August Hermann Francke," *Harvard Theological Review,* LIV (1961), 159–193, shows Mather trying to adapt the German version of "heart religion" to New England. James Truslow Adams, *Revolutionary New England, 1691–1776* (1923), became famous for his criticism of the Puritans. Chard Powers Smith, *Yankees and God* (1954), in pursuing the influence of New England Puritanism from the beginning to the 20th century, is eccentric and disjointed, but offers some insights along the way. Robert G. Pope, *The Half-Way Covenant* (1969),* explains that compromise. Useful biographies of principals are Barrett Wendell, *Cotton Mather, Puritan Priest* (1891), Kenneth B. Murdock, *Increase Mather* (1925), and Ola E. Winslow, *Samuel Sewall of Boston* (1964).

In discussing John Wise, I have followed Raymond P. Stearns, "John Wise of Ipswich was no Democrat in Politics," *Essex Institute Historical Collections*, XCVII (1961), 2–18; the older view is well presented in Clinton Rossiter, "John Wise, Colonial Democrat," *New England Quarterly*, XXII (1949), 3–32, George Cook, *John Wise: Early American Democrat* (1952),* and Paul S. McElroy, "John Wise: Father of American Independence," *Essex Institute Historical Collections*, LXXXI (1945), 201–226. John Wise, *Vindication of Church Government* (1958 edition), has an introduction by Perry Miller.

New England's Early Enlightenment. The early Enlightenment influence on Benjamin Colman is evident in Theodore Hornberger, "Benjamin Colman and the Enlightenment," *New England Quarterly*, XII (1939), 227–240; Charles B. Giles, "Benjamin Colman" diss., UCLA, 1963; and Clayton H. Chapman, "Benjamin Colman and Philomena," *New England Quarterly*, XLII (1969), 214–231. On the general topic of American-English cultural contacts, see William L. Sachse, *The Colonial American in Britain* (1956).

The Anglican penetration of the colonies after the Glorious Revolution is ably discussed by Carl Bridenbaugh, *Mitre and Sceptre* (1962), who devotes chapter 3 to the New England phase. Bruce E. Steiner, "New England Anglicanism: A Genteel Faith?" *William and Mary Quarterly*, XXVII (1970), 122–135, explores the socio-economic status of parishioners. Roland H. Bainton, *Yale and the Ministry* (1955), describes the "Great Apostasy" of 1722. Herbert W. and Carol Schneider, eds., *Samuel Johnson; His Career and Writings* (1929), 4 vols., offer plentiful material on the leading defector. See also Arthur L. Cross, *The Anglican Episcopate and the American Colonies* (1902), Evarts B. Greene, "The Anglican Outlook on the American Colonies in the Early Eighteenth Century," *American Historical Review*, XX (1914), 64–85, and Edmund F. Slafter, *John Checkley* (1897, 1967), 2 vols.

Pennsylvania's Holy Experiment. Rufus M. Jones, *The Quakers in the American Colonies* (1911, 1962), is an old but fair account. The accomplishments of the Quaker aristocracy of Philadelphia are stressed in Frederick B. Tolles, *Meeting House and Counting House: The Quaker Merchants of Colonial Philadelphia, 1682–1763* (1948),* *James Logan and the Culture of Provincial Pennsylvania* (1957), and *Quakers and the Atlantic Culture* (1960). An un-Friendly historian, Daniel Boorstin,

The Americans: the Colonial Experience (1958),* Part Two, finds the Quakers too rigid and prone to martyrdom. Stow Persons, *American Minds: A History of Ideas* (1958), chapter 3, discusses them in conjunction with other colonial sectarians. Edwin B. Bronner, "Inter-colonial Relations among Quakers before 1750," *Quaker History,* LVI (1967), 3–17, finds American Friends' ties with England stronger than among themselves. Joe Lee Davis, "Mystical Versus Enthusiastical Sensibility," *Journal of the History of Ideas,* IV (1943), 301–19, makes some interesting distinctions between the Inner and the New Light.

Women are as conspicuous in Quaker biography as they are at the meeting. See Catherine O. Peare, *William Penn* (1956), Mary Marples Dunn, *William Penn: Politics and Conscience* (1967), and Edward C. O. Beatty, *William Penn as a Social Philosopher* (1939); Amelia Mott Gummere, ed., *The Journal and Essays of John Woolman* (1922), Catherine O. Peare, *John Woolman, Child of Light* (1954), and Ethyn W. Kirby, *George Keith* (1942).

For the journals of English Friends see Luella M. Wright, *The Literary Life of the Early Friends, 1650–1725* (1932, 1966), and the American Friends, Daniel B. Shea, Jr., *Spiritual Autobiography in Early America* (1968), Part I.

Recent studies of Quaker politics are: Gary B. Nash, *Quakers and Politics: Pennsylvania, 1681–1726* (1968); Edwin B. Bronner, *William Penn's Holy Experiment: The Founding of Pennsylvania, 1681–1701* (1962); Joseph E. Ilick, *William Penn the Politican: His Relations with the English Government* (1965); and Robert O. Byrd, *The Quakers and Foreign Policy* (1960), chapter 8.

Chapter 2
The Great Awakening: Revelation and Reason

The interesting phenomenon of the true believers or "saving remnant" has been discussed by Gordon W. Allport in several places but most concisely in "The Religious Context of Prejudice," *Journal for the Scientific Study of Religion,* V (1966), 447–457. Gerhard Lenski, *The Religious Factor* (1961), draws meaningful contemporary results from the distinction between "orthodox" and "devotional" worshippers. A similar distinction, that between "conservative" and "antinomian" pietism —perfect moral order or perfect moral freedom—is made provocatively as a theme in American history by William G. McLoughlin, "Pietism and the American Character," *American Quarterly,* XVII (1965), 163–185. Rodney Stark and Charles Y. Glock, *American Piety: the Nature of Religious Commitment* (1968), offers illuminating statistics on the 20th century that are suggestive for earlier periods.

Stoddard on the Frontier.   Perry Miller, "Solomon Stoddard," *The Harvard Theological Review,* XXXIV (1941), 277–320, stimulated interest in the "Pope" of the Valley. In his *From Colony to Province,* Miller called for a closer examination of Stoddard. The call has been answered by Thomas A. Schafer, "Solomon Stoddard and the Theology of the Revival," in Stuart C. Henry, ed., *A Miscellany of American Christianity* (1963), who explains the influence of Stoddard's evangelical Calvinism on Jonathan Edwards, and by Eugene E. White, "Solomon Stoddard's Theories of Persuasion," *Speech Monographs,* XXIX (1962), 235–259. Norman Pettit, *The Heart Prepared: Grace and Conversion in Puritan Spiritual Life* (1966), chapter 6, compares Stoddard's view of preparation with those of the Puritan fathers. See also, Harvey G. Swanhart, "Solomon Stoddard: Puritan Patriarch," diss., Boston University, 1961.

Edwards and the Frontier Revival, 1734–36.   Scholars in many disciplines have found Jonathan Edwards a challenge and an enigma; the literature about him is immense and growing rapidly. For his life see Ola E. Winslow (1940), and for his ideas, Perry Miller (1949). That Edwards was a tragic anachronism in the 18th century is the influential thesis of Vernon L. Parrington, *Main Currents in American Thought: the Colonial Mind* (1927); Vincent Tomas, "The Modernity of Jonathan Edwards," *New England Quarterly,* XXV (1952), 60–84, and Peter Gay, *A Loss of Mastery; Puritan Historians in Colonial America* (1968), chapter 4, concur. But Edwards continues to attract advocates: Edward H. Davidson, *Jonathan Edwards: the Narrative of a Puritan Mind* (1966), maintains that he has a special cogency for the 20th century; James P. Carse, *Jonathan Edwards and the Visibility of God* (1967), finds modernity in his ideas but faults his style. Claude A. Smith, "Jonathan Edwards and the Way of Ideas," *Harvard Theological Review,* LIX (1966), 153–173, contends Edwards enlarged upon Locke's conception of human experience. The impact of Locke as well as diverse opinions of Edwards are included in John Opie, ed., *Jonathan Edwards and the Enlightenment* (1970).* In studying Edwards' revivalism, Richard L. Bushman, "Jonathan Edwards and the Puritan Consciousness," *Journal for the Scientific Study of Religion,* V (1966), 383–396, and "Jonathan Edwards as a Great Man: Identity, Conversion, and Leadership in the Great Awakening," *Soundings,* LII (1969), 15–46, has applied the insights of Erik Erikson. Edwin H. Cady, "The Artistry of Jonathan Edwards," *New England Quarterly,* XX (1949), 61–72, considers the technique of his most famous sermon, "Sinners in the Hands of an Angry God." See also Gail T. Parker, "Jonathan Edwards and Melancholy," *New England Quarterly,* XLI (1968), 193–212, and David C. Pierce, "Jonathan Edwards and the 'New Sense of Glory'," *New England*

Quarterly, XLI (1968), 82–95. David E. Levin, ed., *Jonathan Edwards; a Profile* (1969), is a good collection of complementary and conflicting views about the man. For additional references to Edwards, see references under Chapter 6.

The Dutch Reformed and Scotch-Irish. In his description of religion in the Middle Colonies, Leonard J. Trinterud, *The Forming of an American Tradition; Colonial Presbyterianism* (1949), makes an excellent case for the influence of Connecticut Puritanism in shaping the faith of the Scotch-Irish. The classic account is Charles H. Maxson, *The Great Awakening in the Middle Colonies* (1920), but Martin E. Lodge, "The Great Awakening in the Middle Colonies," diss., University of California, Berkeley, 1964, is better. See also Dietmar Rothermund, "Political Factions in the Great Awakening," *Pennsylvania History*, LXXXIV (1960), 3–21, and *The Layman's Progress: Religious and Political Experience in Colonial Pennsylvania, 1740–1770* (1962).

The Dutch minister, Theodore Frelinghuysen, is portrayed as an evangelical Calvinist with views quite compatible to the adjacent Puritans in Trinterud, *The Forming of an American Tradition*. James R. Tanis, *Dutch Calvinistic Pietism in the Middle Colonies: A Study in the Life and Theology of Theodore Jacobus Frelinghuysen* (1967), confirms this, using European materials to show that the domine was entirely in the Reformed tradition and owed little to Lutheran pietism. Peter H. B. Frelinghuysen, *Theodore Jacobus Frelinghuysen* (1938), praises his ancestor for Americanizing the Dutch church. Herman Harmelink, 3rd, "Another Look at Frelinghuysen and His 'Awakening'," *Church History*, XXVII (1968), 423–438, is sure that he was a dogmatic troublemaker but doubts that there was much of an awakening in his pastorate.

For Scotch-Irish Presbyterians see, in addition to Trinterud, James G. Leyburn, *The Scotch-Irish: A Social History* (1962), Guy S. Klett, *The Scotch-Irish in Pennsylvania* (1948), and Wayland F. Dunaway, *The Scotch-Irish of Colonial Pennsylvania* (1944). Frederick W. Loetscher, "The Adopting Act," *Journal of the Presbyterian Historical Society*, XIII (1928–29), 337–355, discusses that measure in some detail. See also Charles A. Briggs, *American Presbyterianism; Its Origin and Early History* (1885), George H. Ingram, "William Tennent, Sr., the Founder, 1673–1746," *Journal of the Presbyterian Historical Society*, XIV (1930), 1–27, and Robert F. Scott, "Colonial Presbyterianism in the Valley of Virginia," *Journal of the Presbyterian Historical Society*, XXXV (1957), 71–92, 171–192.

George Whitefield and The Great Awakening. Interesting contemporary accounts of the revival have been made accessible in Alan Heimert and

Perry Miller, eds., *The Great Awakening* (1967). Joseph Tracy, *The Great Awakening* (1842, 1970), is excellent and now accessible again. As the title suggests, Frederick M. Davenport, *Primitive Traits in Religious Revivals* (1910), takes the sceptical view of the early social scientists. In addition, four books with the title *Great Awakening* that combine primary sources with interpretation have appeared in 1970. The editors are: John M. Bumsted, Richard L. Bushman, David S. Lovejoy, and Darrett B. Rutman.

Historians find it hard to describe George Whitefield's personality and style fairly—to empathize with him. The most balanced treatment of the Awakener and his theology is Horton Davies, *Worship and Theology in England; From Watts and Wesley to Maurice, 1690–1850* (1961), chapter 7, where he is compared with John Wesley. Stuart C. Henry, *George Whitefield: The Wayfaring Witness* (1957), is less favorable to his intellect. Luke Tyerman, *The Life of the Rev. George Whitefield* (1876–1877), 2 vols., contains long excerpts from his pen. His personality can be glimpsed firsthand in his *Journals* (1960–1969). William H. Kenney, 3rd, "George Whitefield, Dissenter Priest of the Awakening, 1739–1741," *William and Mary Quarterly*, XXVI (1969), 75–93, attributes the success of the first tour to underlying Anglican-dissenter tensions along the seaboard north of Maryland.

The New England phase of the Awakening has been objectively studied by Edwin S. Gaustad, *The Great Awakening in New England* (1957). Because eastern Connecticut was a special center of religiosity, it has received much attention: Mary H. Mitchell, *The Great Awakening and Other Revivals in the Religious Life of Connecticut* (1934), Ellen D. Larned, *The History of Windham County* (1874), 2 vols., Clarence C. Goen, *Revivalism and Separatism in New England* (1962), and James P. Walsh, "The Conservative Nature of Connecticut Separatism," *Connecticut Historical Society Bulletin*, XXXIV (1969). Thomas H. Billings, "The Great Awakening," *Essex Institute Historical Collections*, LXV (1929), 89–104, notes the weak response in Essex County, Massachusetts. John C. Miller, "Religion, Finance, and Democracy in Massachusetts," *New England Quarterly*, VI (1933), 29–58, connects the revival with disappointment over failure of the land bank scheme. The position various Boston churches took is indicated by Gaustad, "Society and the Great Awakening in New England," *William and Mary Quarterly*, XI (1954), 566–577; he maintains that the Awakening was "great and general," without strong regional and class patterns. Perry Miller, "Jonathan Edwards' Sociology of the Great Awakening," *New England Quarterly*, XXI (1948), 50–77, shows the great theologian capable of more insights than critics suspected. Eugene E. White, "The Decline of the Great Awakening in New England: 1741–1746," *New England*

Quarterly, XXIV (1951), 35–52, describes the rapid withdrawal of the Spirit.

Effects of the Revival. Cedric B. Cowing, "Sex and Preaching in the Great Awakening," *American Quarterly,* XX (1968),* 624–644, demonstrates the strong appeal New Light preachers had for white males as well as for Indians, Negroes and women; he views male converts as strengthening church discipline, congregational polity, and the American-born learned ministry. He also suggests that persons who collapsed in the Awakening may have been altered permanently, and cites William W. Sargant, *The Battle for the Mind* (1957), who endorses both the Whitefield-Edwards and the Wesley revivals as 18th century approximations, on the mass level, of modern psychiatric techniques. The statistics in Emil Oberholzer, *Delinquent Saints: Disciplinary Action in the Early Congregational Churches of Massachusetts* (1956), suggest that the Awakening revived church discipline.

The resistance or indifference to the revival by Anglicans, Quakers, and inward-looking pietists is described in three articles: Leonard W. Labaree, "The Conservative Attitude toward the Great Awakening," *William and Mary Quarterly,* I (1944), 331–352; Gerald J. Goodwin, "The Anglican Reaction to the Great Awakening," *History Magazine of the Protestant Episcopal Church,* XXXV (1966), 343–371; and Frederick B. Tolles, "Quietism Versus Enthusiasm: The Philadelphia Quakers and the Great Awakening," *Pennsylvania Magazine of History and Biography,* LXIX (1945), 26–49.

Richard Hofstadter believes the colonial revival was a major root of *Anti-Intellectualism in American Life* (1963).

Chapter 3
Indians and Negroes: The Heathen in America

Speculation about the origins of races is considered in Margaret T. Hodgen, *Early Anthropology in the Sixteenth and Seventeenth Centuries* (1964); John C. Greene, "Some Early Speculations on the Origin of the Human Species," *American Anthropologist,* LVI (1954), 31–41, and Don Cameron Allen, *The Legend of Noah* (1949).

The impact of the Indians on the intellectual world of the settlers is examined by Roy Harvey Pearce, *The Savages of America; A Study of the Indian and the Idea of Civilization* (1953).* Students of literature and history have explored the implications of the Noble Savage myth; for its effect on Europe in general see Hoxie N. Fairchild, *The Noble Savage* (1928); for Indians in England, Benjamin Bissell, *The American Indian in English Literature* (1925); and in America, Albert Keiser, *The*

Indian in American Literature (1933), although he is concerned chiefly with a later period. The hilarious—and tragic—experiences of Indians who visited Europe are in Carolyn T. Foreman, *Indians Abroad* (1943) and Richmond P. Bond, *Queen Anne's American Kings* (1952). For the period of this book, Arthur R. Buntin, "The Indian in American Literature (1680–1780)," diss., University of Washington, 1961, is pertinent; he construes "literature" to include everything in print.

The Red Man and the Missionary.   The discouraging story of missionary work is told by Robert F. Berkhofer, Jr., *Salvation and the Savage; An Analysis of Protestant Missions and the American Indian Response, 1787–1862* (1965), and with more specific attention to the colonial period in R. Pierce Beaver, "American Missionary Motivation before the Revolution," *Church History*, XXXI (1962), 216–226; and "Methods in American Missions to the Indians in the 17th and 18th Centuries: Calvinist Models for Protestant Foreign Missions," *Journal of Presbyterian History*, XLVII (1969), 124–148. Yet the missionaries were largely successful in imparting their hymnody to the heathen; see Robert Stevenson, *Protestant Church Music in America* (1966),* chapters 1, 9.

The Puritan pioneer in the "Indian Work" has a new biographer: Ola E. Winslow, *John Eliot; Apostle to the Indians* (1967), but see Ezra H. Byington, *The Puritan as Colonist and Reformer* (1899), chapter 3. The long term effort to Christianize the red men is described in William Kellaway, *The New England Company, 1649–1776; Missionary Society to the American Indians* (1962). The Mayhew barony on Nantucket where Calvinism became so benign and ineffective is discussed in Margery R. Johnson, "The Mayhew Mission to the Indians, 1643–1806," diss., Clark University, 1966. Edwards' view of the Indians can be glimpsed in his famous life of the missionary, David Brainerd (included in his works), and for his policy with the Stockbridge Indians, see Arthur M. McGiffert, Jr., *Jonathan Edwards* (1932), chapter 7. Alden T. Vaughan, *New England Frontier: Puritans and Indians, 1620–1675* (1965), is a spirited defense of 17th century Puritan policy toward the aborigines.

The Quakers' part in the Work is discussed sympathetically and at length by Rayner W. Kelsey, *Friends and the Indians, 1655–1917* (1917), and more briefly by Frederick B. Tolles, "Nonviolent Contact; the Quakers and the Indians," *Proceedings, American Philosophical Society*, CVII (1963), 93–101. Marie J. Kohnova, "The Moravians and their Missionaries, A Problem in Americanization," *Mississippi Valley Historical Review*, XIX (1932), 348–361, is a fair account, as is Thomas F. McHugh, "The Moravian Mission to the American; Early American Peace Corps," *Pennsylvania History*, XXXIII (1966), 412–431. Roland H. Bainton, *Christian Attitudes toward War and Peace* (1960), chapter

10, discusses "The Historic Peace Churches and the War with the Aborigines."

Modern scholars, like 18th century readers, have been drawn to the captivity tales. Robert W. G. Vail, *The Voice of the Old Frontier* (1949), sees in their vivid simplicity, the beginnings of our native literature. Phillips Carleton, "The Indian Captivity," *American Literature,* XV (1943), 169–180, notes their usefulness to anthropologists. Roy Harvey Pearce, "The Significance of Captivity Narratives," *American Literature,* XIX (1947), 1–20, describes the trend from religiosity to secular hatred. Firsthand accounts can be gory: Howard Peckham, *Captured by the Indians; True Tales of Pioneer Survivors* (1954), and Charles H. Lincoln, ed., *Original Narratives of Indian Wars, 1675–1699* (1913).

Indian treaties and the procedure of treaty-making have also been favorably viewed: Lawrence C. Wroth, "The Indian Treaty as Literature," *Yale Review,* XVII (1928), 749–766; and A. M. Drummond and Richard Moody, "Indian Treaties: the First American Dramas," *Journal of Speech,* XXXIX (1933), 15–24. For the protocol, see Wilbur R. Jacobs, *Wilderness Politics and Indian Gifts: The Northern Colonial Frontier, 1748–1763* (1966 ed.).

The Noble Savage.   There was a Noble Savage influence in various sections of North America early in the 18th century. For New France see George R. Healey, "French Jesuits and the Noble Savage," *William and Mary Quarterly,* 3rd Series XV (1958), 143–167, and John Hopkins Kennedy, *Jesuit and Savage in New France* (1950); for New York, Frank J. Klingberg, "The Noble Savage as Seen by the Missionaries of the S.P.G. in Colonial New York, 1702–1750," *Historical Magazine of the Protestant Episcopal Church,* VIII (1939), 128–165; for Virginia, Louis B. Wright, "Beverley's History . . . of Virginia (1705); a Neglected Classic," *William and Mary Quarterly,* II (1944), 49–64; for the Carolinas, A. L. Diket, "The Noble Savage Convention in John Lawson's 'A New Voyage to Carolina'," *North Carolina Historical Review,* XLIII (1966), 413–429, and for the frontier, Lewis O. Saum, "The Fur Trader and the Noble Savage," *American Quarterly,* XV (1963), 554–571. See also Richard M. Gummere, *The American Colonial Mind and the Classical Tradition: Essays in Comparative Literature* (1963). There are various editions of accounts by contemporary observers, for example, Robert Beverley, *A History . . . of Virginia;* John Lawson, *A New Voyage to Carolina;* Hugh Jones, *The Present State of Virginia;* Cadwallader Colden, *A History of the Five Nations,* and James Adair, *A History of the American Indians.*

We are constantly more aware of the ramifications of the collison of the two cultures. Wilcomb E. Washburn, ed., *The Indian and the White*

Man (1964), provides a sympathetic introduction and pertinent documents. William N. Fenton, *American Indian and White Relations to 1830: Needs and Opportunities for Study* (1957),* is a plea for an integrated historical-ethnological approach. Bernard W. Sheehan, "Indian-White Relations in Early America: a Review Essay," *William and Mary Quarterly*, XXVI (1969), 267–286, surveys the progress that has been made in this direction. The cultural dimension had been successfully included in an earlier biography: Anthony F. C. Wallace, *King of the Delawares: Teedyuscung, 1700–1763* (1949). Herbert Moller, "Sex Composition and Correlated Cultural Patterns of Colonial America," *William and Mary Quarterly*, II (1945), 113–153, speculates about attitudes toward intermarriage. The most notable assessments of the contribution of red to white civilization are A. Irving Hallowell, "The Impact of the American Indian on American Culture," *American Anthropologist*, LIX (1957), 201–217, and A. Hyatt Verrill, *The Real Americans* (1954).

The Indians and Natural History.   The Scottish Enlightenment that encouraged a stages of civilization theory is best described by Gladys Bryson, *Man and Society; the Scottish Inquiry of the 18th Century* (1945); see also Louis Schneider, ed., *The Scottish Moralists of Human Nature and Society* (1967); Andrew Skinner, "Natural History in the Age of Adam Smith," *Political Studies*, XV (1967), 32–48, and John Clive and Bernard Bailyn, "England's Cultural Provinces—Scotland and America," *William and Mary Quarterly*, XI (1954), 200–213.

The Enlightenment is indicated in Gilbert Chinard, "Eighteenth Century Theories of America as a Human Habitat," *Proceedings, American Philosophical Society*, XCI (1947), 27–57, and reflected in the works of Jefferson and Franklin; see especially the former's *Notes on Virginia,* and Ruth Henline, "A Study of the Notes on Virginia, as Evidence of Jefferson's Reaction against the Theories of the French Naturalists," *Virginia Magazine of History & Biography*, LV (1947), 233–246.

White Over Black.   For the white man's views of the black man in the colonies, Winthrop D. Jordan, *White Over Black* (1968),* is indispensible, as is David Brion Davis, *The Problem of Slavery in Western Culture* (1956).*

The social and literary reaction to the African immigrants is indicated in Katherine George, "Western Civilization Looks at Primitive Africa: 1400–1800; A Study in Ethnocentrism," *Isis*, XLIX (1958), 62–72; J. Robert Constantine, "The Ignoble Savage; the 18th Century Stereotype," *Phylon*, XXVII (1966), 171–179; Milton Cantor, "The Image of the Negro in Colonial Literature," *New England Quarterly*, XXXVI (1963),

452–477; and Louis Ruchames, "Sources of Racial Thought in Colonial America," *Journal of Negro History,* LII (1967), 251–272.

Among the denominations, the Quakers have the most renowned bibliography on slavery and the Negro. See Sydney V. James, *A People Among Peoples; Quaker Benevolence in Eighteenth-Century America* (1963),* the early chapters of Thomas E. Drake, *Quakers and Slavery in America* (1950), Phillips Moulton, "John Woolman's Approach to Social Action, as Exemplified in Relation to Slavery," *Church History,* XXXV (1966), 399–410, and the biographies of John Woolman and Anthony Benezet.

The Anglican effort has also received considerable attention: Frank J. Klingberg, *Anglican Humanitarianism in Colonial New York* (1940), Jerome W. Jones, "The Established Virginia Church and the Conversion of Negroes and Indians, 1620–1760," *Journal of Negro History,* XLVI (1961), 12-23, Mary F. Goodwin, "Christianizing and Educating the Negro in Colonial Virginia," *Historical Magazine of the Protestant Episcopal Church,* I (1932), 143–152, and Faith Vibert, "The Society for the Propagation of the Gospel in Foreign Parts. Its Work for the Negroes in North America before 1783." *Journal of Negro History,* XVIII (1933), 171–212.

In Puritan New England, while Negroes were regarded as economic liabilities, they were not thoroughly isolated from the white population, according to Robert C. Twombly and Robert H. Moore, "Black Puritan: the Negro in 17th Century Massachusetts," *William and Mary Quarterly,* XXIV (1967), 224–242. Lawrence Towner, "The Sewall-Saffin Dialogue on Slavery," *William and Mary Quarterly,* XXI (1964), 40–52, believes Cotton Mather's views of the Negro overshadowed those advanced by Sewall and Saffin. Samuel Sewall, *The Selling of Joseph* (1700), has been reprinted (1969) with an introduction by Sidney Kaplan.

Linnaeus, Jefferson and the Negro.   In the scholarly dispute over which came first, slavery or racial prejudice, the latter view has now prevailed. Oscar and Mary Handlin, "The Origins of the Southern Labor System," *William and Mary Quarterly,* VII (1950), 199–222, has been superseded by Carl N. Degler, "Slavery and the Genesis of American Race Prejudice," *Comparative Studies in History and Society,* II (1959), 49–66. Economic thought had its effects: C. Robert Haywood, "Mercantilism and Colonial Slave Labor, 1700–1763," *Journal of Southern History,* XXIII (1957), 454–464.

The theory of the "numbed" personality offered by Stanley M. Elkins, *Slavery; A Problem in American Institutional and Intellectual Life* (1959), has been challenged by Eugene D. Genovese, "Rebelliousness and Docility in the Negro Slave: A Critique of the Elkins Thesis," *Civil*

War History, XIII (1967),* 293–314; he writes that in practice Latin-American masters, particularly in Brazil, may have been crueler than their Anglo-Saxon counterparts because the gap between the law and practice was greater in Latin America than in England's colonies. Sambo was not a unique product of the American south but existed wherever slavery existed, with dehumanization rising with the amount of commercialism present. For a full discussion see Ann J. Lane, ed., *Slavery and Personality: The Elkins Thesis and Its Critics* (1970).*

The scholars who have compared the institution of slavery in South America so favorably with the North have tended to be critical of capitalism rather than sympathetic to Catholicism. Frank Tannenbaum, *Slave and Citizen; the Negro in the Americas* (1946), was the pioneer; Elkins and Eric McKitrick, "Institutions and the Law of Slavery: the Dynamics of Unopposed Capitalism," *American Quarterly,* IX (1957), 3–21, and "Institutions and the Law of Slavery: Slavery in Capitalist and Non-Capitalist Cultures," *ibid.,* 159–179; Herbert S. Klein, "Anglicization, Catholicism, and the Negro Slave," *Comparative Studies in History and Society,* VII (1965), 289–308, and *Slavery in the Americas; A Comparative Study of Cuba and Virginia* (1967), have followed him. Davis, *The Problem of Slavery,* chapter 8, doubts the extent of the Protestant-Catholic difference; Arnold Sio, "Interpretations of Slavery: The Slave Status in the Americas," *Comparative Studies in History and Society,* VII (1965), 289–308, finds relatively little difference between slavery in Virginia and in ancient Rome. Richard H. Sewell, "Slavery in the Americas: an Essay Review," *Wisconsin Magazine of History,* LI (1968), 238–243, finds that Klein exaggerates legal differences and mistakes law for reality. Laura Foner and Eugene D. Genovese, eds., *Slavery in the New World; A Reader in Comparative History* (1969),* is an excellent collection. Jefferson's early unfavorable comparison of Negroes with Indians is in *Notes on Virginia* and is analyzed skillfully by Daniel Boorstin, *The Lost World of Thomas Jefferson* (1948), chapter 2.

The strong anti-slave views of the Reverend Samuel Hopkins have aroused interest in post-Awakening Calvinistic reformism; see David S. Lovejoy, "Samuel Hopkins; Religion, Slavery, and the Revolution," *New England Quarterly,* XL (1967), 227–243, and David E. Swift, "Samuel Hopkins: Calvinist Social Concern in 18th Century New England," *Journal of Presbyterian History,* XLVII (1969), 31–54.

Some indication of the political activism of blacks outside the plantation country can be gained from Lorenzo C. Greene, *The Negro in Colonial New England, 1620–1776* (1942), Benjamin Quarles, *The Negro in the American Revolution* (1961), and especially Edgar J. McManus, *A History of Negro Slavery in New York* (1966).

Chapter 4
Ben Franklin and the Spirit of "A Rising People"

Joseph Dorfman, *The Economic Mind in American Civilization* (1946), Vol. I, gracefully integrates economics and history in the 18th century. Klaus E. Knorr, *British Colonial Theories, 1570–1850* (1944), is encyclopedic but useful. Virgil G. Wilhite, *Founders of American Economic Thought and Policy* (1958), includes Franklin. William Appleman Williams, *The Contours of American History* (1961),* is a well-written attack on the rise of *laissez-faire* capitalism; he unfairly characterizes Franklin as a "nabob." The best general biographies of the Philadelphia Sage are Carl Van Doren (1938), and Verner W. Crane (1954). Charles L. Sandford, ed., *Benjamin Franklin and American Character* (1955),* shows his many sides as seen by many authorities. John William Ward asks "Who was Franklin?" *American Scholar,* XXXII (1963), 541–553, and answers that we don't know, although Franklin was among the first to ask two perennial American questions: "Who's Who?" and "Who am I?" Richard L. Bushman, "On the Uses of Psychology: Conflict and Conciliation in Benjamin Franklin," *History and Theory,* V (1966), 225–240, finds the young printer learning early in life to get "ego supplies" without hurting people. Latest edition of Franklin's Papers is by L. W. Labaree and W. J. Bell (1959–), and many of his major essays are in Ralph Ketcham, ed., *The Political Thought of Benjamin Franklin* (1965).

Max Weber's specific references to Franklin in *The Protestant Ethic and the Spirit of Capitalism* (1905), should be noted. Two studies that lend support to Weber are A. Whitney Griswold, "Three Puritans on Prosperity," *New England Quarterly,* VII (1934), 475–493, and more recently, Stephen Foster, "The Puritan Social Ethic, Class and Calling in the First Hundred Years of Settlement in New England," diss., Yale University, 1966. The book by Cotton Mather, *Bonifacius; or Essays to Do Good* (1710), that Franklin claimed inspired him has been re-issued, edited by David Levin (1966). The case for continuity in the practical piety of the two men has been made thoroughly and persuasively by Phyllis Franklin, *Show Thyself a Man; A Comparison of Benjamin Franklin and Cotton Mather* (1969).* Gabriel Kolko, "Max Weber on America—Theory and Evidence," *History and Theory,* I (1961), 243–260, registers an ideological dissent from Weber's thesis, and the choice of American Puritans and Franklin to exemplify it. Winthrop S. Hudson, "Puritanism and the Spirit of Capitalism," *Church History,* XVIII (1949), 3–17, speaks for many when he notes that Weber and Tawney overemphasized calling and underemphasized God's sovereignty in Calvinism; because Calvinistic teachings were explicitly antithetical to capitalism, it is easier to argue, he says, that the capitalistic spirit brought changes in religion rather than *vice versa*. See also Robert S. Michaelson, "Changes in the Conception of the Calling or Vocation," *New England Quarterly*, XXVI (1953), 315–336, and Edgar A. J. Johnson, *American Economic Thought in the Seventeenth Century* (1932).

John Hardin Best, ed., *Benjamin Franklin on Education* (1962), provides the pertinent writings and an analysis emphasizing Enlightenment influence. David Tyack, "Education as Artifact: Benjamin Franklin and the Instruction of 'a Rising People,' " *Journal of Education Quarterly*, VI (1966), 3–15, indicates that his educational ideas were designed to facilitate social mobility.

Two informative books on education in this period are Bernard Bailyn, *Education in the Forming of American Society* (1960),* and Robert L. Middlekauff, *Ancients and Axioms* (1963). For Franklin's religion, see Alfred O. Aldridge, *Benjamin Franklin and Nature's God* (1967), and for his science, I. Bernard Cohen, *Benjamin Franklin; His Contribution to American Tradition* (1953),* and *Franklin and Newton* (1956).

Franklin's political and economic views have been the subject of many special studies; Paul W. Conner, *Poor Richard's Politicks: Benjamin Franklin and his New American Order* (1965),* is excellent; others are Malcolm R. Eiselen, *Franklin's Political Theories* (1928); Lewis J. Carey, *Franklin's Economic Views* (1928); Gladys Meyer, *Free Trade in Ideas, Aspects of American Liberalism Illustrated in Franklin's Philadelphia Career* (1954), and W. A. Wetzel, *Benjamin Franklin as an Economist* (1895). Marx's praise for Franklin is in John R. Aitken, "Benjamin Franklin, Karl Marx and the Labor Theory of Value," *Pennsylvania Magazine of History and Biography*, XC (1966), 378–422. E. James Ferguson, "Currency Finance: An Interpretation of Colonial Money Practices," *William and Mary Quarterly*, X (1953), 153–180, explains paper money and Franklin's role in the controversy, as does William R. Riddell, "Benjamin Franklin and Colonial Money," *Pennsylvania Magazine of History and Biography* LIV (1930), 52–64. For his "Manifest Destiny," see Gerald Stourzh, *Benjamin Franklin and American Foreign Policy* (1954), chapter 2, and Leon Dion, "Natural Law and Manifest Destiny in the Era of the American Revolution," *Canadian Journal of Economics and Political Science* XXIII (1957), 227–247.

Interesting articles on population theory are Alfred O. Aldridge, "Benjamin Franklin as a Demographer," *Journal of Economic History*, IX (1949–50), 25–44; Conway Zirkle, "Benjamin Franklin, Thomas Malthus and the United States Census," *Isis*, XLVIII (1957), 58–62; Norman E. Himes, "Benjamin Franklin on Population; a Re-Examination," *Economic History*, III (1937), 388–398, and a new comprehensive work, James H.

Cassedy, *Demography in Early America* (1970).* Philip J. Greven, Jr., "Historical Demography and Colonial America," *William and Mary Quarterly*, XXIV (1967),* 438–454, reviews recent works on England and the colonies.

Chapter 5
Natural Rights and Real Whigs

Leonard W. Levy, *The Legacy of Suppression: Freedom of Speech and Press in Early American History* (1960),* dwells on the limitations that remained in the 18th century. The preface to the 1963 edition contains some caveats by reviewers. Levy, ed., *Freedom of the Press from Zenger to Jefferson: Early American Libertarian Theories* (1966),* collects the classic statements. Lawrence H. Leder, *Liberty and Authority: Early American Political Ideology, 1689–1763* (1968), modifies Levy, discovering signs of increasing libertarianism after the Zenger case. The English background is in Frederick S. Siebert, *Freedom of the Press in England, 1476–1776* (1952). David L. Jacobsen, ed., *The English Libertarian Heritage* (1965), explains the influence of Trenchard and Gordon in Britain and America. Mary P. Clarke, *Parliamentary Privilege in the American Colonies* (1943), is the sole authority on privilege. Editor Stanley N. Katz provides the political setting for a contemporary account of the Zenger episode, James Alexander, *A Brief Narrative of the Case and Trial of John Peter Zenger* (1963). Vincent Buranelli, "Peter Zenger's Editor," *American Quarterly*, VII (1955), 174–181, and *The Trial of Peter Zenger* (1957),* make Alexander the conspicuous hero of liberty as does Henry N. McCracken, *Prologue to Independence; the Trials of James Alexander* (1964). Foster C. Nix, "Andrew Hamilton's Early Years in the American Colonies," *William and Mary Quarterly*, XXI (1964), 390–407, offers evidence of the barrister's legal training in Virginia. Richard B. Morris, *Fair Trial*, chapter 3, covers the Zenger case, adding some colorful details. Elizabeth C. Cook, *Literary Influences in Colonial Newspapers, 1704–1750* (1912, 1966), chapter 5, describes the newspaper war between Bradford's *Gazette* and Zenger's *Journal*. See also Livingston Rutherfurd, *John Peter Zenger* (1904), Harold Nelson, "Seditious Libel in Colonial America," *American Journal of Legal History*, III (1959), 160–172, and Helen Hill Miller, *The Case for Liberty* (1965).

Daniel Boorstin, *The Americans: the Colonial Experience*, Book Three, focuses on rhetoric and the printed word. Arthur M. Schlesinger, Sr., *Prelude to Independence: The Newspaper War with Britain, 1764–1776* (1958),* discusses the role of the press in Revolutionary politics.

The Legal Mind, the Saxon Myth and the Revolution.   The best work on colonial lawyers is still Charles Warren, *A History of the American Bar* (1911, 1966). Anton-Hermann Chroust, *The Rise of the Legal Profession in America: The Colonial Experience* (1965), provides additional details. See also Paul Hamlin, *Legal Education in Colonial New York* (1939), and E. Alfred Jones, *American Members of the Inns of Court* (1924).

The impact of Real Whiggery and the Saxon Myth is thoroughly examined in H. Trevor Colbourn, *The Lamp of Experience: Whig History and the Intellectual Origins of the American Revolution* (1965).* Caroline Robbins, *The Eighteenth Century Commonwealthman* (1959), a pioneer in exploring the dissenter tradition among the British, suggested its importance in America, too. Samuel Kliger, *The Goths in England* (1952), examines the Gothic vogue in English politics and letters during the 17th and 18th centuries. Bernard Bailyn, *The Origins of American Politics* (1968), thinks the extravagant rhetoric of the pre-Revolutionary agitation can be explained by the grip Real Whig ideas already had in the colonies before 1763. He shows that the high standards of the Real Whigs had become something of a reality in the American environment. The difference in social environment between Europe and America from the beginning is also the theme of Louis Hartz, *The Liberal Tradition in America* (1955).

Because the literature on the constitutional quarrel after 1763 is so extensive, only the few titles directly pertinent here will be noted. Borrowing from Britain is emphasized in A. E. D. Howard, *The Road from Runnymede: Magna Carta and Constitutionalism in America* (1968), and Roscoe Pound, *The Development of Constitutional Guarantees of Liberty* (1957); both discuss Sir Edward Coke's influence, but see also Charles F. Mullett, "Coke and the American Revolution," *Economotica* XII (1932), 457–471. Speculation about the separation of powers increased in the mid-18th century; William B. Gwyn, *The Meaning of the Separation of Powers* (1965), traces the origin of the conception to the English civil war.

The beliefs of our statesmen are well surveyed in Randolph G. Adams, *The Political Ideas of the American Revolution* (1922), Clinton Rossiter, *The Political Thought of the American Revolution* (1963),* and Carl Becker, *The Declaration of Independence* (1922). Convenient collections of the colonials' arguments are available in Bailyn, ed., *Pamphlets of the American Revolution*, and Merrill Jensen, ed., *Tracts of the American Revolution, 1763–1776* (1967); Edmund S. Morgan, ed., *Puritan Political Ideas, 1558–1794* (1965), also has some relevance as has John R. Howe, Jr., *The Role of Ideology in the American Revolution.* The works of John Adams, Thomas Jefferson, James Wilson, Benjamin Franklin, and

Samuel Adams are useful. For more extensive treatment of the great figures of political theory, see Correa M. Walsh, *The Political Science of John Adams* (1915), and John R. Howe, Jr., *The Political Thought of John Adams* (1967);* Edward Dumbauld, ed., *The Political Writings of Thomas Jefferson,* Gilbert Chinard, *Thomas Jefferson: Apostle of Americanism* (1939), and Dumas Malone, *Thomas Jefferson* (1948), vol. I; David L. Jacobsen, *John Dickinson and the American Revolution in Pennsylvania, 1764–1776* (1965), Page Smith, *James Wilson; Founding Father, 1742–1798* (1956), Ralph L. Ketcham, ed., *The Political Thought of Benjamin Franklin* (1965), John J. Waters, Jr., *The Otis Family in Provincial and Revolutionary Massachusetts* (1968), and Robert D. Meade, *Patrick Henry* (1969).

The return to the constitutional view of the Revolution, neo-Whiggery with an admixture of religion, is reflected in the selections of Jack P. Greene, ed., *The Reinterpretation of the American Revolution,* (1968). Bernard Bailyn, *The Ideological Interpretation of the American Revolution* (1966), shows how Real Whiggery made American leaders react paranoically to the change of imperial policy after 1763. Richard Buel, Jr., "Democracy and the American Revolution: A Frame of Reference," *William and Mary Quarterly,* XXI (1964), 165–190, finds the colonials applying the political ideas of the dissenting tradition to an unprecedented situation. Merrill Jensen, "Democracy and the American Revolution," *Huntington Library Quarterly* XX (1957), 321–341, notes the emergence of "new men" on the political scene in 1774, and concludes the Revolution was a democratic movement, not in origin, but in result.

Chapter 6
God's Sovereignty and a More Perfect Union

There are at least three important post-World War II books that attempt to fill the gap between the Great Awakening and the 19th century. William W. Sweet, *The Religious Development of American Culture, 1765–1840* (1952),* like his earlier efforts, emphasizes democratic changes, and gives each denomination its due in contributing to the quality of life in the new republic. H. Shelton Smith, *Changing Conceptions of Original Sin; A Study in American Theology since 1750* (1955), traces the vicissitudes of that Calvinistic doctrine—so important to the evangelicals in the 18th and early 19th centuries—all the way to the Neo-Orthodox re-emergence in the 20th century. Alan Heimert, *Religion and the American Mind; From the Great Awakening to the Revolution* (1966),* links the Awakening with the Jeffersonians and Jacksonians despite its subtitle. Compared to Sweet and Smith, Heimert is diffuse and prolix, but I am heavily indebted to him for the insights I have used in this chapter. There have been two lengthy essay reviews of his work by prominent scholars in the field. William G. McLoughlin, "The American Revolution as a Religious Revival: 'The Millennium in One Country'," *New England Quarterly*, XL (1967), 99–110, generally agrees with Heimert's attempt to reassert the importance of Edwardsian Calvinism in Revolutionary politics and the quest for democracy. On the other hand, Sidney E. Mead, "Through and Beyond the Lines," *Journal of Religion*, XLVIII (1968), 274–288, is highly critical of his methods, conclusions, and literary style. He says historians must read the lines before them and not try to go "through and beyond them" as Heimert promises to do in his preface. Gaustad's *The Great Awakening in New England* describes the theological and institutional results of the revival succinctly. Perry Miller, "The Great Awakening from 1740 to 1750," *Nature's Nation*, finds that afterward both sides, New Lights as well as Old Lights, had to shift their focus from the will of God to the nature of man.

New Light in Virginia.   The continuity between the Awakening and the Revolution is fairly obvious in the southern colonies. Ernest T. Thompson, *Presbyterians in the South. Volume I: 1607–1861* (1963), devotes seven brief chapters to the colonial period. Most accounts of Samuel Davies are based upon Wesley M. Gewehr, *The Great Awakening in Virginia, 1740–1790* (1930), and stress his unintended role in furthering religious toleration in Virginia for all the dissenters. George W. Pilcher, "Samuel Davies and Religious Toleration in Virginia," *Historian*, XXVIII (1965), 48–71, notes that Davies was conservative enough not to oppose an American bishop for the Anglicans. Davies' ideas, theological and political, are treated in Robert S. Alley, "The Rev. Samuel Davies; A Study in Religion and Politics, 1747–1759," diss., Princeton University, 1962, and in Pilcher, "Preacher of the New Light, Samuel Davies, 1724–1761," diss., University of Illinois, 1963. Davies is included in Richard M. Gummere, *Seven Wise Men of Colonial America* (1967), chapter 4; his unsurprising finding is that the classicism of Davies' sermons was clearly subordinated to his Christian message.

Separates and Baptists.   There is not a full and satisfactory account of Baptist thought in the colonies. Albert H. Newman (1894), is the best general history, and Robert G. Torbet (1950), the most recent. William G. McLoughlin, *Isaac Backus and the American Pietistic Tradition* (1967), and *The Writings of Isaac Backus,* ed. (1968), indicate the thinking of a New England Congregational convert to the Baptists, as does Thomas B. Maston, *Isaac Backus, Pioneer of Religious Liberty* (1962). Clarence C. Goen, *Revivalism and Separatism* (1962), offers two chapters on Separates who became Baptists. For Baptists in the South see Gewehr, *The Great Awakening in Virginia*, chapter 5; William L. Lumpkin, *Baptist Foundations in the South* (1961); David T. Morgan, Jr., "The Great Awakening in North Carolina, 1740–1775: the Baptist Phase," *North Carolina Historical Review*, XLV (1968), 264–283; George W. Paschal, *A History of North Carolina Baptists* (1930); Leah Townsend, *South Carolina Baptists, 1670–1805* (1935), and among older works, William T. Thom, *The Struggle for Religious Freedom in Virginia; the Baptists* (1900), and Robert B. Semple, *The History of the Rise and Progress of the Baptists in Virginia* (1810, 1894).

Edwards on the Will and Original Sin. The studies of Edwards as a theologian and philosopher are, of course, more numerous than those of him as a pastor and revivalist; the references offered here are in addition to those cited in chapter 2. There have been many editions of his works; the most recent is the most authoritative and begins with Paul Ramsey, ed., *Freedom of the Will* (1957), followed till now only by John E. Smith, ed., *The Religious Affections* (1959). Perry Miller, ed., *Images or Shadows of Divine Things* (1948), Harvey G. Townsend, ed., *The Philosophy of Jonathan Edwards From His Private Notebooks* (1955), and Leon Howard, ed., *"The Mind" of Jonathan Edwards: A Reconstructed Text* (1963), indicate his intellectual preoccupations. Douglas J. Elwood, *The Philosophical Theology of Jonathan Edwards* (1960),* is authoritative. Conrad Cherry, *The Theology of Jonathan Edwards: A Reappraisal* (1966),* emphasizes his Calvinism and theory of faith. Roland A. Delattre, *Beauty and Sensibility in the Thought of Jonathan Edwards* (1968),* expands in detail Perry Miller's discovery that for Edwards the Elect were set off from others by special aesthetic perceptions or sensibilities: spiritual beauty in Being's consent to Being, and natural beauty in order and proportion. Alexander V. G. Allen, *Jonathan Edwards* (1890), is specific and lucid in treating will and sin; Arthur E. Murphy, "Jonathan Edwards on Free Will and Moral Agency," *Philosophical Review*, LXVIII (1959), 181–202, believes that Edwards' brand of determinism does deny the will, and by postulating instead causally necessitated "acts of volition," offers no "intelligible substitute" for it. William S. Morris, "The Reappraisal of Edwards," *New England Quarterly*, XXX (1957), 515–525, takes the occasion of the publication of Ramsey's edition to review the historiography of the controversy on the will.

Other pertinent articles on Edwards' thought are: Alfred O. Aldridge, "Edwards and Hutcheson," *Harvard Theological Review*, XLIV (1951), 35–51; Thomas A. Schafer, "Jonathan Edwards and Justification by Faith," *Church History*, XX (1951), 55–67, and "Jonathan Edwards' Conception of the Church," *Church History*, XXIV (1955), 51–66;

Clarence C. Goen, "Edwards' New Departure in Eschatalogy," *Church History*, XXVIII (1959), 25–40; and Clyde A. Holbrook, "Edwards and the Ethical Question," *Harvard Theological Review*, LX (1967), 163–175.

I. Woodbridge Riley, *American Philosophy; the Early Schools* (1907, 1958), is still the most thorough and readable book on the subject; Vincent Buranelli, "Colonial Philosophy," *William & Mary Quarterly*, XVI (1959), 343–362, laments the lack of a new systematic treatment.

The Arminians and the Enlightenment. Conrad Wright, *The Beginnings of Unitarianism in America* (1955),* describes concisely the reasonable religion of the late 18th century. Joseph Haroutunian, *Piety Versus Moralism* (1932), G. Adolph Koch, *Republican Religion* (1933), and Herbert M. Morais, *Deism in Eighteenth Century America* (1934), err in overestimating the European rationalism and underestimating the residual piety in the colonial figures they discuss. Claude M. Newlin, *Philosophy and Religion in Colonial America* (1962), juxtaposes Edwards and the rationalists. Charles W. Akers, *Called unto Liberty; A Life of Jonathan Mayhew, 1720–1766* (1964), is good; see also Earl E. Lewis, "The Theology and Politics of Jonathan Mayhew," diss., University of Minnesota, 1966. For the other major Liberal, see Harold B. Wohl, "Charles Chauncy and the Age of Enlightenment in New England," diss., University of Iowa, 1956, stressing Chauncy's social conservatism. Edmund S. Morgan, *The Gentle Puritan: A Life of Ezra Stiles, 1727–1795* (1962), is a sympathetic treatment of an Old Light; see also Richard D. Birdsall, "Ezra Stiles versus the New Divinity Men," *American Quarterly*, XVII (1965), 248–258. Carl Bridenbaugh, *Mitre and Sceptre*, Part Two, "No Bishop, No King, 1760–1775," indicates the nature of the episcopal threat in those years and Herbert W. and Carol Schneider, *Samuel Johnson*, is useful.

The Beauty of Union. The similarity between the communal feeling among the awakened in a revival or in closed communion, and of the more radical patriots on the eve of the Revolution has been made quite explicitly but is still not well enough known. Perry Miller, "From the Covenant to the Revival," in *The Shaping of American Religion*, James Ward Smith and A. Leland Jameson, eds. (1961), finds that a belief in a specific bond between God and His people made Americans—in all the colonies, not just in New England—receptive to the Lockean arguments offered by rationalistic leaders in the Revolution. His disciple, Alan Heimert, *The Religious Mind*, shows in detail how the Great Awakening revitalized and extended that bond, and how Edwards' ideal of beauty was transformed to give support to a millennial hope for a more perfect union.

The strength of that hope among the 18th century colonists had been argued persuasively earlier by H. Richard Niebuhr, *The Kingdom of God in America.* Delattre, *Beauty and Sensibility in the Thought of Edwards,* warns that Heimert may have exaggerated the beauty of community in Edwards' thought.

The New Light in Revolutionary New England. For glimpses of the New Light at the first stage of the Revolution in New England, see Edmund S. Morgan, *The Stamp Tax Crisis* (1955). Oscar Zeichner, *Connecticut's Years of Controversy, 1750–1776* (1949), gives a full and objective description of the New Light faction, and Robert Sklar, "The Great Awakening and Colonial Politics: Connecticut's Revolution in the Minds of Men," *Connecticut Historical Society Bulletin,* XXVIII (1963), 81–95, explores the link between the revival and the Revolution. There are also references to the New Lights in Lawrence H. Gipson, *Jared Ingersoll* (1920), and Morgan, *Ezra Stiles.* For Massachusetts, E. Francis Brown, *Joseph Hawley; Colonial Radical* (1931), shows the influence of the New Light lawyer in the east as well as the west; see also Robert J. Taylor, *Western Massachusetts in the Revolution* (1954), and Heimert, *The Religious Mind.* Richard D. Birdsall, "The Reverend Thomas Allen, Jeffersonian Calvinist," *New England Quarterly,* XXX (1957), 147–165, presents another striking case of a Northampton New Light of old family who was converted to radical politics in 1774, and from his pulpit in Berkshire county, fought consistently for the common people and against the Federalists until his death in 1810. The precise nature of the religiosity of Sam Adams, the chief propagandist of the American Revolution, is not yet clear but he was strongly Calvinistic in many respects; see Charles Townsend, "The Thought of Samuel Adams," diss., University of Wisconsin, 1968, chapter 2, and William Appleman Williams, "Samuel Adams, Calvinist, Mercantilist, Revolutionary," *Studies on the Left,* I (1960). *Peter Oliver's Origin and Progress of the American Revolution, A Tory View,* Douglass Adair and John A. Schutz, eds. (1961), offers a different perspective on the role of religion. In Rhode Island, New Lightism must be intuited from the politico-economic studies of David S. Lovejoy, *Rhode Island Politics and the American Revolution, 1760–1776* (1958), and Mack E. Thompson, "The Ward-Hopkins Controversy and the American Revolution in Rhode Island: an Interpretation," *William and Mary Quarterly,* XVI (1959), 363–375; see also Samuel Ward, *The Correspondence of Samuel Ward, 1775–1776* (1952) ed. by Bernhard Knollenberg. Alice M. Baldwin, *The New England Clergy and the American Revolution* (1928), indicates the important role of the pastors in stirring libertarian sentiment but her usefulness for this study was reduced by a failure to discriminate between New Lights, Old Lights, and

Liberals. Peter N. Carroll, ed., *Religion and the Coming of the American Revolution* (1970), contains excerpts from the writings of various clergymen. He allots much space to the controversy over an American bishopric and to the dilemma of Anglicans in the Revolution.

The "Fair Experiment" in Church and State.   The most comprehensive, readable account of church-state relations in this country is Leo Pfeffer, *Church, State and Freedom* (rev. ed., 1967);* this author has also compressed into one volume the diffuse work of Anson Phelps Stokes, *Church and State in the United States* (rev. ed., 1964). Evarts B. Greene, *Religion and the State* (1941), tells the story succinctly and well. John F. Wilson, ed., *Church and State in American History* (1965),* contains many relevant documents and essays. Edward F. Humphrey, *Nationalism and Religion in America, 1774–1789* (1924, 1966), is rich in documentation and describes the adjustment of all the denominations to independence and religious freedom; Sidney E. Mead, *The Lively Experiment, the Shaping of Christianity in America* (1963), somewhat overplays the rationalistic, and underplays the evangelical component as does William W. Sweet, "Natural Religion and Religious Liberty in America," *Journal of Religion* XXV (1945), 45–55. Hamilton J. Eckenrode, *Separation of Church and State in Virginia* (1910), remains the most thorough account of the major church-state conflict; see also Gewehr, *The Great Awakening in Virginia, 1740–1790* (1930), chapter 8.

Three divergent intellectual sources came together and contributed to the separation that occurred in Virginia and became a model for other states and the federal union. The most relevant for the extreme pietistic separationism is LeRoy Moore, "Religious Liberty: Roger Williams and the Revolutionary Era," *Church History,* XXXIV (1965), 57–76, and Edmund S. Morgan, *Roger Williams on Church and State* (1967). For the rationalistic extreme separationists, see Dumas Malone, *Jefferson, the Virginian* (1948), chapter 20, Jefferson's *Notes on Virginia,* Bernard Fabian, "Jefferson's 'Notes on Virginia'; Genesis of Query xvii—the Different Religions Received into the State?" *William and Mary Quarterly,* XII (1955), 126–131, and Frederick C. Luebke, "The Origins of Thomas Jefferson's Anti-Clericalism," *Church History,* XXXII (1963), 344–356. Stokes, *Church and State,* gives Madison his due; Irving Brant, *James Madison; the Nationalist, 1780–1787* (1948), devotes chapter 22 to freedom of religion.

The case for the predominant historical importance of a third position held by the evangelicals, a pragmatic line rather than a high wall of separation, is made forcefully by William G. McLoughlin, "Isaac Backus and the Separation of Church and State in America," *American Historical Review,* LXXIII (1968), 1392–1413, and in his biography of the Baptist leader. See also Lyman H. Butterfield, "Elder John Leland, Jeffersonian Itinerant," *Proceedings of the American Antiquarian Society,* LXII (1952), 155–242, Edwin S. Gaustad, "The Backus-Leland Tradition," in Winthrop S. Hudson, ed., *Baptist Conceptions of the Church* (1959), Edmund S. Morgan, ed., *Puritan Political Ideas* (1965), and William Haller, "The Puritan Background of the First Amendment," in Conyers Read, ed., *The Constitution Reconsidered* (1938).

The ideal standard Backus and his pious followers sought—and the one actually prevailing until the 20th century—seems to have been close to that practiced by the Pilgrims before 1650; see John M. Bumsted, " 'A Well-Balanced Toleration'; Church and State in the Plymouth Colony," *Journal of Church and State,* X (1968), 265–279.

And finally, a skeptical footnote: Perry Miller, in a whimsical essay, "The Location of American Religious Freedom," in *Religion and Freedom of Thought* (1954), seems ready to deny the premise of so many historians—including, to a considerable degree, this one—that the principle of liberty was somehow latent in the Protestant churches of colonial America. In both education and religion, he says, "we didn't aspire to freedom, we didn't march steadily toward it, . . . we stumbled into it. We got a variety of sects as we got a college catalogue: the denominations and sciences multiplied until there was nothing anybody could do about them. Wherefore we gave them permission to exist, and called the result freedom of mind."

Index

PRINTED IN U.S.A.

DATE DUE			
OCT 30 '79			
NOV 11 '80